THE WRITER'S HANDBOOK
A Guide for Social Workers

COMPOSE FEARLESSLY · EDIT RUTHLESSLY · Write to Learn

THE
WRITER'S HANDBOOK
A Guide for Social Workers

COMPOSE FEARLESSLY
EDIT RUTHLESSLY
Write to Learn

Dona J. Young

Contributions by

Andrea Tamburro
Marshelia Harris

The Writer's Handbook – A Guide for Social Workers
Dona J. Young with Andrea Tamburro and Marshelia Harris

Writer's Toolkit Publishing LLC
www.wtkpublishing.com

Valerie Decker, APA Editor

Cover design by Nanc Ashby and Marshelia Harris
www.saveldesign.com

ISBN-13: 978-0615965215
ISBN-10: 0615965210

LCCN: 2014932840

Fifth printing.

To the caring social workers

who dedicate their lives to helping others

About the Authors

Dona J. Young, MA, teaches professional writing at Indiana University Northwest as well as designs and facilitates corporate writing programs. Young earned an MA in education from The University of Chicago, a certificate from the Teacher Education Program at The Chicago Institute for Psychoanalysis, and a BA in sociology from Northern Illinois University. She is the author of *Business Communication and Writing* (Writer's Toolkit Publishing, 2012), *Business English: Writing for the Global Workplace* (McGraw-Hill Higher Education, 2008), and *Foundations of Business Communication* (McGraw-Hill/ Irwin, 2006), among others. Young believes that writing is a powerful learning tool and that learning shapes our lives.

Andrea Tamburro, MSW and EdD, is a member of the Shawnee Tribe and is the Bachelor of Social Work Program Director at Indiana University at the South Bend campus. She teaches policy, research, and practice. She earned her education doctorate from Simon Fraser University in British Columbia, Canada, and her master of social work through the University of Iowa. Tamburro's main research area is indigenous social work education; her practice areas include child welfare, mental health, domestic violence, and criminal justice. In this book, Tamburro wrote Chapter 4, "Literature Review," and also contributed to other chapters.

Marshelia Harris, MSW, is the field coordinator for the Bachelor of Social Work Program in the Indiana University School of Social Work, Northwest campus. She teaches policy, administration, and child welfare across the bachelor and master of social work programs. Harris received her MSW from Indiana University and is pursuing a doctorate in social work at University of St. Thomas and St. Catherine University. She is a licensed child welfare specialist with several years of administrative experience in social services, case management, and clinical services. Harris has also managed parenting and non-parenting youth programs, developed new programs, and facilitated training. In this book, Harris wrote Chapter 2, "Documentation and Forms."

Brief Contents

Introduction

Clear and effective writing is an essential communication skill for social workers. We often share our practice experiences with other professionals through publishing our research, submitting reports to supervisors, judges and doctors, and documenting the experiences of our clients. When a research article or a court report demonstrates critical thinking and is clear, concise, and accurate the reader is more likely to consider the outcomes and recommendations. As a result, our writing impacts countless lives.

Writing is not a gift but a skill that is developed with effort over time. Some people write well because they learned from early training. Others develop those skills later in life. The writing courses required for social work education can help build those skills. Writing, critical thinking, and research are essential skills in the profession.

The Council on Social Work Education (CSWE), which accredits social work programs, has identified several core competencies that support the use of effective writing. Students are expected to demonstrate ethical and professional behavior, including oral, written, and electronic communication (CSWE EPAS, 2015). Communication includes spoken and written communiqués. The ability to write is a necessary skill and part of our professional identity as social workers.

Critical thinking is an essential skill in the profession. Clarifying the importance of critical thinking, the CSWE core competency states that students will achieve the following:

> Social workers understand frameworks of ethical decision-making and how to apply principles of critical thinking to those frameworks in practice, research, and policy arenas. CSWE EPAS, p. 72015).

This competency clearly identifies the importance of written communication in all aspects of service provision.

Academic research leads to evidence-based practice, which is crucial for effective social services. The fourth CSWE core competency directly relates to research. How do we find, understand, and evaluate the evidence that does or does not support a particular policy or treatment approach? This competency states that students will "[e]ngage in research-informed practice and practice-informed research" including the use of "practice experience to inform scientific inquiry and research evidence (CSWE EPAS, 2015, p.8). Academic and professional writing requires an effective argument supported by evidence and explaining counter-arguments.

Practitioners must be able to explain to clients and supervisors the reasons one strategy or approach is encouraged over another. Research can support these recommendations and further our ability to be effective practitioners. However, literature reviews demonstrate gaps in the research, and these need to be filled by social work practitioners. The only way social work practitioners will be considered credible by scholarly journals is by conducting ethical research, guided by sound research principles. There are many important discoveries in the field that must be reported through clear scholarly writing. This text will guide you through the principles of scholarly and professional writing.

Remember, no one starts out being able to write well. Many students struggle to develop writing skills just as they struggle with other skills, such as learning math or using a computer effectively. Do not let your struggles hold you back. Writing is a skill that can be learned and developed, and writing skills are essential to the social work professional.

Andrea Tamburro, MSW, EdD, ACSW BSW
Program Director
Indiana University – South Bend Campus

Note to Students

Different Voices

As you go through your academic and professional career, you must adapt each piece of your writing for your audience. One aim of this textbook is to assist you in developing your voice—or rather, your *various voices*. For example, you will use your *academic voice* for papers and other documents in which your audience expects a formal style. In contrast, you will use your *professional voice* when you write less formal documents such as e-mail messages and letters to clients in which a simple and direct style is more effective. Finally, you will use your *personal voice* for reflective types of writing, such as journals in which you express your feelings and opinions.

An element of voice is formatting: *formatting speaks to your audience at a glance.* Each document that you produce, from a simple e-mail message to an academic paper, must be formatted according to guidelines and protocol. Only by developing expert formatting skills will you be able to adapt each piece of your writing for purpose and audience.

Since your academic papers in social work are formatted in the American Psychological Association (APA) style, Chapter 6, "APA Citation Style," provides information to get you started formatting papers in APA style. (Also note that references at the end of each chapter of this book are formatted in APA citation style.) Moreover, Chapter 18, "Formatting" gives you additional details about APA formatting as well as the guidelines that you need to produce professional letters, memos, and e-mail messages.

Textbook Focus

The Writer's Handbook: A Guide for Social Workers first gives you an overview of the kind of writing that you will do in the field. Then the remainder of the book focuses on principles that lead to correct and credible writing.

Part 1, Academic and Professional Writing, examines the qualities of academic writing as well as the expectations of professional writing in the field. In Chapter 2, you become familiar with forms used in the day-to-day operations of social work, preparing you to document your practice. Chapters 3 and 4 provide the basics of how to evaluate, conduct, and present research, including a literature review. Chapter 5 gives insight into critical thinking; Chapter 6 covers APA citation style, the required style of documentation in your chosen profession.

Part 2, Process and Structure, reviews core principles for composing and revising. Chapter 7 covers the writing process; Chapter 8, the sentence core; and Chapter 9, cohesive, coherent paragraphs.

Part 3, Mechanics of Writing, presents comma and semicolon rules, taking the guessing out of punctuating and reinforcing the sentence core.

Part 4, Grammar for Writing, covers core elements of structure such as verbs, pronouns, and modifiers.

Part 5, Editing for Clarity, presents principles that lead to a clear and concise writing style.

Part 6, More Mechanics, provides correct use of the minor marks of punctuation as well as capitalization and number usage.

Finally, the *Quick Guide for Job Search Tools* gives a step-by-step process so that you can prepare your career portfolio.

Each chapter builds on the previous, so do not take any shortcuts. By learning foundational principles first, complex topics become easy. This book applies the method of *principle and practice*: as you learn each principle, practice it until you integrate it into your writing.

In Part 2, you tune into the process of writing, learning first to push through editor's block. Then in Parts 3 through 6, you learn expert editing skills. Here is your first goal when it comes to the process of writing:

Compose freely and then edit ruthlessly.

By working through each chapter and doing the activities as prescribed, you build your skills, filling knowledge gaps that may keep you from doing your best. To give yourself immediate reinforcement for practice on exercises, refer to **Keys to Activities** located at the back of the book. For additional practice, visit the book's website at **www.thewriterstoolkit.com**.

Learning involves change, and change is challenging, even painful at times. Commit yourself to the learning process as well as the writing process, and you will become an expert editor. *Do the work, and you will see the results!*

Write to Learn—Edit to Clarify

Note to Instructors

The Writer's Handbook: A Guide for Social Workers is designed to prepare social work professionals for all types of writing required in their field. In addition to social work content, *The Writer's Handbook* covers essential writing topics in a user-friendly format: principles are sequenced from the simple to the complex, using a narrative style to engage learners.

While writing is a core activity in all professions, in the field of social work correct and credible writing is critical: at times, people's lives depend on it. Therefore, even those who are challenged by writing must become proficient writers to be effective in the field.

A traditional approach to improving writing skills has been to work with learners individually, giving feedback and coaching. Though time-consuming, this approach is powerful; however, significant accountability seems to remain in the hands of the instructor rather than in the hands of the learner.

As an alternative, *The Writer's Handbook* quickly gives learners a set of principles on which to base writing decisions. Learners also acquire a common vocabulary to discuss editing, making peer editing activities productive and even fun. *The Writer's Handbook* can be used effectively for group instruction or individual study:

- Present chapters in workshop format.

- Encourage learners to work on learning activities on their own or with a peer, using the keys at the back of the book or completing the practice exercises at the book's website, **www.thewriterstoolkit.com**.

The Writer's Handbook charts an instructional design that is in tune with the taxonomy of educational objectives. As a result, learners readily fill knowledge gaps that may have been hindering their progress. For example, the taxonomy reveals why learners have a more difficult time with higher-order principles of writing (such as analysis and synthesis) when they do not first understand lower-order principles (such as summarization). The taxonomy also gives insight into how a graduate student can write an insightful analysis of a complex theory but still have difficulty with run-on sentences or subject-verb agreement.

The Writer's Handbook: A Guide for Social Workers aims to provide writers at all levels the tools that they need to succeed in their academic studies as well as their professional careers.

- **Part 1, Academic and Professional Writing,** sets the tone by giving learners a clear understanding of the types of writing and the quality that is expected in the field of social work.

- **Part 2, Process and Structure,** provides a foundation for composing and editing, from controlling the sentence core to developing cohesive paragraphs.

- **Part 3, Mechanics of Writing,** teaches commas and semicolons while further reinforcing the sentence core, ensuring that fragments and run-ons are no longer issues.

- **Part 4, Grammar for Writing,** fills knowledge gaps, giving learners insights into their own language patterns and control over them.

- **Part 5, Editing for Clarity,** reinforces expert editing skills by having learners apply active voice and parallel structure. Students also learn how to format business documents such as letters, memos, and reports.

- **Part 6, More Mechanics,** covers the fine details of editing, such as word usage, colons, apostrophes, capitalization, number usage, and so on.

The Writer's Handbook also provides instructors and learners with a common vocabulary for punctuation. This approach makes it easier to learn the rules and to provide feedback efficiently. The methodology integrates principles of structure with principles of style so that a learner's writing becomes clear and concise as well as correct.

Another critical element of all writing is *formatting*, which speaks to readers at a glance. To help your students gain control of formatting early on, have them review Chapter 18, "Formatting," and then Chapter 6, "APA Citation Style."

Experiment using individual chapters as workshops or use them for activity-based learning. If your students need additional practice, have them visit the website, **www.thewriterstoolkit.com**, for a full range of interactive activities.

Feel free to contact us through the book's website for additional assessments and other supplemental materials. We will do our best to add resources, examples, and exercises based on your requests. We look forward to hearing your feedback and suggestions.

All the best,

Dona Young

Note about APA Style

The Writer's Handbook: A Guide for Social Workers aims to assist writers at all levels build their skills so that they produce correct, clear, and concise writing. Those aims align naturally with APA style and formatting guidelines. Therefore, principles presented in the book's chapters on grammar, punctuation, style, and tone support guidelines presented in the *Publication Manual of the American Psychological Association, Sixth Edition.*

This book also presents and illustrates basic elements of APA formatting to get learners started. Though covering all elements of APA style is beyond the scope and mission of this book, APA guidelines are noted in various chapters throughout the book. In addition, the following chapters are dedicated to helping students learn APA formatting and citation:

- **Chapter 4, Literature Review,** walks learners through a step-by-step process to write a literature review, providing an example of a student's paper formatted in APA style.

- **Chapter 6, APA Citation Style,** covers basic elements of the style, giving learners another example of APA formatting in which the elements of APA citation style are discussed and illustrated.

- **Chapter 18, Formatting,** includes information about APA formatting that writers struggle with, such as setting paragraph controls and creating a running head; this chapter also contains an APA checklist.

- **Chapter 21, Capitalization and Number Usage,** reviews the differences between title case and sentence case as well as provides basic points about how to display numbers in APA documents.

- The book's website, **www.thewriterstoolkit.com**, provides additional resources.

In addition to APA style, this book aims to prepare social work graduates so that they enter the field well equipped for any kind of writing, from documenting cases to writing e-mail and business letters. Each type of document has its own set of guidelines and formatting standards, and they are all important writing tasks that social workers must perform on a daily basis. Producing these types of documents correctly adds to a professional's credibility in the field.

In fact, social workers rank at the top of professions in which correct and credible writing is critical. Their clients' lives depend on it. When a case goes to court, a judge depends on documentation the social worker provides so that a fair decision can be made.

Though the authors and editors have done their best to ensure accuracy, APA style is complicated and some points may differ due to interpretation. Where you may find differing opinions, refer to the *Publication Manual of the American Psychological Association, Sixth Edition*, for your final answer.

In fact, many books and websites are dedicated to APA style, some which are also published by the APA. This book recommends that writers use those primary sources to research the fine details in APA style and formatting.

Online Learning

Online Classes

Communicating effectively online is a critical element of most professions today, and online classes give you an exceptional opportunity to hone your skills as you prepare for your career. The following information gives you a general idea of how to participate in online classes.

When you arrive to your online class, review the tabs for the various pages at your online learning site. For example, here are some of the tabs for a typical online class:

- Home
- Syllabus
- Announcements
- Discussions
- Modules
- Messages
- Gradebook
- Chat Room

Experiment by navigating to each of the tabs that your instructor has included for your class.

Many online classes work in teams, and a critical component of online classes is the *discussion* (sometimes called a *forum).* In discussions, students post responses to questions and develop dialogues with their teammates.

Discussions

By clicking on the tab marked *Discussions,* you will see the current discussions that your instructor has posted. Each week or so, your instructor will add new discussions for your class. If a discussion is *locked*, it means that your instructor has not yet opened that discussion for your class, or the discussion is completed and thus closed.

In general, a discussion consists of two types of activities: *substantial postings* and *discussion responses.*

- A **substantial posting** is a response to a *discussion question* in which the writer starts a new *thread* for the posting.

- A **discussion response** is a comment in response to a substantial posting.

For each discussion, read the full description so that you clearly understand how to compose your substantial response. Your teammates or classmates will post discussion responses so that together you can develop a dialogue about the topic in that discussion.

For substantial postings, **summarize key points** from your readings. For all postings, use your own words, sharing your insights and giving examples about how you are applying new principles. In other words, do not paraphrase from your readings. By summarizing your own understanding, you are learning principles as well as reinforcing your teammates' understanding of the readings.

Learning online is a team effort, and when all team members participate fully, the outcomes are outstanding.

- *What is an effective **substantial posting**?*

    To write a substantial response, summarize **principles** from your readings along with your insights and how you are applying what you are learning. Your teammates will respond to your posting by validating your points and adding new information.

    | **P** | = | Principle | explain *principles* and *key points* from readings |
    | **E** | = | Evidence | support main points with *facts* and *details* |
    | **E** | = | Examples | give *examples* and share *insights* |
    | **R** | = | Recap | summarize and *recommend outcomes* or next steps |

    The following is the start of a substantial response:

    Chapter 1 covered principles about academic writing, which is also known as scholastic writing because of the stringent requirements for using research effectively and writing in the correct style. For example, in the field of social work, writers must use the American Psychological Association (APA) citation style. Also, when referring to an author, use the author's last name. Never refer to an author by only his or her first name.

Before reading the next example, use the PEER model to analyze the above: can you find *key points*, *facts*, *details*, or *examples*?

*The following is **not** a substantial response:*

I liked reading the chapter about academic writing because I learned a lot about how to write a paper, which can really be hard at times. Academic writing is important because that's the kind of writing that is expected in our classes, but I've never been really good at writing papers but now I feel more confident.

Can you see the difference between the two postings? In the first example, the writer explains a key principle. In the second posting, the writer does not tie his or her experience to a principle from the chapter.

Substantial postings are generally two to three paragraphs or longer. Effective substantial postings spark a discussion among teammates.

- *What is an effective **dialogue posting or response**?*
  As you respond to your teammates, validate points that resonate with your own experience. Add new information to extend the reader's knowledge, and share how you are applying what you are learning.

S	=	Support	*support* teammates by making thoughtful postings
A	=	Apply	*apply* key points and explain your results
V	=	Validate	*validate* points by sharing your own experiences
E	=	Extend	*extend* learning by including new information that adds value
R	=	Respect	*respect* others and the learning environment: learn what is expected, follow best practices, and do the work on time

Support the learning environment by giving feedback without being critical. Be accepting and forgiving, and your teammates will respond in kind.

More about Discussions

Even after reading the above, you may still be confused about discussion postings and responses and how to navigate your online class. Your instructor understands that you may feel confused and will patiently guide you through the process.

Do your part by reading course materials and thinking things through. Any new experience is difficult in the beginning—that is why you need to give your best until you understand what is expected. It may take as long as a week to feel comfortable at your class site: every time that you go back, you will feel more confident. The following is an example of a discussion assignment.

Here are some questions you might examine in discussion:

- **Discussion 1: Introduction and Advocacy Interests**
  Instructions: In this discussion, you will get to know your classmates. Since supporting social and economic justice is an essential aspect of social work, in your response include information about an issue you advocate.

  1. Share general background information about yourself—what things would you like for us to know about you?
  2. What areas of social work practice interest you and why?
  3. What is an issue that you want to advocate for or against? Please explain the issue and describe how you might do this.

- **Discussion 2: Creating a Safe and Respectful Environment**

In some ways, interacting on the Internet is different from interacting in person; however, all communication has some elements in common.

How can we co-create a respectful and productive learning environment in class and online?

  1. What can classmates do to help you feel safe to express yourself?
  2. What can you do to provide feedback in a supportive and respectful way?
  3. What can classmates do to help you hear and understand their feedback?
  4. If you were to write a list of rules for online etiquette, or "netiquette," what would be some of your rules?
  5. Finally, describe three ways to have a discussion online that enable members of the discussion to disagree respectfully.

In each discussion, for your **substantial response**, start a new **thread**. Please post one paragraph for each topic. Once you have posted your discussion, respond to other postings.

Online Classroom Management

Though e-communication is different from face-to-face communication, keep the human elements of communication in mind: your online class is an interactive process among people who have feelings and expectations. Communication is about building relationships based on trust and respect.

Stay in tune with your teammates' and professor's expectations by respecting ground rules and following best practices. Manage deadlines by setting internal due dates in advance of the deadlines your professor establishes.

Best Practices Online

To support the context of building relationships based on trust and respect, here are some **best practices** for online classes.

1. For all e-mail messages, use a *greeting* that includes the recipient's name; also include a *closing*.

```
┌──────────────────────────────────────────────────────────────┐
│  ┌────────┐   To ...      Professor Harris                    │
│  │  Send  │   Cc ...                                          │
│  └────────┘   Subject:    APA Formatting                      │
│  ───────────────────────────────────────────────────────     │
│                                                                │
│  Hi Professor Harris,                                          │
│                                                                │
│   Attached is my paper that I revised to demonstrate APA formatting. │
│                                                                │
│  Thank you for your assistance with this assignment.           │
│                                                                │
│  All the best,                                                 │
│                                                                │
│  Jasmine                                                       │
└──────────────────────────────────────────────────────────────┘
```

2. Always follow standard rules of grammar, punctuation, spelling, and capitalization.

3. Avoid using abbreviations and never use text message language in e-mail messages.

4. When you reply to a message, do not delete the *thread*. By leaving the history, your reader understands the context in which to reply to your message.

5. Update the subject line so that the recipient can file your message effectively.

6. When you send assignments as e-mail attachments, label your work correctly.

7. Respect all due dates: if you are not able to meet a due date, ask *in advance* for an extension.

8. Before you ask for help, read your syllabus, reading schedule, assignments, e-mail messages, and discussion descriptions ***two* or *three times***.

9. Read discussion instructions *before* you read an assigned chapter. Then read the chapter thoroughly, highlighting key points, taking notes, and jotting down your insights.

10. If you wish, compose your discussion response in Word and then copy and paste it to your online discussion.

11. When you save an assignment to Word, use the following format to label it: *your last name* and the specific assignment; separate each part with a dot (no spaces needed); for example:

Jordan.APA Formatting

12. Proofread and edit your writing carefully *before* you post.

13. Proofread and edit your writing carefully *again* after you post.

14. *Work independently*: try to figure things out on your own before asking questions. This approach prepares you for what will be expected in your profession.

15. Build your expertise in formatting; review Chapter 18, "Formatting" early on, paying special attention to setting paragraph controls and learning spacing guidelines.

16. Save and file all class communications; keep track of all of your assignments and grades.

17. Finally, keep human elements of online communication alive by respecting your classmates and professor: following protocol is one way to show respect.

In summary, adapt to what is expected:

o Know best practices and follow them.
o Use greetings and closings when you write an e-mail.
o *Never use text message language.*
o Label your assignments correctly.
o Try to figure things out before you ask for help.
o Post *in advance* of due dates.

Become confident in your ability to communicate effectively—the more you put into class, the more value you gain.

Contents

PART 1: ACADEMIC AND PROFESSIONAL WRITING

Throughout your career, you need to shape your writing for your reader, which includes adapting to the style that your audience expects.

In fact, unless you adapt your writing for your audience, you are not likely to achieve the best possible outcome. For example, you can write an outstanding paper full of insight and cutting-edge research; but if your paper is not properly *formatted*, your reader may give it only a passing glance and possibly not even a passing grade. That does not sound fair, does it? However, when you adapt your presentation (formatting) for your audience (readers), you are engaging in their system according to the rules defined for all. You are no exception.

To adapt your writing for your audience, you must become proficient in the different styles of writing and types of formatting that the various genres demand. In Chapter 6, "APA Citation Style," you learn how to format academic papers for your social work coursework. Later in this text, in Chapter 18, "Formatting," you learn how to format various types of business documents, such as e-mail, letters, memos, and reports—documents that you will use throughout your career.

Each of these first six chapters gives insight into how to adapt your writing and presentation (formatting) for the academic arena of social work.

Chapter 1, Academic Writing, examines scholastic writing and discusses the different modes of writing, from informative to argumentative writing.

Chapter 2, Documentation and Forms, reviews critical elements of documenting, including the types of information collected in the field and meeting the professional standards of governmental agencies and the legal system.

Chapter 3, Research and Evidence-Based Practice, provides insight into quantitative and qualitative research, going into detail about how to conduct and collect research as well as display it.

Chapter 4, Literature Review, offers a process for reviewing articles, indicating some of the details that need to be examined. Also included are templates for summarizing, comparing, and contrasting research articles.

Chapter 5, Critical Thinking and Reflective Practice, gives insight into the thinking-learning process and provides tools to enhance the learning process throughout academic studies and professional careers.

Chapter 6, APA Citation Style, explains and illustrates many elements of APA citation style. Guidelines and examples in this chapter (as well as Chapters 4, 18, and 21) demonstrate how to apply APA citation style to social work papers.

1

Academic Writing

Academic writing is a broad and varied topic: every discipline has its own culture, and writing at the undergraduate level differs somewhat from writing at the graduate level. However, in important ways, academic writing is no different from other types of writing: you shape your writing for purpose and audience, applying conventions for consistency and ease of communication.

Be aware that writing skills are a bit fickle: when you start writing in a new field, such as social work, you are likely to feel as if you are starting all over again. Even if writing feels challenging, with each document that you write, your social work terminology, documentation, and research skills become stronger.

As a social work student, you will learn to adapt your voice for the purpose of your writing and, in the process, develop various types of writing styles.

- *Reflective writing* includes case notes, academic conclusions, and journals; you include your own perceptions and insights. Some reflective writings also require you to support your thoughts and conclusions with evidence.

- *Informative or descriptive writing* summarizes information, decisions, positions, questions, and actions. Use descriptive writing when you write reports, summarize client interactions in case notes, and give details of research outcomes. Informative writing conveys complex ideas in a dispassionate style.

- *Persuasive writing* is analytical and aims to influence the reader and, at times, argues a position: the writer attempts to bring the reader to agree with his or her position. Most advanced academic writing is persuasive and adheres to a traditional format in the form of an *argument*.

Along with persuasive writing, all academic writing has an element of *analytical writing:* you are taking ideas and concepts apart, analyzing data, decisions, positions, and actions as well as asking questions in a dispassionate, non-adversarial way. Analytical writing involves coming to conclusions based on evidence, and *analytical thinking is a precursor to most academic writing*.

Let us now look further into the qualities of academic writing.

Academic Writing and Purpose

Academic writing is *scholastic or scholarly writing*; it is the most formal type of writing, adhering to high standards of accuracy. In the social sciences, writers must rigorously apply correct research and citation standards.

Academic writing strives for clarity and follows a traditional format in which the writer:

- Offers a central idea through a clear *introduction*,

- Develops the idea through well-supported *body paragraphs*, and

- Provides resolution in a *conclusion*.

Beginning academic writers practice their skills by writing essays and summaries. More advanced writing includes analysis, which prepares the way for analytical writing, arguments, and research papers. Before tackling an assignment, make sure that you understand the *purpose* of your assignment. Otherwise, you may write an exceptional paper, but one that does not meet your professor's criteria. For example, if your assignment calls for an *argument*, and instead you write an excellent *summary*, your grade is not likely to reflect your efforts.

Writing in academic disciplines fills many purposes, such as writing to inform, to analyze events and processes, to propose solutions, to examine varied concepts or viewpoints, to narrate events, and to argue positions. However, academic writing is not expressive writing: *at those times when you may share your emotions in your papers or reports, edit out your feelings.* In other words, in academia, the place for expressive writing is in your journals. (And a word of caution about writing expressively online: be selective about what you post, as your words may follow you throughout your career, costing you credibility and opportunity.)

Argumentation has a formal structure that appeals to logic and reason. When writing an argument, use evidence to develop a position that leads logically to a conclusion. However, every story has at least two sides; and at some point, a convincing argument must evaluate the strengths of the opposing view or views. Finally, the writer must provide *evidence* that demonstrates the opposition's weaknesses or flaws, revealing how the opposing view is inferior.

Some types of persuasive writing do not argue a point. Your aim may be to show only one side of a topic, convincing your reader to think the way that you do or persuading the reader to take action about an idea, a product, or a service. Persuasive writing uses reason, taps into the reader's emotions and, at times, involves ethics. *From a social work perspective, people need to be provided information and make their own decisions.*

In social work, you are expected to see various perspectives of an issue. For example, a parent may see drug use differently from the way her teenage child sees it. Or a politician's perspective on poverty may differ from the view of a client who receives financial assistance.

Though the substance of your writing is always more important than its form; if submitted in an incorrect form, documents can lose credibility or even be dismissed without being read. For academic papers, use APA citation style (see Chapter 6, "APA Citation Style"; also see Chapter 18, "Formatting").

Next, let us review how to develop a strategy to respond to questions.

Response Strategy

When you write papers or essays, you can shape an effective response by understanding what is expected on the basis of how a question is formulated. For example, the following key words indicate how to shape an effective response:

Analyze: Break into parts and show how they relate to the whole.

Argue: Give reasons for or against. Assess the strength of evidence on all sides, using examples and other criteria to back up your points.

Comment on: Write about main issues but avoid personal opinion.

Compare: Show the similarities and the differences. Is one more effective than the other?

Contrast: Show only the differences. Are the differences significant? Is one preferable over the other?

Describe: Write about a subject in detail, giving the main characteristics and features. Give enough detail so that your reader can develop a visual image.

Define: Give the exact meaning of something.

Discuss: Write about a subject in detail, giving reasons and examples.

Evaluate: Assess and give your opinion about something: does it work or not? Is it important or not? Are there gaps? Use evidence to support your judgment.

Explore: Examine thoroughly from various viewpoints.

Illustrate: Give details, examples, and evidence.

| *Justify:* | Give evidence to show why a conclusion was reached; answer objections. |
| *Summarize:* | Give the main points only; omit details and examples. |

Part of your writing strategy will be to use **transitions** effectively, which means using *conjunctions* effectively. Conjunctions give your reader signals about how to interpret the words that follow them.

Here are words and phrases that signal transitions for your reader:

Compare:	in the same way, in a similar fashion, likewise, as well as
Contrast:	however, in contrast, on the other hand, on the contrary, conversely, otherwise, nevertheless, still, yet, instead, although, while, but, even though
Cause and effect:	as a result, consequently, thus, therefore, for this reason, so
Illustrate:	for example, for instance, hence, in general, thus, mostly, specifically, to illustrate
Show results:	fortunately, unfortunately, consequently, as usual, of course, in fact, even more important, above all
Summarize:	finally, in brief, in closing, in summary, as a result, thus, therefore, hence, in short
Sequence:	first, second, third, finally, meanwhile, in the meantime, to begin with
Show time:	currently, earlier, immediately, in the future, in the meantime, in the past, later, meanwhile, previously
Conclude:	finally, in conclusion, in summary

As you give your essay a final edit, add these and other words to show transitions, making it easier for your reader to follow your line of thought.

Another element of academic writing is viewpoint.

Viewpoint and Voice

Viewpoint relates to *pronoun* usage and emanates from one of the following points of view: *first person, second person,* or *third person*; singular or plural.

As it applies to viewpoint and voice, here are some points about APA style (2010):

- If you are the sole author of a paper, you may refer to yourself as "I." If you coauthor a paper, you and your coauthors may refer to yourselves as "we."

- When referring to the author of a study, book, or article, use only the author's last name to avoid gender bias.

Though you may be comfortable writing in the first person (I, we) or second person (you), much of your academic writing will occur in the third person. For example, when you are summarizing an article, you are not speaking from *your* point of view; you are speaking from viewpoint of the *article's author*.

Let us say that you are writing a paper about sociologist Talcott Parsons. As you discuss Parsons, you would most effectively write from the *third person singular point of view*. In addition, when you discuss related topics, the *third person plural point of view* would be most effective (for example, *social systems*), for example:

Parsons argues that social systems are . . .

Parsons further concludes . . .

He maintains . . .

Social systems remain the central focus . . .

In the above, the reader is not addressed directly. Instead, the third person viewpoint focuses on the topic and what the article's author says about it. Writing from this viewpoint, you are limited in giving personal feelings or beliefs about a topic; you would connect to the reader in an indirect way, not a direct way.

For the most part, avoid using pronouns such as *I* and *you* in academic papers unless you are writing about your own research or the response part of a **summary-response essay**. When you speak from a personal viewpoint in an academic paper, take special care to edit out your personal opinions unless your views are part of a response or are supported by evidence.

As a result of not speaking from a personal voice, writers commonly use *passive voice*, and passive voice is widely accepted in academic writing. However, APA style recommends the use of the *active voice*, which becomes more easily accessible when writer are allowed, and even encouraged, to speak from the first person viewpoint, using the pronouns "I" and "we," as appropriate.

Extensive use of passive writing is also found among scientific writing. However, even scientists are turning to a more concise, active style, relying on the passive voice only to describe how an experiment was conducted, but otherwise applying the active voice (Tischer, 2009).

Be aware of your voice: Even for academic writing, use simple constructions for readability, keeping your writing clear and to the point. Rest assured, you will still sound intelligent, and even esteemed professors appreciate receiving papers that are readable.

Verb Signals

As you edit, make special effort to use strong verbs to signal an author's position. Here are some strong *signal verbs* to add variety to your writing:

admits	creates	organizes	remarks
argues	denies	observes	reports
asserts	emphasizes	persuades	solves
charges	expresses	points out	shows
claims	maintains	promotes	speculates
complains	finds	proposes	states
concedes	implies	proves	stresses
concludes	insists	refutes	suggests
conducts	interprets	reinforces	summarizes
contends	justifies	rejects	supports

Notice that the above verbs are listed in the third person singular, which is the $-s$ form, the most common viewpoint of academic writing.

Verb Tenses

Verb tense is used slightly differently in academic writing than writing in real time. For example:

- You could be citing research that was conducted decades ago and still make a comment such as, "Parsons *concludes* . . . ."

- As you write a description of your paper, stay in the present tense: instead of stating, "This paper *will explore* . . . ," instead state, "This paper *explores* . . . ."

In a literature review, if the discussion is of past events, stay within the chosen tense. Use past tense, such as "productivity increased" to describe the results. However, report *your* conclusions in the present tense, such as "The outcomes of the pilot indicate . . . ." Here are some points to consider:

- When emphasizing the findings of research, use the present tense:

    o   Jones shows . . .

- When emphasizing how the author conducted the research, use the past tense:

    o   Jones surveyed 20 participants . . .

- When contrasting research from different periods, use the past tense for older research and present tense for current research:

    o   Martin (2002) supported Jones' findings that training is a worthwhile investment for companies in transition.

- When describing situations that are conditional (which involve modals such as *would* or *could*), use the *subjunctive mood*:

    o   If the pilot *were* not conducted on site, the results *would* differ.

Use verbs to create smooth transitions among past, present, and future events. When you edit, screen your use of verb tense.

Structure for Academic Papers

Academic papers follow the general format of *introduction*, *body*, and *conclusion*. (See Figure 1.1, page 10.)

If you use anything more complicated as a framework, do not be obvious about it. For example, many students have successfully written the traditional 5-paragraph essay. This model is excellent for beginning writers, but college writing is more complex than the structure of a 5-paragraph essay can support.

As a writer, you need to speak from your own voice. Most topics cannot be plugged into tidy frameworks and still express an authentic perspective. College writing demands original, organic thinking that does not fit into a tight mold. Writing at its best is messy; and when writers clean up their work as they edit and revise, they do not seek parallel structure at the level of idea, insight, or concept.

Another element of structure is *formatting*. Always format papers precisely according to guidelines of the required style. For social work classes, format most papers according to APA citation style.

Figure 1.1. Structure for Academic Papers

Academic Papers

Introduction

In your introduction, state your purpose, making it relevant to your audience.

- Give an overview of the topic and state your thesis.
- Connect your topic to your audience.
- Pose questions about your topic:

    What am I writing about and why?

    What is my general purpose . . . my specific purpose?

    What are my main points?

    Who are my readers?

    How can I shape my writing for my audience?

Body

In the body of your paper, provide evidence. Focus on key points and give concrete examples; avoid generalizations not substantiated by fact.

- Break your topic into component parts.
- Provide evidence / examples / explanation.
- Support all main points thoroughly.

Conclusion

In your conclusion, restate your thesis and provide resolution for the problem that you are addressing. Answer the questions that you may have posed in the introduction, drawing conclusions for your reader. Finally, make sure that your conclusion sounds fresh, glancing forward to next steps, if relevant.

Note: Formatting is an important element of structure. Your final step in adapting your paper for your audience is formatting it according to the standards required for the project. Any paper that is not formatted correctly loses credibility *at a glance*. See Chapter 6, "APA Citation Style," and Chapter 18, "Formatting."

Thesis Statements

A **thesis statement** presents a paper's purpose, clarifying the problem that is being written about or the argument that is being made.

The thesis statement—generally a one- or two-sentence summary—unifies the content of the entire paper. The thesis statement is often presented toward the end of the first paragraph, which gives an overview of the paper. The body paragraphs present evidence to support the thesis, and the conclusion summarizes the results, tying back to the introduction and the thesis statement.

To identify your purpose, start by defining your problem:

What is my core question?

For example, let us say your task is to show how Jean Piaget's theory of cognitive development deepens your understanding of social work. Start by stating the problem as a question:

Thesis Question: How does Piaget's theory relate to social work?

Next, turn your question into statement:

> Piaget's theory of cognitive development reveals his perspective of the stages of human development in social environments that are nurturing and supportive.

Finally, once you understand some of the broader implications of your question, draft a statement that reflects your response:

Thesis Statement: Piaget's theory of cognitive development is a critical tool in developing social work theory and practice.

As you write about your purpose, avoid using the word *purpose*. For example, your first draft might include a statement such as the following:

> The purpose of this paper is to discuss how Jean Piaget's theory of cognitive development has influenced the field of social work.

When you revise your purpose statement, remove the word *purpose*:

> Jean Piaget's theory of cognitive development has influenced social work theory, in part, because it identifies four developmental stages of human development.

Let us turn one more problem into a thesis statement. For example, here is how you could work through the topic *alcohol addiction*:

Thesis Question: What does it mean to have an addiction to alcohol?

Thesis Statement: An addiction or dependence on alcohol affects many aspects of a person's life.

The thesis statement typically occurs somewhere in the first paragraph, which develops the thesis and gives an overview of the paper. (For more on paragraphs, see Chapter 9, "Cohesive Paragraphs and Transitions.")

Remain flexible with your writing. Your purpose is likely to change as your thinking becomes deeper and clearer. Writing is thinking on paper: as your thinking evolves so does your writing.

A tool to use to structure your ideas is the *peer model* described below. Use the model to stay focused on elements that you need to provide for your readers.

The PEER Model

The **peer model** helps you focus on the purpose of each part of your essay or paper. Use the model to ensure that you have developed all relevant aspects.

P   What is the *purpose*?
     What are the *key points* and why are they relevant?

E   What *evidence* demonstrates the main points?
     What are the facts and details?

E   What *explanation* or *examples* do readers need to understand the evidence and its significance?

R   How can you *resolve* your thesis for your readers?
     What key points provide a *recap*?
     What are your conclusions and *recommendations*?

If you loosely apply the peer model as you compose, your content will be somewhat structured before you revise. When you are composing, use these parts as side headings to rough out your ideas.

When you are revising, evaluate whether you have developed your topic adequately with specific evidence and examples. Would your evidence convince a person who was undecided about the topic?

Next are guidelines about how to shape an introductory paragraph for an academic paper.

Introductory Paragraph

The type of introductory paragraph that you write depends largely on the type of paper that you are writing.

In an introductory paragraph, state your purpose and give an overview of your paper. In addition, you may wish to pose questions about your topic to awaken your reader's curiosity, use a quotation to draw interest, or include another sort of attention-getter to engage your reader.

When you are writing a summary of another writer's work, give a complete reference in the introductory paragraph. For example, include the author's last name, the name of the article or book, and its purpose. The following is one possible template to use:

> In the article entitled "Facebook Addiction," Jones argues (or *asserts* or *reveals*) that ego casting is more prevalent than authentic communication.

Your introductory paragraph is one of the most important paragraphs of your paper or essay: first impressions make a difference. If the reader is immediately engaged, he or she will look to confirm a good impression while reading the remainder of the work. However, the opposite is also true. An unfavorable initial impression leaves the reader looking to confirm his or her original reaction.

Many writers find writing an introduction a difficult way to start the process and instead work through the body and conclusion first. Without giving too much thought, you might not see the value of this approach.

However, since the introduction gives an overview of your paper, an introduction is naturally easier to write once you have developed your line of thought. By writing your introduction as a last step, you can incorporate the insight that you gained as you worked through the body and conclusion.

Latin Terms for Academic Writing

Writers have traditionally used Latin terms in academic writing; in fact, Latin terms have played a major role in citation systems.

However, currently the APA (2010) advises that, other than *et al.*, Latin abbreviations should be used only in parenthetical material. Otherwise, the English translation should be used.

For your reference, here are a few commonly used Latin terms:

cf.	*confer:* compare to
e.g.	*exempli gracia*: for example, for instance
et al.	*et allii*: and others
	When listing only one author for a work with multiple authors, use *et al.* to indicate other names were omitted.
etc.	*et cetera:* and the others; and other things
ibid.	*ibidem*: in the same place
	In older articles, when citing the same source consecutively, *ibid.* was written directly under the citation which gave the author's name (or other identifying information).
i.e.	*id est*: that is; in other words
[*sic*]	so, thus, in this manner
	The term *sic* is placed within brackets to indicate that the error that occurs in a text was made by the original author, not the current writer. (Brackets [ ] are also used around words or letters added to another's quotation.)
viz.	*videlicet:* namely, that is (that is to say), as follows

In general, Latin terms are italicized because they are part of a foreign language. However, APA style does not recommend italicizing commonly used Latin terms.

Also, avoid using Latin abbreviations in other types of writing, such as business writing. In fact, using a term such as *among others* instead of using *etc.* gives writing a smoother, reader-friendly style.

Since professionals need to adapt their writing for various domains, the following discusses differences between academic writing and business writing.

Academic Writing Versus Professional Writing

Whereas academic writing is highly formal, professional writing is less formal, often labeled as business writing.

In academic writing, process is critical: process reveals to the reader how ideas are formed and explored. Defining for readers how a study was conducted contributes to its credibility. In contrast, in business and professional writing, data is almost always summarized concisely. In business, the details about how a writer arrives at outcomes are considered background thinking; those types of details are cut so that readers can get to the point and take action, as needed.

Professional writing in social work is primarily informative and includes process recordings, forms, reports, and social histories. For academic writing in social work, APA citation and formatting requirements are detailed and must be followed precisely.

In professional writing, the context of the situation defines the problem. When you write in business, you are writing as one human being to another, connecting on a personal level. Readers expect you to speak from your own voice, use evidence to support your views, and be respectful.

In academic writing, formality establishes a tone that contributes to the audience's ability to connect to the writing and the writer. The formality of academic writing gives readers shared expectations about quality and credibility and sets the tone that builds acceptance for your work.

Since professional writing (or business writing) is less formal, feel free to use contractions in e-mail, as long as they are spelled correctly. However, for formal academic writing, avoid using contractions, such as "don't" or "can't." As you can see, adapting to a specific audience aids you in shaping your writing to meet your readers' expectations.

Note: When using contractions for informal writing, *spell them correctly*; for example, leaving out the apostrophe for a contraction, such as spelling "can't" as "cant," is a serious misspelling that causes the writer to lose credibility instantly.

Recap

Academic writing requires that you write about topics for their merit, someone else's requirement, and their relevance to the profession. If you can embrace this requirement rather than resist it, writing becomes less stressful. In addition, by writing about a variety of topics, you become a more versatile writer and thinker.

Here are some of the points stressed in this chapter:

➢ Understand your assignment before you start writing.

➢ Write in the third person for most academic papers.

➢ Use strong verbs to signal an author's position.

➢ Use conjunctions and transitions to bring your reader's thinking along with yours.

➢ Follow a traditional format: present your central idea through a clear introduction, develop the idea through well-supported body paragraphs, and provide resolution in a conclusion.

➢ Allow time to edit your work, even when your writing is timed.

Writing Workshop

Part 1. Instructions: Select a paper that you wrote or exchange papers with a peer. Analyze the paper for *content*, *structure*, *style*, and *format* by answering the questions posed below.

Content

What mode of writing was applied: informative, expressive, persuasive, or a combination? Give reasons or examples to support your claim.

What was the original question? Did the paper answer that question effectively? Please explain.

Structure

What was effective about each part of the paper?

• Introduction

• Body

• Conclusion

What could the author do to improve each part?

Style

Comment on the author's use of each of the following:

• Signal Verbs

• Point of View

• Transition Words

Format

- Does the paper follow APA guidelines?
- Are the title page, running head, abstract, and reference page done correctly?
- Does the document reflect good use of white space and formatting features, as appropriate?

Take notes as you do your analysis so that you are prepared to complete part 2 of this assignment. (See *process message* below.)

Part 2. Instructions: Write your instructor a message describing what you discovered from analyzing your essay or paper.

This type of message is called a **process message** because you discuss your learning process, sharing insights you gleaned from completing the assignment. In short, you can also think of a process message as a *progress message*.

You can send your message through an e-mail. Make sure to use a greeting and a closing; for details about how to format your message, see pages 310 to 311.

Send	To ...	Professor Tamburro
	Cc ...	
	Subject:	Paper Analysis – Process Message

Hi Professor Tamburro,

For this week's assignment, I worked on a paper that I had written for my Introduction to Sociology class.

Some of the ways that I could have improved my paper would have been to state my purpose more clearly in the introduction and then to provide more evidence to support my thesis. These changes would have led to a stronger conclusion that tied back into my introduction.

I made some errors in the APA style, which could easily be corrected by revising my headings and correcting some of my references. In addition, other ways to improve the paper would include . . .

References

American Psychological Association [APA]. (2010). *Publication manual of the
American Psychological Association* (6th ed.). Washington, DC: Author.

Tischer, M. (2009). *Scientific writing booklet*. Department of Biochemistry
and Molecular Biophysics, University of Arizona. Retrieved from
http//www.biochem.arizona.edu/marc/sci-writing

Andrea Tamburro, MSW, EdD, contributed to this chapter.

COACHING TIP

Finding Your Voices:

Personal, Professional, and Academic

To adapt your voice for your audience, tune in to *pronoun viewpoint.*

- When you write from your *personal voice*, you are expressing your feelings and opinions. Use your personal voice when you write in a journal or use the DEAL Model (see pages 84-85). When you speak from your personal voice, feel free to use the personal pronoun "I" (which, by the way, is always capitalized).

- When you write from your *professional voice*, you are connecting with your clients through simple, clear, concise writing. Use your professional voice when you write e-mail messages, business letters, and memos. Limit your use of the *I* **point of view**, shifting to the *you* **point of view** when possible. (See Coaching Tip, page 226.)

- When you write from your *academic voice*, you are writing in the most formal way, taking ideas and concepts apart, analyzing data, decisions, positions, and actions as well as asking questions in a dispassionate, non-adversarial way. For the most part, use the **third person point of view**.

As you see, an element of voice is pronoun usage. In addition, for professional and academic writing, *formatting is also an element of voice: formatting speaks to readers at a glance.* Learn early on how to format e-mail messages so that you connect effectively with your reader; also learn early on how to cite and format in APA style.

➢ For more information on *pronoun viewpoint and consistency*, see Chapter 13, "Pronouns."
➢ For more information on formatting, see Chapter 6, "APA Citation Style," and Chapter 18, "Formatting."

Compose freely—clarify your voice when you edit.

2

Documentation and Forms

By Marshelia Harris, MSW

In social work, the saying, "If it is not written, it did not happen," speaks to the urgency of maintaining strong documentation in the field.

Social workers must have strong writing skills to document formally their experiences and interactions with clients. Recording information professionally is a critical part of the job. Social workers are placed in several roles when assisting clients with services. To keep a good record of these interactions and roles, social workers must submit well-written forms and documents for the agency and for external service providers and collaborators.

Depending on the case, social workers are required to submit formal written reports to various entities. Routinely these reports are sent to the courts, medical community, criminal justice department, and other agencies as part of a case file that serves as an official document. The reports are used to assist in decision making for the client's well-being and to provide services or resources.

Formal reports may include a written document or a form, such as a client treatment plan, a social history, an integrated assessment, a clinical summary or recommendations, and general case notes. These reports and forms may be based on observations, theories, and behaviors as well as mental, physical, and health issues about the client.

In most states, the guidelines of the accreditation or governing body require social workers to update the client's file continually until the client is no longer eligible for services or the client's case is officially closed. However, closed records can be subpoenaed by the courts, and documents can be reviewed as required.

Social workers must provide professionally written documentation in the beginning of their career because it remains as a permanent record and may be reviewed in later years.

National Association of Social Work (NASW)

The social work profession is guided by the NASW *Code of Ethics*. These professional ethics are at the core of social work. The profession has an obligation to articulate its basic values, ethical principles, and ethical standards.

The NASW *Code of Ethics* sets forth these values, principles, and standards to guide social workers' conduct. The code is relevant to all social workers and social work students, regardless of their professional functions, the settings in which they work, or the populations they serve (NASW, 2008).

Let us review a few of the standards that support the need for professional documentation when providing services to a client.

Note: The word "clients" refers to individuals, families, groups, organizations, and communities.

NASW Standards

Several of the NASW standards that apply directly to documenting in the field are presented and discussed on the following pages. In the field of social work, the importance of correct, clear writing cannot be overemphasized, as people's lives depend on the accuracy.

NASW Standard 1.01. Commitment to Clients

> Social workers' primary responsibility is to promote the wellbeing of clients. In general, clients' interests are primary. However, social workers' responsibility to the larger society or specific legal obligations may on limited occasions supersede the loyalty owed clients, and clients should be so advised. (Examples include when a social worker is required by law to report that a client has abused a child or has threatened to harm self or others.)

Social workers must submit a written report to the court detailing the client's progress and making recommendations on the client's behalf.

On the next page is a court summary that a social worker presented on behalf of a client.

Figure 2.1. Court Summary

Social workers submit a written report to the court detailing the client's progress and making recommendations on the client's behalf.

Court Summary

Janet Swanson is a 17-year-old African American female, date of birth January 7, 1996. Janet is currently residing in a foster care placement at 1234 Main Street, with Sally Jackson, foster caregiver.

Janet entered the foster care system at the age of 10 when her parents died in a tragic car accident on January 30, 2006. Janet was placed in two foster care placements prior to being placed with Ms. Jackson. Each of those placements was disrupted due to Janet's anger issues and her threatening behavior towards the foster caregivers.

Janet was placed in an older teen foster home with Ms. Jackson on May 1, 2012 and was required to attend anger management therapy. Ms. Jackson reports that Janet's anger issues have decreased and the communication between the two of them has increased. Ms. Jackson is working directly with Janet's school counselor to prepare Janet for college enrollment in fall 2013. Janet has expressed interest in attending state university, and Ms. Jackson has agreed to allow Janet to return to her home on school breaks and holidays.

The agency supports Ms. Jackson's request for Janet to return to her home on school breaks and holidays, and to remain as the foster care placement for Janet until she turns 21.

NASW Standard 1.07. Privacy and Confidentiality

a. Social workers should respect clients' right to privacy. Social workers should not solicit private information from clients unless it is essential to providing services or conducting social work evaluation or research. Once private information is shared, standards of confidentiality apply.

b. Social workers may disclose confidential information when appropriate with valid consent from a client or a person legally authorized to consent on behalf of a client.

c. Social workers should protect the confidentiality of all information obtained in the course of professional service, except for compelling professional reasons. The general expectation that social workers will keep information confidential does not apply when disclosure is necessary to prevent serious, foreseeable, and imminent harm to a client or other identifiable person. In all instances, social workers should disclose the least amount of confidential information necessary to achieve the desired purpose; only information that is directly relevant to the purpose for which the disclosure is made should be revealed.

d. Social workers should inform clients, to the extent possible, about the disclosure of confidential information and the potential consequences, when feasible before the disclosure is made. This applies whether social workers disclose confidential information on the basis of a legal requirement or client consent.

Before disclosing any confidential information about a client, a social worker would obtain a signed *consent form* from the client. For example, disclosing confidential information without a signed consent form would not only be a breach of confidence but also possibly a breach of the law.

NASW Standard 1.08. Access to Records

a. Social workers should provide clients with reasonable access to records concerning the clients. Social workers who are concerned that clients' access to their records could cause serious misunderstanding or harm to the client should provide assistance in interpreting the records and consultation with the client regarding the records. Social workers should limit clients' access to their records, or portions of their records, only in exceptional circumstances when there is compelling evidence that such access would cause serious harm to the client. Both clients' requests and the rationale for withholding some or all of the record should be documented in clients' files.

b. When providing clients with access to their records, social workers should take steps to protect the confidentiality of other individuals identified or discussed in such records.

The information provided in the client's file should be truthful and documented correctly. The file must be edited to protect the confidentiality of other individuals identified or discussed before it can be provided to the client for review. The client can review the file in the office but should not leave the office with the file.

NASW Standard 3.04. Client Records

a. Social workers should take reasonable steps to ensure that documentation in records is accurate and reflects the services provided.

b. Social workers should include sufficient and timely documentation in records to facilitate the delivery of services and to ensure continuity of services provided to clients in the future.

c. Social workers' documentation should protect clients' privacy to the extent that is possible and appropriate and should include only information that is directly relevant to the delivery of services.

d. Social workers should store records following the termination of services to ensure reasonable future access. Records should be maintained for the number of years required by state statutes or relevant contracts.

Let us next examine some of the forms and reports used in a case file that social workers may be required to complete when working with the client. Suggestions are provided on how to write detailed notes and collect correct information from the client.

Social History

The *social history* is the client's formal record that details background, family relationships, special needs, mental illness or medical conditions. It explains in great detail how the client came into the system and the presenting issues.

The social history can be used in several ways, such as tracking the number of placements and providing critical data about the family. The primary use is for placement agencies to make a decision on whether or not the client is suitable for services available through the agency. This decision is based on fit and availability as well as the client's physical, emotional, and medical needs.

Figure 2.2. Social History

Social workers write up a social history. Below is an example of the "Hale" family's social history.

The Hale family first came to the attention of the Department of Children Services in 1987 when natural mother Janet Hale gave birth to Adrianna Smith, who was born drug exposed. In September 1991, Janet gave birth to Helen Johnson, who was also born drug exposed. Followed by these two births, two more children were born drug exposed, Terrence Johnson in 1994 and Trent Davis in 1995. The drugs of choice for Janet Hale are cocaine and heroin.

The four children were placed in the home of Beatrice Grambling, paternal grandmother, in 1999 and she was later granted guardianship in 2000 of all of the children. In 2003, Adrianna Smith was sexually molested by Mr. Booth, the paramour of Ms. Grambling, and living in the home with all of the children. When Janet Hale learned of the incident, Ms. Hale took Adrianna to the police station, where it was discovered that Adrianna had belt welts and bruises all over her body. It was also discovered later at the hospital that Adrianna had been sexually molested as originally stated. The hotline was called and the case was indicated. All of the children, Adrianna Smith, Helen Johnson, Terrence Johnson, and Trent Davis were removed from Ms. Grambling's home in September 2003. The children were placed in the home of an Aunt, Jackie Collins, the sister of Janet Hale.

According to Adrianna, she had "a great relationship with Aunt Jackie." Things began to change as Adrianna began to develop a "womanly shape" and the arguments began. Jackie eventually accused Adrianna of flirting with her paramour, Jim Scott. Adrianna stated, "I could not take it anymore so I ran away." Adrianna is now 16 years old, 3 months pregnant, and homeless. She is in need of immediate shelter and services.

After reading the social history, the social worker must determine the immediate needs of the individual identified as the client. In the case discussed in Figure 2.2 on page 25, *the client is Adrianna, and her immediate needs are a home, prenatal care, medical services, possibly education, and support.* Once Adrianna's needs are determined, the social worker must select an agency that can provide effective services for Adrianna.

New Client Intake

The new client intake form requires the social worker at the new placement agency to complete basic identifying information such as name, birthdate, age, gender, weight, height, address, parents' names and ages, and sibling data along with a basic description of the presenting problem or need. (See Figure 2.3 on page 27.)

New clients are assigned to a case worker who will review the client's file, take the social history, and create a plan of action with the client. The case worker may also work with the therapist to develop a treatment plan. A treatment plan will identify goals, objectives, and tasks that should be completed within a certain timeframe, such as 30, 45, 60, or 90 days, based on the agencies policies and procedures.

Figure 2.3. New Client Intake Form

New Client Intake Form

Client Name Adriana Smith   Case No. AS1234567   Age: 17

Date of Birth _____ Ethnicity _____

Gender _____ Pregnant / Parenting _____ Number of Children _____

Weight _____ Height _____ Eye Color _____ Hair Color _____

Identifying Marks or Scars: _____

Parents Name and Age: _____

_____

Number of Siblings	Sibling Names	Sibling Ages	Sibling Placement/Address

Current Address: _____

_____

Previous Placement Address: _____

_____

Immediate Needs or Presenting Problems: _____

_____

_____

Staff Completing Form   Date

Treatment Plan

The next step in the process involves developing a treatment plan in conjunction with the client. To record the results in a uniform way, social workers fill out a treatment plan that becomes part of the client's records.

Figure 2.4. Treatment Plan

Client Name: Adriana Smith	ID No.: AS1234567	
Date of Birth:	Age: 17	
Case Worker:	Date of Plan:	
Goal 1 – Prenatal Care / Medical Services	**Target Date**	**Outcomes / Results**
Task 1: Locate free medical clinic for prenatal care	Within the month	
Task 2: Schedule regular appointments with clinic	Within the month	
Task 3: Take prenatal vitamins	Immediately	
Goal 2 – Increase Parenting Skills	**Target Date**	**Outcomes / Results**
Task 1: Attend parenting classes	Within 3 months	
Task 2: Create a birthing plan	Within 3 months	
Task 3: Learn information about stages of child development	Within 6 months	

Case Notes

Case notes are professional records of the case worker's interaction with the client, providing a documentation of what was discussed, agreed upon, or unresolved with the client. Case notes serve as proof of the case worker's contact with the client and whether or not the client is compliant with services.

Within the last few years, case notes have moved from being handwritten to being documented using a computerized template. This change allows the case worker to be more efficient when writing notes.

Figure 2.5. Case Notes

Client Name:	
ID No.	Date of Birth
Case Worker Name: Date of Interaction:	
Case Notes:	

The client's file is a permanent record that is fluid and moves with the client to each new placement or location. The file is used to document various types of information, such as the client's history, diagnosis, treatment plan, medications, and progression toward goals.

Great documentation can assist the court with making good decisions on behalf of the client. However, poor documentation may result in the court making uninformed decisions that may eventually hurt the client.

In the case study above with Adriana Smith, poor documentation resulted in the case being handled differently. For example, rather than documenting the case as presented in Figure 2.2, page 25, the social history was written as follows:

> The four children were placed in the home of *B. Grambling, grandmother*, in 1999 and she was later granted guardian-ship in 2000 of all of the children. In 2003, Adrianna Smith stated she was sexually molested by Mr. Booth, the paramour of Ms. Grambling, and living in the home with all of the children. *Ms. Grambling did not believe Adrianna and told this worker that Adrianna "lies often." Adrianna seems to be well taken care of and does not seem to suffer from any problems at this time.*

Based on the above, the court found this placement to be suitable for Adrianna and allowed her to stay in the home for two more years, where she was repeatedly sexually abused by Mr. Booth.

Now compare the documentation in Figure 2.2, page 25, with the above documentation. What problems can you identify in the above information?

1. The full name of the grandmother was not listed.

2. The relationship of the grandmother was not identified.

3. There was not a formal report of sexual abuse made by the case worker.

4. Neither the case worker nor the grandmother took the client to the hospital for a physical exam to confirm the sexual abuse.

5. The case worker did not call the hotline to report the sexual abuse or discuss it further with the client.

6. The court was unaware of the allegations and the sexual abuse due to the poor documentation by the case worker.

Once the case was transferred to a new worker, Adrianna was properly examined and immediately moved to a new foster care placement. By then, Adrianna had experienced serious psychological and emotional damage resulting from Mr. Booth's sexual abuse and Ms. Grambling's denial. The case worker's poor documentation and incompetence resulted in damaging the client unnecessarily.

Recap

Accurate, complete documentation is essential in the field of social work. The paperwork tells the story of the client by advocating for services and showing progression towards the identified goals. Strong and thorough documentation is used as a measure for great and efficient social workers.

Writing Workshop

Part 1. Instructions: Write your instructor a message describing what you learned about documentation in the field. Also discuss the role that writing plays in the profession.

You can send your message through an e-mail or write a memo and print it out. (For details about how to format your message, see pages 310 to 312.)

This type of message is called a **process message** because you discuss your learning process, sharing insights you learned from completing your assignment. You can also think of a process message as a *progress message*.

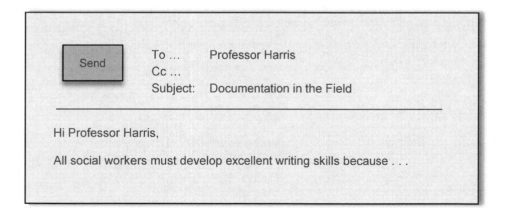

Send

To ...   Professor Harris
Cc ...
Subject: Documentation in the Field

Hi Professor Harris,

All social workers must develop excellent writing skills because . . .

Reference

National Association of Social Workers [NASW]. (2008). *Code of ethics of the*

National Association of Social Workers. Retrieved from

http://www.socialworkers.org/pubs/code/code.asp

Marshelia Harris, MSW, wrote this chapter.

COACHING TIP

Use Gender-Neutral and Unbiased Language

The NASW Press Guidelines for Describing People (2011) advises how to use language to respect diversity and avoid bias:

1. Do not specify sex unless it is a variable or is essential to the discussion.
2. Do not label people; refer to people as *people*, not as objects; for example, *people with disabilities*, not *the disabled*.
3. Be specific about age, race, and culture.

Outdated	Revised or Alternative
policeman	police officer
waiter/waitress	food server or wait staff
stewardess	flight attendant
salesman	sales representative
mankind	humankind
chairman	chairperson

Biased Language	Revised or Alternative
schizophrenics	people who have schizophrenia
challenged	people who have challenges
high-risk groups	high-risk behavior
AIDS victims	people with AIDS
minority	*state what the population prefers to be called*

Labels	Revised or Alternative
wheelchair-bound	uses a wheelchair
the elderly or the aged	elderly people
the lower class	people who are poor
the blind	people who are blind

For more information, see *NASW Press Guidelines for Describing People*: http://naswpress.org/authors/guidelines/08c-tools.html

3

Research and
Evidence-Based Practice

Evidence-based practice is essential for effective social services. Through research, you gain a better understanding of the needs of the communities and client systems, people you will work with. Through research, you also find resources to help your clients.

You can research information about their cultures and effective approaches for treatment through literature reviews on a particular topic. For example, you are working with a native *Hawai'i an* family. They talk about the island that was their home as well as some of the problems that they experience adjusting to your community, which is on the mainland.

Through research you can learn more about their homeland, how other native *Hawai'i an* people have adjusted to living on the mainland, and what community resources are available. You can also review specific approaches that social service providers have found to be effective in helping native *Hawai'i ans* adjust to their new homes.

Some information you need to help this family may not be in the literature. Now you have found a gap in the literature, and your experience with the family may help fill it. Thus, once you have worked with this family, you may want to share what you learned with the academic and service provider community. With their permission, maintaining confidentiality, you write about your experience helping this family. As a result, your experience might help the next practitioner provide more effective services to another *Hawai'i an* family who is relocating.

Research

Research is an organized attempt to answer a specific question: *the goal of scientific research is to explain, predict, and/or control phenomena.* Valid and reliable research is respected by professionals because the results provide accurate information, reduce misleading assumptions, and point social service providers onto a more genuine and accurate path.

While this chapter provides a brief overview of research, additional research courses will provide more in-depth knowledge and experience in the area. This chapter introduces these elements of research:

- *Collecting research* through a review of the literature.

- *Conducting research* through quantitative, qualitative and mixed (using both) methods.

- *Displaying research* through graphs and charts.

Acquiring new knowledge requires suspending beliefs and opinions and looking for evidence to help better understand a situation or dilemma. In part, the process involves becoming a self-reflective, critical thinker who questions and avoids assumptions and personal biases.

When you use research and evidence to shape the way you think and act, your decisions become clearer; your outcomes become more helpful to clients. The key is letting the research lead you to your conclusions rather than having your opinions, faith, or beliefs determine the conclusions of your research.

The scientific method of research relies on logical reasoning, supported by evidence. The Council on Social Work Education (CSWE), the accrediting body for social work programs, has identified research as an essential core competency.

> Engage in research-informed practice and practice-informed research. Social workers understand quantitative and qualitative research methods and their respective roles in advancing a science of social work and in evaluating their practice. Social workers know the principles of logic, scientific inquiry, and culturally informed and ethical approaches to building knowledge. Social workers understand that evidence that informs practice derives from multi-disciplinary sources and multiple ways of knowing. They also understand the processes for translating research findings into effective practice. Social workers:
> - use practice experience and theory to inform scientific inquiry and research;
> - apply critical thinking to engage in analysis of quantitative and qualitative research methods and research findings; and
> - use and translate research evidence to inform and improve practice, policy, and service delivery. (CSWE EPAS, p. 8, 2015)

Therefore, learning to understand, engage in, and write about research in a professional social work program is essential.

Collecting and Conducting Research

There are three types of research: *observation* along with *quantitative* and *qualitative methods*. Here is a brief explanation so that you can understand the basics of each.

- *Observation* involves directly observing to better understand a situation or circumstances. For example, observing a student in a classroom gives insight into the context, the interaction among the students and teachers, and the behavior of the child.

- *Quantitative research* collects numerical data to explain, predict, and/or control phenomena of interest. This form of research utilizes deductive reasoning and empirical methods to explore human experiences. For example, you decide you want to know more about how people recover from an alcohol addiction. Let us say your research includes surveying 1,000 people who were once addicted to alcohol and have been sober for at least a year. If they use a numerical scale (1-5) to rate methods of recovery, you have numerical data to find which methods these people found the most effective.

- *Qualitative research* collects narrative data to gain insight into phenomena of interest. This form of research utilizes inductive reasoning. For example, after you have surveyed the group of people who have recovered from alcohol addiction, you realize that the numerical outcomes have provided an overview but have not answered all of your questions. So you interview 25 of these people to explore in more detail how and why some of the methods of recovery worked better than others.

The primary goal of social work research is to understand and have an impact on individuals, groups, families, communities, and society. Understanding research methods is essential for evaluating academic journal articles that guide your practice.

> Think of the last quantitative or qualitative research journal article that you read.
> - *Did you agree with the findings?*
> - *Did you find flaws in how the research was conducted or fallacies in conclusions the authors made?*
> - *How did the research help shape your thinking?*

Quantitative Research

Quantitative research uses numbers to interpret information (data); for example gathering and analyzing information to decide which policy to support, what treatment approaches to use, or which method might be most effective.

Quantitative research includes experiments, polls, and questionnaires that include a large number of people, and the results can be generalized (applied to larger groups of people). Some quantitative research involves predictability: did an event happen by chance or does a causal relationship exist? To determine probability, research starts with a question, which when turned into a statement can become a *hypothesis*:

- A **hypothesis** is an explanation that can be tested.

Let us assume you are exploring methods to help smokers quit smoking. Two popular methods include nicotine replacement and the use of antidepressants. Your basic question might be, *which treatment method is most effective for smoking cessation?* Here is one way your hypothesis could be written:

Hypothesis: Nicotine replacement is more effective than antidepressants in helping smokers stop smoking.

Researchers use *probability theory* (a branch of statistics) to test a hypothesis to determine if a causal relationship exists. According to probability theory, research can support that it was *unlikely* something happened due to chance, but not the likelihood. Therefore, to conduct research, a researcher needs to nullify the hypothesis, which does not support the positive statement. As a **null hypothesis**, our example could be written in either of the following ways:

Null Hypothesis: Nicotine replacement is not more effective than antidepressants in helping smokers stop smoking.

Null Hypothesis: Nicotine replacement is equally effective as antidepressants in helping smokers stop smoking.

When the probability level (usually preset at 95 or 99 percent) shows that our null hypothesis can be rejected, our hypothesis is supported: the higher the probability, the stronger the correlation. (You can find a statistical table that lists probability levels in any statistics book or online by searching "probability table.")

To identify predictability, quantitative researchers often apply the **scientific method** to design an experiment. This experiment would include a control group and an experimental group.

For example, let us suppose that you are working with teens who have been suspended from school for fighting at least three times. To half of the group, you will teach communication and problem-solving skills; the other half of the group will participate in a support group.

The researcher would write a hypothesis theorizing (predicting) expectations from the study. The hypothesis could be stated as follows:

Hypothesis: The students who are taught communication and problem-solving skills will gain more effective anger management skills and have a lower percentage of suspensions for fighting than the students in the support group.

Then the hypothesis would be turned into a null hypothesis stating that differences were *not* expected:

Null Hypothesis: The students who are taught communication and problem solving skills will gain less effective anger management skills and receive the same or greater percentage of suspensions for fighting as the students in the support group.

Here are the basics of the experimental design:

1. The record for the number of suspensions in each group would be determined.

2. Both groups would take a **pretest** to measure their anger management skill level.

3. One group would meet for six weeks to learn communication and problem-solving skills. The other group would meet in a support group.

4. After six weeks, each group would take the **posttest** to measure their anger management skills. Pretest and posttest results would be tabulated and analyzed.

5. After the six-week treatment, the number of suspensions in each group would be tracked for the next two months. After the frequency of suspension for fighting data is analyzed, the suspension rates would be compared.

If the experimental group scored significantly lower, probability would help determine if the differences occurred due to chance or were a result of the treatment. (Of course, the research design would be more detailed than what is given here, but these are the basics.)

Quantitative research is rigorously applied in social work, health care, sociology, psychology, education, the social and physical sciences, business, and economics.

Qualitative Research

Qualitative researchers gather information through observations, focus groups, interviews, historical data, and stories. Qualitative research identifies beliefs, experiences, and perceptions.

Social workers may use qualitative research to better understand a particular client population, such as Hispanic teens under the age of 14 who are pregnant. Qualitative research does not try to determine a cause and effect relationship but instead seeks to explore, describe experiences, and identify patterns.

As a result of client feedback, agencies may design or alter their services and change their policies. Qualitative research provides rich descriptions of a particular event, population, or situation. The outcomes cannot be generalized to other groups or populations. However, the *reliability* of the research can be evaluated by sharing the outcomes with the people who were interviewed and including their interpretation of the data that is published.

Reliability and Validity

Social workers look for studies that are reliable and valid. R*eliability* and *validity* are basic to understanding the quality of research.

- *Reliability* relates to consistency of measure; for example, if the same study is repeated several times and the outcomes are the same, then it is reliable.

- *Validity* refers to whether the study examines what it is intended to examine.

The previous example of research on smoking cessation can give insight into the meaning of reliability and validity. Let us say that a researcher found that in the first group or sample of 100 smokers, that 75 percent successfully used nicotine replacement to stop smoking; and then, the same study was repeated two, three, or more times on other sample groups. If the results were similar, the results would be *reliable*.

To assess validity, questions on the survey would be tested to verify if the questions actually revealed whether those surveyed had actually stopped smoking, had used nicotine replacement products, and had not used other methods of smoking cessation.

Also, validity might be tested by measuring the information using a different method and comparing the results. For example, you might use the survey and also have participants keep a journal. Since the participants might forget details in the time between a pretest and a posttest, they would describe the methods they used and the effectiveness of each method in the journal. If the outcomes from the journal are similar to the outcomes of the survey, then your survey is *valid*.

Here are examples of how these two terms are used:

- Our research results are *reliable*: we are confident that you can test a larger population and get the same results.
- The questions on our survey have been tested extensively and have been shown to be *valid*.
- When research results are *reliable* and *valid*, they can be reproduced and used with confidence.
- Qualitative research may have internal validity due to rigorous research methods. However, the same study may not have external validity because few people participated in the study. As a result, the results could not be generalized to different groups.

In addition to reliability and validity, another critical factor is *credibility*.

Credible Research

A goal of all research, quantitative or qualitative, is an attempt to obtain clear outcomes that are supported by the data.

- Credible research does *not* take a position and then seek evidence to confirm it.
- Credible research asks a question and then attempts to evaluate if the evidence and data support the conclusions.

The key to valid research starts with an open mind about a topic. A researcher may have a hunch or gut feeling (which may be the catalyst for the research); but to be valid, outcomes must be supported by the data. You are most likely to find credible research in academic journals that have peer-evaluated (juried) articles.

Everyone has biases, and it is not always easy to identify them. Peer review and discussion help identify biases in writing as well as strengths and weaknesses of each project.

Thus, do not take research data at face value. To challenge research findings, examine the research for biases. Also see if the authors identify any biases or promote specific perspectives.

Can you identify your biases? Social workers are expected to become aware of their biases and manage them effectively. For example, if a researcher who supports the use of birth control engages in research that demonstrates the positive and negative effects of birth control, her or his biases are likely to be integrated into the article. If that article is sponsored and placed on Planned Parenthood's website, the bias becomes clear, and the reader needs to consider those biases. Comparing the outcomes of several studies can help identify biases.

Here are the types of questions to ask:

- Could intervening variables (other people, things, or events) have interfered with the research, leading to inaccurate results?

- Were the samples (people surveyed or items examined) an accurate representation of the people being studied?

- Did the researcher identify the strengths and weaknesses of the research?

- Was the research poorly constructed, biased, contaminated, and thus invalid?

- Could a profit motive be involved? For example, who paid for the research of the smoking cessation experiment?

Even theories confirmed through the best quantitative research are useful only to the extent that current knowledge confirms their effectiveness; they are not final truths. As knowledge changes over time, some theories fall to the wayside. Have you ever seen the results of research confirmed only to find out later that the research was inaccurate or invalid?

Though the Internet has valuable resources, you do not have access to older research online, and not all online sources are credible. In fact, anyone can say anything through a website without evidence to support views or information. The value of information relates to the credibility of the author or organization publishing it, but no authority screens information posted on the Web.

The biggest issue related to a website's credibility is bias (which is the same issue that invalidates research findings). The most used websites for social work research include governmental and social service websites; for example, census results.

Here are some ways that bias misleads:

- For financial profit, a site may present or highlight only select research; in other words, the site leaves out research that negates the site's position. For example, the tobacco industry reported many studies that smoking was safe before the Surgeon General and unbiased researchers were able to show that it was not safe.

- The author may present opinions and beliefs but not evidence based on research.

- The site may represent a conflict of interest without making the conflict known.

Therefore, you cannot be sure that every website or news report provides a balanced, accurate perspective on your topic. This skewed information can affect your views, especially if you were leaning in that direction already. Use academic literature to decide which sources to use and which ones to avoid.

To be credible, your research must include information from academic sources, reputable and *established* publishing houses, juried journals, associations, organizations, and governmental reports.

A thorough review of the literature includes all types of sources. Use print and electronic sources as well as microfilm or microfiche.   In addition to books and periodicals, many websites contain important and useful information. However, *some* online sources are not credible: for the most part, anyone can post anything on the Web; it is up to the reader to use discretion and be selective.

To ensure the credibility of online sources, follow these tips:

1. Look for governmental and academic sites such as the U.S. Bureau of Labor Statistics. (In other words, individuals or private organizations are likely to have biases.)

2. Identify how long the site has been in operation; the longer, the better.

3. Identify how often the site is updated. Some sites are posted and left unchanged for years.

4. Check to see if the site is linked to other sites that you consider reputable.

5. Evaluate whether the site provides information to answer your questions accurately and objectively.

6. If you use a site such as Wikipedia, which can be helpful as an overview, make sure to examine and read the original documentation that supports what is stated; cite original documentation in your research, not Wikipedia.

7. Non-profit sites, which often end in "org"; they may provide useful information but check out the accuracy through academic sites.

8. Avoid blogs, opinion sites, and for-profit sites (ending in "com").

Also consider the following:

1. Use sources your library has already screened *before* you put your topic into an outside search engine. (Your library has screened many sources through online subscriptions, data bases, and CD-ROMs.)

2. Compare how information on a website meshes with the print materials in your research. (Since print materials are scrutinized heavily during the publishing process, online sources that validate those sources can be considered more seriously.)

3. Discuss your source with your local librarian if you have a question.

Though you may start your research online, use your online sampling as an entrée to books and periodicals that provide substance and balance. What your library does not carry in hard copy or online subscriptions, it may carry in the form of microfilm or microfiche. Libraries also request material for you through inter-library loan—one more reason to start your research early.

Action Research

The types of qualitative research that you are likely to use are *surveys*, *focus groups*, and *interviews*. A qualitative approach to research can be used as *action research*. Action research is a method which assists the researcher in collecting information to use in an immediate application. Thus, the researcher takes action as the improved understanding (or research) occurs.

According to Gay and Airasian (2003), action research is carried out in a *cyclical* manner; here are the four basic steps of action research:

1. *Identifying a problem* or question,
2. *Conducting a meeting* or brainstorming session to gain information,
3. *Analyzing research data* or information, and
4. *Taking action* to help resolve the problem or better understand the question.

In addition to the four steps above, action researchers use an additional step: *evaluating how effective their efforts were to make change and determining their next steps.*

Action research provides feedback to assist in making decisions that lead to effective change. In addition, action research can involve both quantitative (numbers, statistics) and qualitative (feelings, beliefs, opinions) data.

To improve results, consider ways you can include action research in your personal and professional life. For example, to improve team communications, ask for feedback about what works well and what creates barriers to progress. This informal type of exploration can make a difference.

> *How does conducting action research differ from problem-solving in general? What are ways that you can incorporate action research into how you solve problems or make decisions?*

Interviews

Individual interviews consume more time than other types of qualitative research and provide information only within the context of the circumstances; in other words, the information generated relates to only a few people.

The purpose of the interview is to gain better understanding of the experiences, interests, and perceptions of the people being interviewed. The interviewer listens and accurately reports the voices of the people whose stories they are compiling, analyzing, and perhaps publishing.

Interviews are useful when working with a small population of 20 or fewer people. For example, assume you are working with a group of volunteers and you want to better understand why they volunteer in your agency. You would talk to (interview) each volunteer asking the same questions. Once you had interviewed them, you would look for themes and interests, organizing the data in a way that would work best for your agency. You could also use what you learned to enhance the volunteer experience, helping to retain volunteer participation in the agency.

Effective listening skills are at the core of interviewing skills. An interview is not a two-way conversation; for example, an academic interviewer uses scripted questions that are sometimes approved by the review board of an academic institution. The research is designed to protect the rights of interviewees.

At the end of this chapter, you may apply your interviewing skills in an activity entitled *The Research Interview*. That activity includes displaying information through the use of a chart, graph, or table, which are all reviewed next.

Displaying Research

Displaying research spans different levels of complexity: you are displaying research when you put someone else's words in quotation marks or when you turn complicated data into charts, graphs, or tables. Displaying numbers and other concepts in charts and graphs clarifies meaning at a glance.

To create effective charts, graphs, and tables, you may need to become more familiar with formatting options that your software avails you. For example, with Microsoft Word, go to the *Insert* tab to find options for making various types of charts, graphs, and tables.

The type of data that you are displaying will help determine the kind of visual to create. For assistance in creating a visual, do an Internet search; many helpful explanations and tutorials are available on the Web. For example, by searching "how to create graphs in Word," many informative sites will pop up.

In addition, charts and graphs can also be developed in Excel by highlighting a group of titles and numbers and using the *Insert* function.

Graphics: Charts, Graphs, and Tables

At times, visual displays are more effective than descriptions. Words can include excuses or explanations mixed in with the numbers, thus making it difficult to illuminate real trends.

As you display your research, remain aware that the information is the important issue, not the fancy display. Do not place your energies on trying to impress your audience with *smoke and mirrors*. Let your concepts and ideas lead the way with displays remaining secondary to the information they support.

On the next few pages, you will see examples of the following types of charts:

- Bar Chart
- Pie Chart
- Line Graph
- Table

Bar Charts   Use a bar chart to compare and contrast up to six different items. You can show relationships over a period of time by clustering several different groups in the chart. The following guidelines apply to any type of bar chart:

- Display relationships horizontally or vertically.
- Make sure bar widths and the space between them is equal.
- Arrange bars in a logical order (by length, by age, by date) to make comparisons easier.

Figure 3.1. Projected Social Work Job Growth (2010-2020)

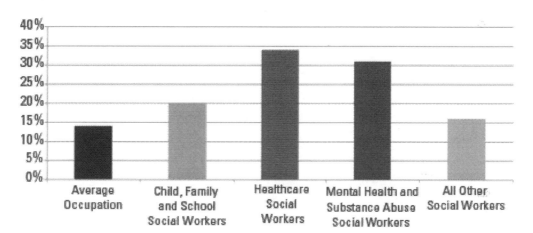

Source: National Bureau of Labor Statistics.

Pie Charts   Use pie charts when the various components add up to 100 percent.

- Limit the number of categories to six; if you have more than six, combine them.
- Label categories directly and add percentages.
- Place the most important section at the 12 o'clock position to emphasize a point.

Figure 3.2. Facts and Figures About Social Security 2010

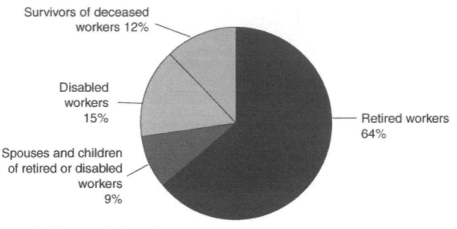

Source: Social Security Administration.

Line Graphs — Use line graphs to show trends.

- Use left-justified, 10- or 12-point bold for line graph titles.
- State what data the graph illustrates.
- Label each axis clearly.
- In a time graph, indicate time on the horizontal axis, and display units of measurement on the vertical axis.

Figure 3.3. Time Spent on E-Mail

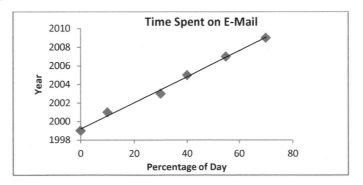

Tables   Tables should have enough information so that readers who look at them will be able to interpret the findings without explanation. *What conclusions are you able to draw by reviewing the tables below?*

Figure 3.5. Quick Facts About Social Workers

2012 Median Pay	$44,200 per year $21.25 per hour
Work Experience in Related Occupation	None
Number of Jobs, 2012	607,300
Job Outlook, 2012 – 2022	19% (Faster than average)
Employment Change 2012 – 2022	114,100

Source: Bureau of Labor Statistics

Figure 3.4. Change in Hourly Wages by Education, 1973-2001

Change in real hourly wages for all workers by education, 1973-2001					
	Less than high school	High School	Some college	College	Advanced degree
Hourly wage					
1973	$11.66	$13.36	$14.39	$19.49	$23.56
1979	11.62	13.04	13.94	18.27	22.31
1989	9.99	12.17	13.67	19.16	24.71
1995	9.04	11.95	13.37	19.84	26.18
2000	9.40	12.65	14.3	22.10	27.9
2001	9.50	12.81	14.60	22.58	28.14
Source: *The State of Working America 2002/2003* by Mishel, Bernstein, and Boushey.					

Recap

For some people, research is the most exciting aspect of their work and life. Even if you have not yet reached that point, you have to admit that research adds direction and power to the way that you make decisions or form an argument.

Use action research to reach clear and accurate understanding: focus on identifying relevant questions that keep a situation alive rather than relying on neat and tidy answers that soothe the emotions but offer little substance. Good research applied in the right way not only enriches life but also helps alleviate human suffering.

Writing Workshop

The Research Interview[1]

Instructions: For this activity, you examine the role that research plays in how decisions are made in a social service agency. Interview a social worker, exploring the kinds of research he or she does, the amount of time spent reviewing research, and other relevant information.

As you complete the research interview, collect data that you can use to construct a table, chart, or graph. Therefore, as you plan your interview, analyze elements about the job that you can quantify.

Below is a list of questions you may use during the interview; however, *feel free to add to these.* Your interview may be conducted over the phone or in person. Let your interviewee know that it may take 20 to 30 minutes.

Requirements:

- Format your report in APA style (see Chapter 6, "APA Citation Style," pages 89 to 107, for formatting instructions.)
  - o Include a title page, abstract, and reference page. (See Note 1 below.)
  - o Use a running head throughout your paper.
- In the opening paragraph, explain the purpose of the report and introduce the person whom you have interviewed.
- Format your interview summary in paragraphs, not in the question/answer format sometimes used for interviews.
- Include an original graphic—a chart, graph, or table—incorporating it into your paper according to APA guidelines. (See Note 2 below.)

[1]*The Research Interview* was adapted from *The Writing Interview*, designed by Lou Ann Karabel, English Professor, Indiana University Northwest.

Note 1: APA citation style does not call for referencing an interview that is not documented and available for others to read. However, since a reference page is required for this assignment, here is one way to format your reference for this paper.

If "J. Smith" were the person whom you interviewed, you could format your reference as follows:

J. Smith (personal communication, February 12, 2014)

Note 2: Graphics do not always explain numerical data. If you cannot create a chart or a graph, make a table. (In Microsoft Word, options for making charts, graphs, and tables are available at the *Insert* tab, located next to the *Home* tab.)

To create your visual, use data from your questions. For assistance in making a graphic, contact technical support at your university do a search to find an online tutorial.

Questions for the interview:

1. What is your position, and how long have you held it?
2. What kinds of research do you review or apply in social work?
3. Are you required to do research? If so, what kind?
4. How heavily do you rely on research?
5. What kinds of problems do you address in your day-to-day operations?
6. Do you use visuals for documents or presentations?

Make sure that you ask these two important questions:

7. Do you feel that you were adequately prepared by your education to do the work required of you?
8. If you could give one piece of advice, what would it be?

For a final touch, as a result of doing the interview, what did you learn? What insights did you have about your future profession?

References

Council on Social Work Education [CSWE]. (2015). Educational policy and

accreditation standards. Retrieved from http://www.cswe.org/

Accreditation-Process/2015-EPAS.aspx

Gay L. R., & Airasian, P. (2003). *Educational research: Competencies for analysis

and applications.* Upper Saddle River, NJ: Merrill Prentice Hall.

NASW. (2008). *Code of ethics of the National Association of Social Workers.*

Retrieved from http://www.socialworkers.org/pubs/code/code.asp

Andrea G. Tamburro, MSW, EdD, contributed to this chapter.

4

Literature Review

By Andrea Tamburro, MSW and EdD

The first part of any research involves collecting, synthesizing, and critiquing what others have already written on the topic.

By reviewing the current academic literature, you are able to define the problem and put it in context. By identifying what others have researched, you establish a credible base of evidence: the work of experienced practitioners provides a springboard for your thesis. You can move forward by extending established knowledge and by showing the strengths, gaps, weaknesses, and inaccuracies in the literature.

The Process

A thorough review of the literature includes all types of academic sources. A balanced search includes using books and juried academic journals and online sources found through credible websites and databases. Be sure to include social work journals. Her e is how to get started:

Select a topic that interests you.

Next identify what you want to know about the topic.

Then form questions based on what you want to know.

Before you write a literature review, however, read a few well-written examples that are published in academic journals. Each academic journal article provides a literature review.

The rest of this chapter walks you through a process for doing an academic literature review. Let us get started, walking through the process step by step. *What topic would you like to research?*

Journal Article Review

Here are the steps to follow when reviewing a journal article.

Step 1: Select an article.

- When you review an academic article, begin by looking at the credentials and academic affiliation of the author or authors. One way to do this is to search the Web to find out more about the authors and other articles they have written.

- Next, look at the references. Do the authors mostly use their own work, or do they cite articles from other mainstream academic journals? While checking out the references, see if any of the other articles relate to your questions.

- Read the abstract, introduction, and conclusion of the article to see if it informs your thesis or other themes and topics in your literature review.

- Begin to critique the article.

Step 2: Analyze a literature review in the article.

Using the same article, examine how the authors structured the literature review. Take notes, especially about the following:

- Did they use headings to identify each theme of the review?
- How did they integrate the literature within each theme?
- How did they present points of agreement in the literature?
- How did they present points of conflict or disagreement in the literature?

(Follow the above process with each article that you include in your review.)

Step 3: Read the *content* of the article.

Note how the *themes* are foregrounded and how the articles, websites, and books provide support for each theme.

- How did the authors connect each book or article to the *thesis* of their research article?

- What information did the literature review provide for the research question in the article?

- How did the authors integrate (synthesize) the various articles into themes?

- How do you connect the literature reviewed in the article to *your thesis*?

- Which topics in your literature review did the article inform?

Critique of the Literature

Once you have reviewed the structure and content of a juried academic journal article or a book, the next step is to critique the content. Critique one piece of literature at a time.

Identify the strengths and weaknesses of the document, including research methods, characteristics of participants, methods of data analysis, outcomes, and conclusions. For example, did the study include people from diverse populations, or did it focus on one particular segment of the population?

For example, if the study focused on only one segment of the population, such as white males, ages 18 to 25, the outcomes cannot be generalized to other populations. If a study includes equal numbers of both women and men and include equal numbers of white, African-American, Hispanic, Asian, and American Indian people who are ages 18 to 25, the outcomes are more likely to provide insights into diverse populations of people within that age range.

Once you have critiqued the literature, decide which articles are credible and useful for your topic. Next, divide the articles into *themes* or *topics*. Use an analytic chart to help you identify which articles address key topics or themes in your literature review. You can also use a spreadsheet, if that works for you.

Figure 4.1. Analytic Chart

Name of Article	Topic 1	Topic 2	Topic 3	Topic 4	Topic 5

When you begin to write the review, make each topic a heading in your document to help you organize the articles. Now you are ready to integrate the literature.

- Which articles agree on the topic?

- Which articles provide new insights or multiple perspectives that are worth considering?

- Which articles contradict the findings of other articles and why?

The example on the next page explains different perspectives of the same topic.

Figure 4.2. Example of Analytic Chart

Analytic Chart*

In the example below, assume that you are interested in child neglect. You have found 4 articles so far and have put the content into a grid to analyze the content and keep the articles organized.

*Note: The articles discussed in this example are fictitious.

Article	Topic 1	Topic 2	Topic 3	Topic 4	Topic 5
	Define neglect	Ways to identify neglect	Reasons for neglect	Interventions for neglect	Outcomes
Smith (2008)	X – agree		X	X	
Jones (2010)	X – disagree	X			
Johnson (2013)	X – agree		X	X	X
Thigpen (2012)	X brief		X	X	X

Interpreting the chart:

Smith (2008) and Johnson (2013) used similar definitions of neglect. However, Jones' (2010) definition was from a U.S. Department of Health and Human Services website and is used nationally by social service agencies.

If you search *child neglect* on the Web, you are likely to find information from sources that are not academic. However, the Child Welfare Information Gateway through the U.S. Department of Health and Human Services provides useful and relevant information and can be included in an academic literature review.

Examine the similarities and differences. How does Thigpen's (2010) definition fit in? If you find disagreement among authors (and you will), go to the *Encyclopedia of Social Work*, which is electronic. Check your library for access, or check the *Social Work Dictionary* (2003).

When you write your literature review, be sure to use the *thesis statement* or *question* in both the *introduction* and *conclusion* (see page 9). When you describe your findings, support your topics with evidence from the literature.

As you collect research on various topics, you may find yourself wishing to go beyond the literature to conduct your own qualitative research. If so, review how to conduct *action research,* which is discussed in Chapter 3, "Research and Evidence-Based Practice."

Social Workers, Ethics, and Research

The NASW *Code of Ethics* (2008) requires the use of evidence-based social work practice. However, Gambrill (2003) questioned whether there would ever be enough credible research evidence to support effective practice.

Gambrill's (2003) research indicates many gaps exist in the literature. Therefore, social workers must be actively involved in conducting and publishing research to fulfill their ethical obligation.

Example of Literature Review

On the following pages, an example of a literature review written by social work student Leigh Westergren is provided. On page 56, you find the "Literature Review Analysis Table" (Figure 4.3); then on pages 57 through 68, part of the paper, "Self-Esteem in Adolescents" (Figure 4.4).

As you read through Westergren's paper, notice that the paper is formatted in APA citation style, which is the required style for papers written in your chosen field of study, social work.

To read Westergren's entire paper, go to **www.thewriterstoolkit.com**; click on the *social work* tab and then *student samples*.

Figure 4.3. Example of Literature Review Analysis Table

Literature Review Analysis Table: Self-Esteem in Adolescents

Author: Leigh Westergren, Master of Social Work student, Indiana University Northwest

Authors	Belong/ Relatedness/ Peers	Healthy Human functioning/ indicator of well-being	Family climate vs. Family structure effects SE	Internal resources/ process to cope with stress/life	High Risk Youth/ Drug use/ homeless	Related to depression
Bagley, et al.			Parents caretakers create conditions for positive SE		Positive SE "freedom from delinquency"	
Bronson, et al.	X		Parental empathy key component	Sense of self		
Drukker, et al.	Social environ. impacts SE; goes up with positive peer influence		Trust equates to higher SE	Life events and developmental tasks in early adolescence		
Flanzer & Seurkle	More aggression w/ low SE	Contradiction: adult victims of martial violence have high SE	Maltreated children have low SE		X	Feelings of unworthiness "adolescents emotionally vulnerable"
Itzahaky Lipschitz				"One of most substantial contributors to adjustment" *vice versa*	X	
Lev-Wiesel	Low SE = societal alienation; working in groups increased SE	Intervention during adolescence is critical		Personality resource, potency	X	
Liem/Martin				X		
Maccio, Schuler	Secure attachments can increase SE			"personal strength" sense of control: high risk coping behaviors	Suicidality in girls: High SE negates effects of drug use (less guilt)	
Phillips						
Searcy	SE through associations; identification generates status and SE		Positive reinforcement generates SE: Aural SE (what one hears about oneself)	SE through activities achievement and *vice versa*		

Running head: SELF-ESTEEM IN ADOLESCENTS 1

Self-Esteem in Adolescents

A Review of the Literature

By Leigh Westergren

Indiana School of Social Work

Scholarly Writing Seminar

Andrea Tamburro, MSW, EdD

December 11, 2013

Figure 4.4. Example of Literature Review in APA Style

Abstract

Self-esteem is a person's self-judgment relating to general worth and

importance in society and may have an impact on a person's life and

functioning (Searcy, 2007). This literature review examines 10 social work

articles on self-esteem that provide evidence for social work practice. The

articles are predominantly research studies on adolescents and adults who are

struggling to cope with their lives, and the studies include exploration of

family structure and climate, socioeconomic status, and other environmental

factors. Several of the articles measure self-esteem levels, attitudes about life

in general, activities, habits, and outcomes. In short, this study explores the

recommendations generated by research on the development of self-esteem

and the concept of self-esteem as an internal resource that can help mediate

difficulties experienced by adolescents. The review is conducted in two parts.

The first part is an annotated bibliography of ten research articles. The second

part is a synthesis and analysis of the articles

Keywords: self-esteem, adolescents, family structure, social work

practice, high-risk youth, research, literature review

Self-Esteem in Adolescents

A Review of the Literature

This literature review examines and synthesizes10 social work articles on self-esteem that helps guide social work practice. This study explores the importance of self-esteem and recommendations generated by research on the development of self-esteem. This research supports the premise that self-esteem is an internal resource that can help mediate difficulties experienced by adolescents.

Analysis--Article 1

Bagley, Bertrand, Bolitho, and Mallick (2001) wrote an article entitled, "Discrepant parent-adolescent views on family functioning: Predictors of poorer self-esteem and problems of emotion and behaviour in British and Canadian adolescents." The article was published in *Journal of Comparative Family Studies*, *32(3),*394-403.

Summary of Article

Bagley et al. (2001) view self-esteem as an internal resource culminated via the family climate. Parents/caretakers are those who can help to create the conditions for positive self-esteem in the individual. To better understand the effects of a high or low self-esteem,
Bagley et al. (2001) used a self-reporting questionnaire with Canadian high school students; the questionnaire focused mainly on maladaptive behaviors, such as substance use and insufficient adjustment.

The researchers also used a parent questionnaire in their study to measure the family climate and gauge the effects of self-reported parenting style upon adolescent self-esteem. The findings of this study indicate that positive self-esteem supports the adolescent's ability to avoid delinquent behavior and other self-harmful activities. The findings also indicate that the underlying factor of low self-esteem is a negative family climate.

Assessment. The article details succinctly the study performed and samples utilized; yet the results of the study of parental and adolescent views of family life leave room for speculation based upon several observances of potential bias.

One such bias is that the respondents, both parents and adolescents, were asked to share their views on the quality of family life within the home. The evaluation is based on perception. Bagley et al. (2001) notes that the differing views between the parents and adolescents might be better attributed to differences in maturity levels and value systems than an overall lack of self-esteem of the adolescents. While the article reveals certain correlations between delinquent behavior, attitudes, and low self-esteem, the authors note a potential bias because the sample of parents were predominantly middle class females; thus the results of the study may not apply to other groups. There is also an absence of similar trials; as a result, the reader does not have like studies to compare against. However this is an important initial study for others to attempt to duplicate. Also, since this article was written in 2001, other literature may be available that was not included in this review.

Reflections. The article is useful to my literature review because it addresses a commonly considered theme in the social work field regarding family structure and the growing trend of single-parent families' effects on adolescent development. Having little or no control over family structure, the observation of family climate instead, having the more profound effect on adolescent self-esteem is a beneficial point to illustrate and creates opportunity for the social worker in practical applications.

Note: Nine other articles were reviewed using the three criteria noted previously: summary, assessment, and reflection. To review the complete paper, go to the *Social Work Resources* tab at www.thewriterstoolkit.com.

Synthesis of the Literature

The following discussion integrates the findings of the ten articles discussed in this review of the literature on self-esteem in adolescents.

Self-Esteem as an Internal Resource

Self-esteem is an internal resource that equips the individual with skills to handle the stressors and difficulties of life. Self-esteem develops during childhood and adolescence: The ideal development is a fully-functioning, emotionally and mentally healthy adult. In the study of high-risk youth, Lev-Wiesel (2009) describes self-esteem as a resource of the personality that increases the individual's *potency* to cope with life's stressors.

According to Phillips (2012), self-esteem can be an indicator of well-being; a positive self-esteem in adolescence is equated with higher optimism, lower hopelessness, less potential for delinquency, and greater satisfaction with family. Maccio and Schuler (2012) define high self-esteem as a personal strength creating an internal sense of control for the individual and a mediator between the sense of hopelessness that many high-risk adolescents demonstrate. They indicate that low self-esteem is linked to substance use, depression, self-injurious behaviors, general delinquency, and for female adolescents, an increase in suicidality. Maccio and Schuler (2012) find that among adolescent drug users, high self-esteem actually negated the emotional effects, such as guilt, of that drug use.

Another sign of low self-esteem in adolescents is aggression towards peers (Flanzer & Sturkle, 1987). Bagley, Bertrand, Bolitho, and Mallick (2001) note that high self-esteem increases healthy sexuality, successful academic achievement, and entry into the employment later in life. Liem and Martin (2011) refer to high self-esteem as something that is created through an internal process of acceptance and rejection, culminating in a sense of belonging and ability to relate to the world.

Self-Esteem Through Achievement

Self-esteem is developed in three ways: activities, feedback, and associations. Activities that generate positive reinforcement increase self-esteem, and there are several ways to garner this reinforcement. Those who perform well in sports and academics have been found to have higher self-esteem, if they can see tangible results. Searcy's (2007) study indicates that while cognitive achievement, measured through academics, can foster positive reinforcement and increased self-esteem, sports and illegal activities tend to have a greater influence on self-esteem than achievement in academics.

Research indicates that students who have poor performance in school have low self-esteem, and low self-esteem is related to poor performance in school. Thus, while self-esteem affects academic performance, academic performance also impacts self-esteem (Itzhaky & Lipschitz-Elhawi, 2005; Liem & Martin, 2011; Searcy, 2007). A student's peer connections were also found to be a mitigating factor for academic achievement (Liem & Martin, 2011).

Self-Esteem Through Feedback

What a child or adolescent is told will have an effect on his or her self-esteem, depending on who is providing the feedback. What a child hears through words or actions from significant others, including parents, teachers, caretakers, or peers will have a positive or negative impact or both on the development of self-esteem, described as social learning (Searcy, 2007).

Social learning theory indicates that if a person that a child or adolescent regards highly gives positive reinforcement, that adolescent feels valued and thus self-esteem is positively affected. Flanzer and Sturkle (1987) illustrate that children who are maltreated and told they have no value by significant others develop low self-esteem. Bronson and Dick (2005) and Bagley et al. (2001) maintain that parents and caretakers create the conditions in the adolescent's environment to foster self-esteem–positive or negative.

Some studies illustrate a positive correlation between self-esteem development and the structure of the family; for example, one-parent, two parents, or divorced parents. However, Bagley et al. (2001) find that a negative family climate is more relevant and fosters low self-esteem in the adolescent. Bronson and Dick (2005) studied the influences of the paternal relationship on self-esteem and find that parental empathy for the adolescent's inner emotional self influences development of high self-esteem.

Self-Esteem Through Associations

While self-esteem issues are present in adolescents from every type of family and environment, the social environment is an important factor in determining self-esteem. Drukker, Feron, Kaplan, Schneiders, and Van Os (2006), define social capital as the features of an organization, environment, family, and so on, that create resources for the individual. They maintain that a strong identity in adolescence is related to high self-esteem, while social alienation and/or lack of secure attachments relate to low self-esteem. Maccio and Schuler (2012) support these findings; they indicate low self-esteem is highly correlated with a lack of attachment and belongingness.

Liem and Martin (2011) document the increased functioning of adolescents who had positive connections with peers and that "satisfying interactions with others" create positive capacities for adjustment (p. 198). Lev-Wiesel's (2009) study shows an increase in self-esteem among youths working in group therapy.

Conclusion

Life's challenges and stressors are more easily navigated when the adolescent and adult has the necessary skills and internal resources to handle those challenges. Self-esteem is an internal resource that is developed through experiences and interactions. High self-esteem can help mediate the difficulties and challenges that adolescents will experience in their lives.

Liem and Martin (2011) describe self-esteem as the internal process of self-acceptance and rejection giving a person a sense of belonging with the world. As indicated through the literature, self-esteem is developed in several ways. First, self-esteem is learned through a person's activities, as illustrated by Searcy (2007), Itzhaky and Lipschitz-Elhawi (2005), and Liem and Martin (2011). Second, self-esteem is developed through verbal feedback, as illustrated by Bagley et al. (2001), Bronson and Dick (2005), Flanzer and Sturkle (1987), and Searcy (2007). Third, a person's peer groups or associations impacts self-esteem (Drukker et al. 2006; Lev-Wiesel, 2009; Liem & Martin, 2011).

Childhood and adolescence are key time periods for the development of self-esteem and high or low self-esteem may have resonating effects on many different aspects of an individual's life, including the capacity for optimism and satisfaction with her or his life (Phillips, 2012). The literature has shown a positive correlation between harmful behavior and low self-esteem. Searcy's (2007) research shows that when adolescents have high self-esteem, they are better prepared to make helpful life decisions. These decisions include whether to participate in sexual or criminal activities.

The literature contains gaps because several of the studies used samples that only included adolescents already in high-risk environments, and developing high self-esteem would have additional challenges (Maccio & Schuler, 2012; Itzhaky & Lipchitz-Elhawi, 2005). Also additional discussion in maintaining a high self-esteem is needed in the literature. The topic has obvious relevance to the social work field and further research on the efficacy of self-esteem development and maintenance activities such as group therapy, skill building, and leadership initiatives would be beneficial. Given the outcomes of this research, effective community programs addressing the importance of self-esteem development would then have greater chance of success in their creation and implementation.

References

Bagley, C., Bertrand, L., Bolitho, F., & Mallick, K. (2001). Discrepant parent-adolescent views on family functioning: Predictors of poorer self-esteem and problems of emotion and behaviour in British and Canadian adolescents. *Journal of Comparative Family Studies*, *32*(3), 394-403.

Bronson, D., & Dick, G. (2005). Adult men's self-esteem: The relationship with the father. *Families in Society*, *86*(4), 580-588.

Drukker, M., Feron, F., Kaplan, C., Schneiders, J., & Van Os, J. (2006). The wider social environment and changes in self-reported quality of life in the transition from late childhood to early adolescence: A cohort study. *BMC Public Health*, *6*, 1-11.

Flanzer, J., & Sturkle, K. (1987). Depression and self-esteem in the families of maltreated adolescents. *Social Work*, *4*, 491-496.

Itzhaky, H., & Lipschitz-Elhawi, R. (2005). Social support, mastery, self-esteem and individual adjustment among at-risk youth. *Child & Youth Care Forum*, *34*(5), 329-346.

Lev-Wiesel, R. (2009). Enhancing potency among male adolescents at risk to drug abuse: An action research. *Child Adolescent Social Work Journal*, *26*, 383-398.

Liem, G., & Martin, A. (2011). Peer relationships and adolescents' academic and non-academic outcomes: Same-sex and opposite-sex peer effects and the mediating role of school engagement. *British Journal of Educational Psychology, 81*, 183-206.

Maccio, E., & Schuler, J. (2012). Substance use, self-esteem, and self-efficacy among homeless and runaway youth in New Orleans. *Child Adolescent Social Work Journal, 29,* 123-136.

Phillips, T. (2012). The influence of family structure vs. family climate on adolescent well-being. *Child Adolescent Social Work Journal, 29,* 103-110

Searcy, Y. (2007). Placing the horse in front of the wagon: Toward a conceptual understanding of the development of self-esteem in children and adolescents. *Child and Adolescent Social Work Journal, 24*(2), 121-131.

Project-Based Learning

Projects such as literature reviews provide an opportunity for students to apply what they are learning, making the experience relevant (Bell, 2010; Gardner, Tuchman, and Hawkins, 2010; Hartsell and Parker, 2008; Nielsen, Du, and Kolmos, 2010). Thus, projects not only enhance learning but also prepare students for social work practice.

As part of your social work studies, you are likely to receive projects as assignments, which have a multitude of learning outcomes. During the process of developing the project, you develop a better understanding why certain knowledge and skills are useful and necessary. For example, when you do a literature review, you build skills in research, critical thinking, writing, and synthesis. All of these skills are used in social work practice.

The writing workshop in this chapter contains your first project-based learning assignment, which is a review of the literature of a topic that you choose.

Recap

One desired outcome of all research is that outcomes be applied to further mankind. However, though research can illuminate even the most difficult and controversial issues, often what is learned through research is not applied.

Next in Chapter 5, "Critical Thinking and Reflective Practice," you examine the various levels of learning, which gives you deeper insight into writing about research. You also develop a broad context to evaluate what you are learning and how to apply it in your life and profession.

Now get ready to hone your research and critical thinking skills by reviewing the literature. By following the process presented in the writing workshop, you have expert guidance as you complete this project-based learning assignment.

COACHING TIP

Literature Review Pre-work

Examine a social work journal article. Read the introduction and the conclusion; identify the thesis statement and consider how the article is summarized:

- *How do the authors present their evidence?*
- *What do the authors include in their literature review?*
- *In the literature review section, how are the various authors introduced?*
- *How is the data analyzed and presented?*

Writing Workshop

Project-Based Learning: Literature Review

A literature review is an essential component of many advanced social work projects, such as a research project or legislative advocacy. In addition, reviewing literature enhances knowledge and skills in several areas.

In the process of completing a literature review, you tap into a multitude of skill sets: writing, organizational skills, and presentation skills. As you write your paper, you also use evidence-based research and online library resources as well as apply APA writing style.

Using a problem-based learning approach, you are able to complete this literature review step by step. However, receiving feedback as you complete each step is essential; thus, if you are able to discuss this process with your peers in class or online, you will increase learning, incorporating various perspectives.

Note: This literature review project is adapted from a social work scholarly writing course at Indiana University modified by Andrea Tamburro.

Step 1: Thesis Statement or Question

Purpose: Step 1 assists you in identifying an area of interest.

Instructions: Write a thesis statement based on your area of interest (which you may modify as the review continues). When you write your thesis statement, focus on the following:

- Being specific.
- Covering only what you plan to discuss in your paper.

As you write your thesis statement, keep in mind that you need to support it with evidence. You may also modify your thesis statement or question as your research progresses: Research is a process, and your original ideas may change as new data emerges. (*Note*: See pages 11-12 for information on writing thesis statements.)

Step 2: Introduction and Review of Two Articles

Purpose: Step 2 gives you practice *drafting* a review of literature in preparation for your paper; step 2 also ensures that enough literature for a comprehensive review for your area of interest is available.

Instructions: Select two social work articles. Review and incorporate the intellectual standards of critical thinking (see page 83 in this text or go to www.criticalthinking.org; select the *Universal Intellectual Standards* tab).

Organize information for each article using these three categories: *summary*, *assessment*, and *reflection*. These categories should appear as subheadings under each source in your bibliography.

- The **summary** describes the main points presented in the article.

- The **assessment** is your evaluation of the article. Is the information trustworthy, why or why not?

- The **reflection** identifies how you intend to apply the information to your work or your review. You can also use the reflection to make personal notes to yourself such as how an article compares or contrasts with other articles, books, or documents.

Step 2 should be about 6 pages in length. After receiving feedback on this step, you are ready to complete subsequent steps.

Summary

Be as objective as possible, giving a brief overview: you do not need to restate detailed information.

- What are the basic details of the article, including the *purpose*, *methods*, and *conclusions*?
- What information does the article provide?
- Who is the article about?
- What do the authors do? How do they do it? Why do they do it?

Assessment and Critique

- How do I know that I can trust the information in the article?
- What is it about the article that suggests that the information is reliable? (Look for evidence on Figure 5.1, "Universal Intellectual Standards," page 83, or go to **www.criticalthinking.org**; select *Universal Intellectual Standards* tab.)
- Which critical thinking standards do the authors demonstrate?
- Which critical thinking standards are missing or are not fully implemented?

Reflection

- Is the article useful to my study? If so, how?
- What themes does this article inform?
- How does information in the article compare, support, or contrast with information in other scholarly articles or books?

Step 3: Complete Annotated Bibliography of 10 Articles

Instructions: Organize information for each article using the three categories: *summary*, *assessment*, and *reflection*. These three categories should appear as subheadings under each source in your bibliography.

Step 4: Synthesis of 10 Articles

Purpose: Gain practice focusing on synthesis and integration skills.

Instructions: Now that you have identified and annotated (summarized) 10 social work articles, synthesize the articles by doing the following:

1. Integrate the articles by theme. (Keep in mind the themes must support the thesis statement or question.)

    For example, "Several authors support *Theme A* (citation here)."

2. As you review the articles, also notice how they synthesize the literature. What can you learn from the approach these authors take?

3. Use a chart similar to the one below to analyze and condense the data that you have found. (Modify the chart as needed; an analytic chart is only an analysis tool, and you do not need to include it in your assignment.)

4. Be sure to edit and proofread your work thoroughly.

Analytic Chart

Use an analytic chart to identify which articles address specific topics, or use a spreadsheet in Excel, if that works better for you.

Name of Article	Topic 1	Topic 2	Topic 3	Topic 4	Topic 5

At this point in the process, can you see the "big picture" and how the steps are integrated?

Step 5: First Draft – Focus on Conclusions

Purpose: Focus on the outcomes and meaning of the literature.

Instructions: Write the first draft of your conclusions; include the following:

1. Your thesis statement or question and how the literature addressed your topic.
2. Your conclusions based on data from the research (statements supported by data).
3. Your recommendations for actions needed.
4. What you have learned.

When your first draft is complete, visit your college's writing center or have a peer read your work for clarity, correctness, and logic.

Step 6: Second Draft – Rethink, Revisit, and Revise

Purpose: Rethink, support conclusions with data, incorporate feedback, and revisit your introduction.

Instructions: Based on your feedback, revise your literature review; compare your conclusion with your introduction.

1. Does your conclusion include your thesis statement or question and how the literature addressed your topic?
2. Are your conclusions based on and supported by data?
3. Can you describe your findings more clearly?
4. What actions are needed based on your research?
5. What have you learned?

Step 7: Presentation of Literature Review

Purpose: By developing a presentation of the review and findings to a group of peers, you solidify arguments. Questions from the group provide alternate perspectives as well as identify strengths, weaknesses, and gaps in rationale.

Instructions: Develop a 10-minute presentation of your literature review; include a PowerPoint. In the review, include the following:

1. Introduction that includes thesis statement
2. Synthesis of your review
3. Conclusion

After your presentation, immediately write a reflection that includes new questions and insights for your final paper.

Step 8: Literature Review

Purpose: Integrate the various pieces of the literature review that you have completed in previous steps.

Instructions: Now you are ready to write a literature review that includes at least 10 scholarly social work sources, peer-reviewed journal articles; you may include one or two scholarly books.

Your literature review should be approximately 28-34 pages in length, including the title page and references. Here is an outline to follow:

1. Title Page
2. Abstract
3. Introduction, including thesis statement or question
4. Annotated bibliography for each article, including the following:
   a. Summary
   b. Assessment and critique
   c. Reflection
5. Synthesis
6. Conclusion
7. References

By using this step-by-step process, you should be less overwhelmed and more able to focus on the various pieces of the project.

Process Message

Instructions: Write your instructor a **process message** describing what you discovered about reviewing literature, critical thinking, and your learning process.

Send	To ...	Professor Tamburro
	Cc ...	
	Subject:	Paper Analysis (Process Message)

Professor Tamburro,

My review of the literature is coming along nicely. The topic that I chose to explore is mentoring systems for young adults.

Some of the things that I learned as I was working on this paper are . . .

References

Bell, S. (2010). Project-based learning for the 21st century: Skills for the future. *Clearing House, 83*(2), 39-43. doi: 10.1080/00098650903505415

Gambrill, E. D. (2003). Evidence-based practice: Sea change or the emperor's new clothes? *Journal of Social Work Education, 39*(1).

Gardner, D. S., Tuchman, E., & Hawkins, R. (2010). Teaching note: A cross-curricular, problem-based project to promote understanding of poverty in urban communities. *Journal of Social Work Education, 46*(1), 147-136.

Hartsell, B. D., & Parker, A. J. (2008). Evaluation of problem-based learning as a method for teaching social work administration: A content analysis. *Administration in Social Work, 32*(3), 44-62. doi: 10.1080/03643100801922456

Nielsen, J. D., Du, X. Y., & Kolmos, A. (2010). Innovative application of a new PBL model to interdisciplinary and intercultural projects. *International Journal of Electrical Engineering Education, 47*(2), 174-188.

Westergren, L.[1] (2013). *Adolescent development of positive self-esteem and healthy human functioning: A review of the literature.* Unpublished manuscript, Indiana University, Northwest, Gary, Indiana.

Andrea G. Tamburro, MSW, EdD, wrote this chapter.

---

[1]Leigh Westergren graduated from the MSW program at Indiana University Northwest. We appreciate her willingness to share her research. This paper fulfilled a 10-article literature review assignment, which was written over several weeks. The paper is the outcome of a project-based learning approach in which students were provided feedback about the thesis statement or question; the introduction, summary, and analysis of three social work journal articles related to the thesis statement; the synthesis of 10 articles related to the thesis statement or question and conclusion.

5

Critical Thinking and
Reflective Practice

You are investing a large amount of your time, effort, and resources into achieving your academic goals, which includes getting a degree. However, the most important outcome of your academic studies is enhancing your thinking skills so that you solve problems effectively.

Critical thinking is a common term, but what does *critical thinking* mean to you? What are some qualities that would demonstrate your ability to think critically? *Reflective practice* adds a dimension to reflective thinking: by applying reflective practice, you add a step to your learning process that can keep you grounded and have a direct impact on your actions and thus your achievements.

Let us review critical thinking first and then move to reflective practice.

Critical, Creative, and Reflective Thinking

To think in critical and creative modes, you must first develop an ability to reflect, an ability that is never mastered and even challenging to access. That is, in part, because life moves quickly, and immediate answers bring comfort (though not necessarily solutions).

The following quote by Dewey (1933) gives insight into why reflective thought is such an uncommon and difficult achievement:

> One can think reflectively only when one is willing to endure suspense and to undergo the trouble of searching. To many persons both suspense of judgment and intellectual search are disagreeable; they want to get them ended as soon as possible. They cultivate an over-positive and dogmatic habit of mind, or feel perhaps that a condition of doubt will be regarded as evidence of mental inferiority. . . . To be genuinely thoughtful, we must be willing to sustain and protract that state of doubt which is the stimulus to thorough inquiry . . . . (p. 16)

As you immerse yourself in reflective thought, you reach deep levels of understanding. Reflective thought is the mode of thinking in which you "connect the dots" so that you can apply what you are learning to your life and practice.

To gain an understanding of the learning process, let us examine the various levels of learning identified by *The Taxonomy of Educational Objectives* (1984), which breaks learning into various levels of complexity.

Note: The taxonomy was developed by a committee of college and university examiners through a series of conferences between 1949 through 1953, and Benjamin Bloom was the editor of the book that resulted from their work.

The Taxonomy of Educational Objectives

The Taxonomy of Educational Objectives (1984) identifies these six levels learning:

1. Knowledge
2. Comprehension
3. Application
4. Analysis
5. Synthesis
6. Evaluation

Each of these levels of learning gives insight into the thinking process and what is involved to gain insight and learn new skills.

Reflective thought occurs at the higher levels of critical thinking; however, all levels of learning are vital in developing skill and insight that lead to critical thinking. In fact, the foundational levels of learning provide a scaffolding for critical thinking; when *learning gaps* occur, skill development is inhibited.

As you read through each level, relate it to your own learning experience. Let us look at each level to understand how it fits into your learning process.

Knowledge   From the simple to the complex, knowledge is the foundation of learning. Knowledge involves simple recall; for example, even with complex theories you start your learning process by knowing the meaning of terms, principles, and other theories. Knowledge is information.

- o   Knowing common terms
- o   Knowing specific facts
- o   Knowing methods and procedures
- o   Knowing basic concepts
- o   Knowing principles

That knowledge is the base of all other levels of the taxonomy validates why certain types of rote learning is important during certain stages of the learning process.

Repetition is a valuable learning tool: the more you repeat something, the more automatic your responses become. For example, if you want to expand your vocabulary, you first must know what a word means before you are ready to use it in context in a meaningful way. The first few times you use a new word may feel awkward; however, the more you use the new word, the more natural it feels.

Comprehension   To comprehend is to understand; *understanding* comes after *knowing*. In other words, you can know the meaning of a word without understanding the meaning.

- o   Understanding facts and principles
- o   Interpreting verbal material
- o   Interpreting charts and graphs
- o   Translating verbal material to mathematical formulas
- o   Estimating future consequences implied in data
- o   Justifying methods and procedures

As a learner, you experience different levels of understanding, from the superficial to the profound. Once you comprehend the meaning of a word, principle, or theory, are you able to see deeper complexities.

Application   When you can apply information, such as a concept, theory, or principle, you have reached a critical level of learning, for example:

- o   Applying concepts and principles to new situations
- o   Applying laws and theories to practical situations
- o   Solving mathematical problems
- o   Constructing charts and graphs
- o   Demonstrating correct use of a method or procedure

You may have heard the saying, "If you don't use it, you lose it." That saying refers directly to application, and educational research has shown it to be true.

In fact, in addition to being a critical level of learning, application may also be an overlooked and undervalued link in the learning process. A great deal of complex information learned at the levels of knowledge and comprehension is not applied. And it is only when someone applies knowledge that what is learned becomes truly meaningful.

For example, how many people who know that smoking is linked to cancer continue to smoke? What are some things that you know would be beneficial to apply but do not?

Application equates to action, to results. Application may sound easy on the surface, but application can be difficult to achieve. However, application is a tipping point in the learning process. By applying what you are learning, you are creating value to yourself and possibly others.

Analysis   When a learner can identify component parts or see how ideas are connected, analysis becomes possible. Here are some skills and qualities associated with analysis:

- o   Recognizing unstated assumptions and logical fallacies in reasoning
- o   Distinguishing between facts and inferences; evaluating relevancy of data
- o   Analyzing organizational structure of a work (art, music, writing, design)
- o   Identifying characteristics and components; comparing and contrasting
- o   Conducting an observation; setting criteria
- o   Categorizing; ranking prioritizing, and sequencing
- o   Determining cause and effect
- o   Thinking deductively

Synthesis   Synthesis is associated with creating, innovating, and inventing. Synthesis involves putting together elements or parts to form a whole, arranging or combining pieces, parts, elements, and so on, to develop a pattern or structure that was not clearly there before, for example:

- o   Writing a well-organized theme or creative composition
- o   Presenting a well-organized speech
- o   Proposing a plan for an experiment
- o   Integrating diverse elements into a plan for solving a problem
- o   Formulating a new scheme for classifying objects, events, or ideas

Evaluation   Evaluation involves judging the value of material and methods for given purposes, assessing the extent to which material and methods meet criteria quantitatively and qualitatively, such as:

- o   Judging the logical consistency of written material
- o   Judging the adequacy with which conclusions are supported by data
- o   Judging the value of a work by use of internal/external criteria

Thus, when you reach the point at which you can make educated judgments on the basis of criteria, you are using what is considered the highest level of your critical thinking skills.

In general, here are some of the qualities that demonstrate critical thinking:

- Being open-minded about a topic; not jumping to conclusions
- Interpreting evidence accurately
- Basing decisions on evidence
- Justifying conclusions on the basis of evidence
- Explaining assumptions and reasons
- Identifying relevant arguments
- Analyzing and interpreting data correctly

Elder and Paul (2006) have developed standards for critical thinking that include the following (also see Figure 5.1 on page 83):

- Clarity
- Accuracy
- Precision
- Relevance
- Depth
- Breadth
- Logic
- Fairness

In addition, here are some qualities that demonstrate a *lack* of critical thinking:

- Basing views on self-interests or pre-conceived ideas and beliefs
- Misinterpreting evidence
- Using irrelevant reasons and unwarranted claims
- Presenting biased interpretations
- Exhibiting closed-mindedness
- Ignoring or superficially evaluating alternative points of view
- Acting negative or hostile to reasonable arguments

At times a weak foundation of the basics within one field inhibits a learner's ability to apply principles and synthesize information in another. For example, if a learner has poor writing or grammar skills, demonstrating synthesis within a content area such as social work becomes more difficult.

You can apply the taxonomy to your own learning process by identifying your *learning gaps* and then taking steps to build your skills. For example, Chapters 7 through 22 in this textbook cover the mechanics, grammar, and editing principles needed to produce professional-quality writing. As you work on your learning gaps, you bring your overall performance to a higher level, leading to increased confidence and credibility in the professional world.

As mentioned previously, the critical step in the taxonomy is *application*: as a learner, if you do not use what you are learning, the learning will be quickly lost. One way to gain insight and foster the application of new learnings is through *reflective practice*.

Reflective Practice

Reflective practice is a form of "reflection on action" (Schön, 1983).

Practicing any profession in this fast-paced, ever-changing world demands "thinking in action," which textbook learning is limited in providing. Reflective practice helps fill the gap between theory and practice.

The challenge for the social work practitioner is to take the time to reflect on your actions and interactions with clients so that you gain insight into becoming ever more effective. Reflective practice involves recording your experience as objectively as possible.

Reflective learning is a source of personal professional development and an element of lifelong learning.

Reflective practice entails the following:

- o Analyzing your experiences, drawing lessons out of them
- o Retelling, rethinking, and evaluating
- o Using experience as a source of learning by connecting it to theory
- o Integrating theory with practice
- o Expressing your own story; reflecting on the story of your clients
- o Developing a coherent understanding of a possibly disjointed series of events
- o Becoming increasingly conscious of what you do and why you do it

Reflective practice includes writing about your own feelings and emotions, which generally are not part of an academic learning environment but are nonetheless a critical element of your experience.

Now take a moment to review Figure 5.1 on page 83, which applies standards for critical thinking.

Figure 5.1. Universal Intellectual Standards (Elder & Paul, 2010)

Critical Thinking Standard	Description	Questions to check for building your critical thinking skills
Relevance	Are all of my statements relevant to the question at hand? Does what I'm saying connect to my central point?	How does this relate to the issue being discussed? How does this help me deal with this issue?
Accuracy	Are all of my statements and all of my information factually correct and/or supported with evidence?	How do I know this? Is this true? How could I validate this?
Precision	Are all my statements discussed in enough detail and examples with enough specifics?	Could I be more specific? Could I give more details?
Clarity	Do I expand on ideas, express ideas in another way, and provide examples or illustrations where appropriate?	Did I give an example? Is it clear what I mean by this? Could I elaborate further?
Depth	Do I explain the reasons behind my conclusions, anticipate and answer the questions that my reasoning raises, and/or acknowledge the complexity of the issue?	Why is this so? What are some of the complexities here? What would it take for this to happen?
Breadth	Am I considering alternative points of view? Have I thought about how someone else might have interpreted the situation?	Would this look the same from the perspective of my client? Someone else? Is there another way to interpret this?
Logic	Does my line of reasoning make sense? Do my conclusions follow from the facts and/or my earlier statements?	Does what I said at the beginning fit with what I concluded at the end? Do my conclusions match the evidence?
Significance	Do my conclusions or goals represent a major issue raised by my reflection on experience?	Is this the most important issue on which to focus? Is this the most significant problem?
Fairness	Do I have a vested interest in this issue? Am I sympathetic to others' viewpoints?	Do I use inclusive language? Do I consider power differential?

DEAL Model

The **DEAL Model** is a three-step process to enhance critical reflection on experiences to gain deeper insight (Ash & Clayton, 2004). One goal is to reveal how experiences are integrated with principles gained from academic content.

Here are the three steps:

D =   **Describe** a specific experience.

E =   **Examine** it closely.

AL =   **Articulate Learning** – *What did I learn? How will I apply it?*

By applying this model, as a learner you reflect on an experience; and in the process, gain access to developing the higher levels of learning as defined by the taxonomy of educational objectives. Here is more about the model:

Step 1: Describe

Your first step is to identify a significant or peak learning experience that you will describe in detail; your ultimate goal will be to connect your experience to social work principles or other academic content that you are studying.

By summarizing an experience in writing, you reach a deeper level of clarity than if you simply thought about the experience without putting words to paper.

To start the process, think about a class discussion, lecture, topic, or service-learning event. Can you identify a peak learning experience? What about the learning experience stood out for you? Can you connect your learning to *specific academic content or social work principles?*

Step 2: Examine

Next, examine the experience that you identified in Step 1: *Examining* an experience involves analyzing or breaking down the experience into smaller parts.

As you examine your learning, identify principles that relate to it: *how can you integrate your learning experience with principles that you are studying?* As you integrate your experience with principles, cite relevant sources.

Step 3: Articulate Learning

As you write about your experience, ask yourself, "What did I learn and how will I apply it?" As you gain deeper insight, you move that much closer to turning your experience into an important life lesson.

At the end of this chapter, you are given an opportunity to apply the DEAL Model: see Writing Workshop, Part 1, page 86.

Figure 5.2. Student Sample of DEAL Model

Describe

This day was spent by responding to a medical emergency in the band room at school, alongside the guidance secretary and school nurse for a female who twisted her ankle. After the medical emergency, I followed up with the part-time MSW about upcoming 12-step programs and discussed prior student sessions.

Later in the morning, my supervisor and I met with a male student about rumors spreading around school regarding his sexuality. Following this, I co-facilitated a PEP session with the part-time MSW, Iva, where we covered tips for successful test taking. Ending the day, my supervisor and I met with a female student about bullying because a male student was calling her trailer trash and saying inappropriate sexual comments. We tried to discuss ideas to prevent further issues and to solve the situation, but the female student was very combative and unwilling. . . .

Throughout this week of internship, I learned that it is important always to get all sides of the story when there are multiple students involved. At times, I felt very useless as much of what I did was observe. However, I realized afterwards, it is important for me to observe the skills to successfully demonstrate them myself.

This week, what I did for myself was sleep a little more than usual! With my work schedule, internship, and classes finally starting to even out, I decided to catch some extra z's to let my body rest! I also made a goal to eat a little healthier for the week (let's see if I can keep it up!).

Examine

After this week of internship, I feel like my challenge was that I had to sit back and observe my supervisor giving presentations. I did not want to overstep my boundaries and take over what she was trying to teach, as she knew the new state laws, and I was unaware of them. For this week, my learning successes included being able to observe the skills of my supervisor and the other social worker, and being able to demonstrate them. I feel I did a good job co-facilitating a presentation that I was not necessarily prepared for.

Articulate Learning

To help alleviate some of my stress, I have tried using my planner much more than I have in the past. I tend to get overwhelmed when I do not have all the due dates of assignments sitting right in front of me. Being organized is an important part of being a student in the BSW program as it will help my learning process progress smoothly. Being organized is also important for my future career in social work as every client's notes have to be kept separately as well as personal resources to connect clients to.

What I learned about myself is that I like to be a leader. I've noticed lately that I tend to take a more dominant role, which is bad, because that means I'm having a hard time accepting that I am in my internship to LEARN. In working with clients, I still get a little nervous because I don't feel confident at this point that I will always provide the best options. Like previously stated in my journals, these realizations are going to be important for my growth as a social worker because if I do not handle them appropriately now, it will only become more difficult later on.

Recap

In this chapter, you have learned tools to assist you in developing your critical and reflective thinking skills.

Reflective practice includes writing about your own feelings and emotions, a critical element of your experience. As you become more reflective, you transition from being a person whose thinking is reactionary, based on your immediate needs and wants, to a person who puts educated, informed, and reflective thought into solving problems.

Application—applying what you are learning—is the critical link between theory and practice. By applying principles to practice, you gain tangible benefits resulting in lifelong learning.

Writing Workshop

Part 1: Applying the DEAL Model

Instructions: Identify an experience and use the DEAL Model as a reflective practice tool.

Once again, here is the three-step process:

D = **Describe** a specific experience.

E = **Examine** it closely.

AL = **Articulate Learning** – *What did I learn, and how will I apply it?*

Step 1: Describe

Think about a class discussion, lecture, topic, or service-learning event. Describe it in detail, focusing on what stood out for you as a learning experience. As you reflect, connect your learning to *social work principles or specific academic content.*

Step 2: Examine

Examining involves analyzing your experience, breaking it down into smaller parts. *Which social work principles can you apply to help understand or explain your learning experience?*

By integrating your experience with principles gained from formal social work study, you deepen your understanding and your ability to apply what you learn. As you integrate your experience with principles, cite relevant sources.

Step 3: Articulate Learning

1. *What did I learn about myself as a social worker or about clients, colleagues, communities, agencies, and so on?*

2. *How did I learn it?*

3. *Why is this learning important for me as a developing social worker?*

4. *What will I do in my future practice in light of this learning?*

As an adjunct to the DEAL Model, consider starting a *work journal*. Your work journal can provide excellent support in applying the DEAL Model (see below).

Part 2: Keeping a Work Journal

Instructions: A work journal and a personal journal are similar; however, with a work journal, you focus specifically on writing about work experiences.

Journaling is an informal method of writing that you can use to capture your insights. Use your work journal in conjunction with the DEAL Model; for example, by journaling freely about your experiences as you have them, you can later select specific entries in which you describe peak learning experiences and then analyze them through the DEAL Model.

Note: For detailed information on starting a journal, see Activity 2, page 128.

Part 3. Writing a Process Message: Critical Thinking

Instructions: Visit the website for *The Critical Thinking Community* and explore the site freely: **www.criticalthinking.org**. Then write your instructor a **process message** describing what you discovered about yourself and the topic.

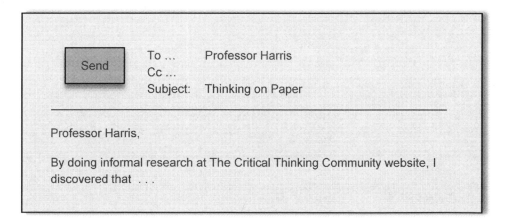

Send

To ...　　Professor Harris
Cc ...
Subject:　Thinking on Paper

Professor Harris,

By doing informal research at The Critical Thinking Community website, I discovered that . . .

References

Ash, S., Clayton, P., & Moses, M. (2006). *Excerpts from teaching and learning through critical reflection: An instructor's guide*. Raleigh, NC: Author. [Model modified for social work by Lisa E. McGuire, Ph. D. & Kathy Lay, Ph.D. Indiana University School of Social Work.]

Bloom, B. (Ed.). (1984). *The taxonomy of educational objectives*. Boston, MA: Addison Wesley Publishing Company.

Dewey, J. (1933). *How we think*. Boston, MA: D.C. Health and Company.

Elder L., & Paul, R. (2010). Foundation for critical thinking. http://www.criticalthinking.org/pages/universal-intellectual-standards/527

Schön, D. A. (1983). *The reflective practitioner: How professionals think in action*. New York, *NY:* Basic Books.

Andrea G. Tamburro, MSW, EdD, contributed to this chapter.

6

APA Citation Style

In the social sciences and related fields, writers use the APA writing style and citation system. In the field of social work, you too will format your papers according to guidelines in the *Publication Manual of the American Psychological Association,* currently in its sixth edition.

APA format is unique, and any kind of distinct formatting style presents challenges the first few times you apply it. APA style is no different: after you have formatted a few papers, you will reach a comfort level in how you set margins, tabs, and spacing as well as how you format headings, citations, and resource lists.

Think of APA as a code that you are sending to your reader, much like texting codes. When abbreviations are used in texting, they are short-cuts to convey meaning without spelling out a whole explanation. APA quotations, paraphrases, and citation formats are similar. When quotation marks are added, you are telling the reader that you did not write this section. The citation tells the reader who did write the quote, and the reference at the end gives information on how to find the original resource. When you paraphrase, your citation tells readers the original source, adding richness and credibility to your work.

Citing your research validates your findings and provides information so that others can find your source and read it in its entirety. In addition, a consistent citation system gives professionals a shared language or code so that they have a common understanding, enabling them to review literature effectively.

This chapter gives you an overview of select elements of APA style to get you started. If you need pre-work in how to set your margins, spacing, and tabs as well as how to create your header, see pages 305 to 307 in Chapter 18, "Formatting."

After you finish this chapter, you will be able to access an abundance of other resources to help you use APA style with confidence. Once you gain skill in using the system, you will appreciate the consistency that APA style provides when you write and review literature in social work. However, let us first review plagiarism, a topic that goes hand in hand with citing sources. In fact, citation prevents plagiarism while adding credibility to your research.

Plagiarism

If you use someone's work without giving proper credit, you must ask yourself *why*. Plagiarism robs the plagiarist more than anyone else, even if the ethical violation is never discovered. Students plagiarize for various reasons, such as fear and anxiety along with poor writing skills. The *dilemma* is that plagiarism feeds the dynamic that keeps students from developing their writing skills, robbing potential as it pulls down confidence and self-esteem.

When novice writers cut and paste another's words into their work, they are giving themselves a message that is loud and clear: *Good writing and insightful thinking are out of reach for me*. The irony is that effective writing is a skill that is *not* out of reach for anyone who actually does the work.

Writing effectively has never been more important than it is today: technology has fueled the importance of writing and, at the same time, made plagiarism easier to accomplish. Instructors can often spot plagiarism, becoming familiar with a student's vocabulary, spelling, grammar, and syntax through only one writing sample. To identify plagiarism, instructors can also use software: with only a sentence or two, the real source can be identified immediately. In fact, many instructors screen for plagiarism *before* they even read a paper.

Students need to learn how to write effectively when they have the chance, not waste their educational experiences on cutting and pasting. Though every writer must grow through the pain and uncertainty on the road to building skills and confidence, the payoff is incredible.

Place process above product—focus more on what you are learning than your final grade. In the *real world*, grades are not nearly as important as the ability to solve problems. In fact, the last time you are likely to be asked your GPA is *before* you secure your first job. After that point, your career is about your skills and accomplishments. Without effective writing skills, you significantly limit your opportunities: ask and you will find the help that you need to improve your writing skills.

What to Credit

Not all information needs to be documented. For example, you do not need to cite information that is considered common knowledge or facts that are available from a wide variety of sources. According to *The New St. Martin's Handbook*, here is a list of information that needs to be documented:

1. Direct quotations and paraphrase.
2. Information that is not widely known or claims that are not agreed upon.

3. Judgments, opinions, and claims of others.
4. Statistics, charts, tables, and graphs from any source.
5. Help provided by friends, instructors, or others.

In academic settings, you must also cite your own work from another course or article. Also be careful when turning in group projects that you do not claim the writing of another group participant as your work. For example, identify who provided information on each presentation slide.

The two most common types of references are *direct quotations* and *paraphrase*.

Direct quotation	Using someone else's exact words requires that the words be set off. For short quotes, use quotation marks; for quotes of 40 or more words, set off the quotation by indenting the left margin 0.5 inches. You can use an in-text reference along with a citation on the reference page. If you use a quote, be sure to explain how it helps explain your topic.
Paraphrase	Paraphrasing is putting someone else's ideas in your own words. When you paraphrase and cite your source, you add credibility to your work. *Note:* Making a few changes in word order, leaving out a word or two, or substituting similar words is not paraphrasing— it is plagiarism.

When students first begin scholarly writing, they often have difficulty with paraphrasing. True paraphrasing occurs when you read material, assimilate it, write about the concepts in your own words, and credit the original author. If you have trouble paraphrasing, try explaining to someone what you think the writer means and then write it in your own words.

Academic standards require you to provide evidence to support a position; outside sources add credibility. However, use quotations selectively. Just as quotes in exactly the right places can enhance your work, too many quotes or unnecessary ones distract your readers and lead them to believe you may not fully understand the topic. Aim for flow, be selective.

Working Bibliography

Citing research can be challenging because it involves details. Therefore, as you collect and use what others have discovered, compile a *working bibliography*. Though each system of documentation has slight variations from the others, they all contain similar information. Use note cards, a small notebook, or a special file on your computer as you collect your research. More advanced writers may want to use a bibliographic database that helps you organize your resources. Databases such as *RefWorks* and *Endnote* will also insert citations into your document as you write, as will Microsoft Word. If you use these aids, be sure to set the software to *APA6*. Also be sure to learn how to insert page and paragraph numbers into the citation for when you cite quotes.

Here is the kind of information you need to collect:

For Books:
- Author, title, and page number
- Publisher, location, and year of publication

For example:

Young, D. J., Tamburro, A. G., & Harris, M, (2014). *The writer's handbook: A*

   guide for social workers. Ogden Dunes, IN: Writer's Toolkit Publishing.

For Periodicals:
- Author, title of article
- Journal title, date of publication, volume and issue number

For example:

Manese, J. E., Wu, J. T., & Nepomuceno, C. A. (2001). The effect of training on

   multicultural counseling competencies: An exploratory study over a ten-

   year period. *Journal of Multicultural Social Work, 29*(1), 1-12.

For websites:
- Author (if known) and title
- Uniform Resource Locator (URL) network address, which includes path and file names and which are enclosed in angle brackets
- Date website was established (if available, located at the bottom of the home page)
- Date the source was published in print (if previously published)
- Paragraph number, if you quote from the website
- Date on which you accessed the information

For example:

National Association of Social Workers. (2008). *Code of ethics of the National*

        Association of Social Workers. Retrieved from http://www.socialworkers.org/

        pubs/code/code.asp

Because electronic sources are ever changing, print a hard copy of the material you are referencing or download the accessed information. To make citing your sources manageable, keep a working bibliography. Alternatively, Microsoft Word, Endnote, and RefWorks Software allow you to cite while you write. Endnote also allows you to save electronic documents, your comment notes, and keywords to enable searches.

APA Citation System

All citation systems, including APA style, require that sources be referenced both in the text and at the end of the work. Both references together provide the reader with complete information through cross-referencing.

- **APA citation style** requires *in-text citation* and *references*.

If you are writing a document in which you want to comment or provide parenthetical information related indirectly to your text, APA allows that through *footnotes* and *endnotes*.

You may cite one resource several times in your manuscript; however, you only need to include identifying information about the book (author, publisher, location, and date) one time in your reference list. Though you may refer to a variety of sources as you do your research, for APA style, list only references on your *reference page* that you cite in your work.

The following page contains a summary of major points from APA style, which you can use somewhat like a checklist. Then on pages 95 through 102, Figure 6.1, Quick Guide to APA Style, walks you through key information about APA style as it displays APA formatting.

As mentioned, to do some pre-work with setting paragraph controls and creating a header, see pages 307 to 308 in Chapter 18, "Formatting." In addition, make use of the many excellent resources online to assist you with the fine details that are not covered here.

Note: Also see Figure 4.5, Self-Esteem in Adolescents, an example of a student paper in APA citation style, pages 57 through 68.

APA Style

APA citation style is used in the social sciences. Here are some elements of the style.

Sections	**Title page** (title of paper, by line, running head/page number)
	Abstract (between 150 and 250 words, keyword summary)
	Main body (introduction, methods, results, and discussion)
	Reference page (titled, "Reference" or "References")
Authors/editors	Use last name and first initial (do not use first names)
	List all authors on the reference page
Titles	On title page and in text, use *title style* (upper and lower case)
	On reference page, use *sentence style* (capitalize first word only)
Publisher	Use full name; list city names and state abbreviations

Format:

- Use 1-inch margins (top, bottom, left, and right)
- Double space entire document, including block quotes
- Indent paragraphs 0.5 inches (0.5")
- Block margins at the left (leave *ragged edges*)
- Insert a *running head* in a header that contains the following:
  - On title page, at left margin: Running head: YOUR TITLE IN 50 CHARACTERS OR LESS; at the right margin, the page number 1
  - On second pages, format the running head with the *title only* in all capital letters in the upper left corner and the page number in the upper right corner
- On the title page, center the title and by line on the upper half of the page; use up to 12 words for the title (also include other information that your professor may require)
- Begin numbering on the title page
- Use a serif font such as **Times New Roman**, **12-point**
- Use up to 5 levels of headings
- Integrate short visuals with the text but put large visuals on separate pages
- Space two times after a period and one time after other marks of punctuation
- On the *reference page*:
  - Alphabetize by last name of authors; use last name and first initial; list all authors
  - If you cite two articles by the same authors, list the oldest article first
  - Block the first line of an entry at the left margin; indent second lines
  - Italicize titles of books and journals, capitalizing only the first word of titles

Quick Guide to

American Psychological Association (APA) Citation Style

Dina Studentessa

Best University

Author Note

A typical author's note would include acknowledgments, departmental

affiliations, disclaimers, and contact information. However, an author's note

is not required, even for theses and dissertations. If you include an *author's*

note, place it on your title page, as demonstrated here.

Figure 6.1. Quick Guide to APA Style

Abstract

An abstract is a one-paragraph summary of your paper that is between 150 to 250 words in length. An abstract summarizes the key ideas of your paper and may be the single most important paragraph of your paper. However, an abstract is *not* your introduction. Place the abstract on the second page, right after your title page. Notice that the section title, *Abstract*, is not presented in boldface type; section titles are different from headings. Also, though paragraphs throughout your paper are indented one half inch, *do not indent the first line of your abstract*. This paper also gives other tips about formatting APA style; however, when you have a detailed question about style, go right to the source and consult the *Publication Manual of the American Psychological Association, Sixth Edition* (2010) or visit the APA's website at www.apastyle.org.

Keywords: apa style, apa formatting, running head, apa example, apa title page, abstract, reference page

Quick Guide to APA Citation Style

Since APA style is used extensively for papers in social work, this guide introduces you to common elements of APA style, providing some formatting guidelines.

Your paper will include five main sections: the *title page*, *abstract*, *introduction*, *body*, and *reference page*. Start the abstract, introduction, and reference page each on a new page.

The introduction is the first section of your paper; start it on page 3; include the title of your paper (not in boldface because the title of your introduction is a section title, not a heading). However, you can start the body of your paper on the same page as the introduction.

In your introduction, discuss the problem and its importance as well as your process or research strategy, presenting your thesis or hypothesis.

General Guidelines

On the upper half of the title page, double space and center the title of your paper and your name. Use up to two lines for the title of the paper. Also, ask your professor for specifics about other information to include on the title page. If your title contains more than 50 characters, abbreviate your title for your *running head*.

Following the title page, write an abstract in one paragraph between 150 and 250 words. Do not indent in your abstract but do indent your keyword summary: Type "*Keywords:*" and follow it with several words in lower case that would identify your paper in a search.

Formatting

For your entire document, use 1-inch top, bottom, and side margins. Use a 12 point serif font, such as 12-point Times New Roman. Also double space your entire document, including your title page and reference pages.

However, for your spacing to be correct, you also must first set your *paragraph spacing* at 0 for spacing *before* and *after*. Therefore, when you set your *line spacing* on *double spacing*, also set *spacing* for *before* and *after* at 0; all of these controls are at the *Paragraph* tab.

Indent each paragraph 0.5 inches (one-half inch), and block your lines at the left margin. In other words, your right margins should have ragged edges (as shown here). Space one time after all punctuation marks except the period: Space two times after the period. On the reference page, however, space only one time. Number all of the pages of your document, starting with the title page.

Headings and Subheadings

APA guidelines provide five levels of headings. For example, the heading at the top of this page (Formatting) is a Level 1 heading; Level 1 headings are centered and presented in bold typeface. The heading immediately above this paragraph is a Level 2 heading; Level 2 headings are flush with the left margin and in bold typeface. Table 1 below displays the various headings, describing whether each is centered, blocked at the left, indented, or presented in boldface type or italics. Note that Levels 3 through 5 are paragraph headings, with the text following the period after the heading.

Table 1.1. Five Levels of Headings

Level 1 Centered, Boldface, Upper and Lower Case
Level 2 Blocked at Left Margin, Boldface, Upper and Lower Case
Level 3 Indented, boldface, and lower case. (Start text.)
Level 4 indented, italicized, boldface, and lowercase. (Start text.)
Level 5 indented, italicized, and lowercase. (Start text.)

Also note that *headings* are different from *section titles*. Levels 1 through 4 are in boldface type; however, these section titles are not in boldface type: *title of your paper*, *title of your introduction*, *abstract* and *references*.

In-Text Citations

Use the author-date citation system to identify your sources, crediting authors whether you quote them directly or put their ideas and research in your own words. For indirect references (paraphrased statements), cite the author's last name and the publication year; for direct quotes, include the page number. Put this information in parentheses at the end of the quotation.

However, if you use the author's name in your text, do not repeat the author's name in the parentheses.

For signal verbs, APA style recommends using the past tense (such as, "stated") or present perfect tense (such as, "has stated"), for example: "Tyler (1988) stated, '[a]ll students can learn what the schools teach if they can find an interest in it' (p. 45)."

For a citation that has only one author, list the author's last name and the year of the publication. If you are giving an exact quote, also list the page number, as shown above. For a citation with two authors, list both authors for all citations; for example: "Winger and Ginther (1992) developed the method."

For citations with three to five authors, list all authors for the first citation, as follows: "Ginther, Tyler, and Winger (2001) supported their research." For the second citation of the same work, cite the first author's surname and add *et al.* (the Latin abbreviation for *and others*). Put the year of publication in parentheses; for example: "Ginther et al. (2001) broke down the groups based on level of experience (p. 5)."

Reference List

Place the reference list at the end of the paper on a separate page. Begin the page with the word "Reference" or "References" centered at the top in bold typeface. For each reference, double space and do not indent the first line; however, indent the second lines 0.5 inches (hanging indent).

List only those works that you cite in the text (APA, 2009). References include the following: author name (or names), publication date, title of work, and publication data. Arrange the citations in alphabetical order by surname.

Each kind of reference requires a specific form, so refer directly to the rule that discusses the type of source that you are citing.

Resources

Doing anything new for the first time is difficult. After you have formatted your first few papers in APA citation style, you will feel much more confident. In the meantime, refer to the latest publication and website provided by the APA. Also refer to other websites, such as Purdue Online Writing Lab (OWL), which is a valuable resource for many types of writing questions, including APA style.

Every detail makes a difference. In fact, most professors can tell *at a glance* if a paper is formatted correctly, and any type of error could affect your grade. Proofread and edit your papers thoroughly, then compare your paper side by side with a model based on APA's latest guidelines. In other words, if you are using an outdated source, your formatting will be incorrect no matter how vigilant you are when you format your text.

References

American Psychological Association [APA]. (2009). *Concise rules of APA*

    style. Washington, DC: Author.

APA. (2010). *Publication manual of the American Psychological Association*.

    (6th ed.). Washington, DC: Author.

Purdue University Online Writing Lab (OWL). May 2011. APA formatting and

    style guide. Retrieved from http://owl.english.purdue.edu/owl/

Stevens, A. (2009). *Some guidelines from the publication manual of the*

    American Psychological Association. Gary, IN: Indiana

    University Northwest.

COACHING TIP
And & the Ampersand

For in-text citations using signal phrases, use the word *and*; for in-text

citations that do not use signal phrases, use the ampersand (&):

Jones and Smith (2007) agree that research is important.

Research is important (Smith & Jones, 2007).

For your reference list, use the ampersand instead of the word *and*:

Jones, R., & Smith, C. (2007). *Research is important: Do your research now.*

    Chicago, IL: Action Research Publishers.

Quotations

Here are guidelines for displaying long and short quotations.

Short Quotations   Incorporate direct quotes *less than 40 words long* into your narrative and set them off by using quotation marks.

Example 1:

"Understanding the context of practice is an essential component of social work practice as is providing service that respects diversity" (Green, Gregory, & Mason, 2009, p. 413).

Example 2:

According to Nixon and Murr (2006), "the development of professional practice is based on practice learning, yet there is no consensus about its definition" (p. 798).

Long Quotations   Display quotations of *forty or more words* in block-quote format. Display the quotation separately from the text by doing the following:

- Indent the quote 0.5 inches from the left margin. (Do not use quotation marks; the indentation signals the reader to the quote.)
- In APA style, double space the body of your paper as well as your quotation.
- Place the period at the end of the quote, not at the end of the citation.

Example:

> Although beginning practitioners often think that methods, approaches, or skills are the critical factors in achieving good client outcomes, clients surveyed in many research studies reported that the relationship qualities of warmth, respect, genuineness, empathy, and acceptance were most important. (Chang et al. 2009, p. 72)

Quotations within Quotations

For short quotes (less than 40 words of quoted material within text):

- Display the main quote between double quotation marks.
- Display the internal quote with single quotation marks.

Example 1:

According to Kegan (1983), "Carl Rogers's 'client-centered' or 'nondirective' therapy has had an enormous influence on the training and practice of three generations of counselors and therapists" (p. 302).

Example 2:

According to Cummins, Byers, and Pedrick (2011) "[l]ong-time policy practitioners realize that 'it is really all about relationship'" (p. 19).

Indirect Quotes or Paraphrasing

When you paraphrase, you express an author's ideas in your own words and should not use quotation marks. However, you must credit the source by using the author's last name and date. By citing the resources that informed your statement, you ensure the reader that you understand the information and how it relates to your topic.

For example, here is a paraphrase of the quote above by *Chang, et al.*:

According to Chang, Scott, and Decker (2009) and several other authors, clients thought the most helpful part of social services was the warm, accepting, respectful, genuine, and empathetic relationship with the practitioner.

Omissions in Quotations

Use ellipsis marks to show omission of a word or words. An ellipsis mark consists of three spaced periods. If the omission comes at the end of a sentence of quoted material, add one more period to indicate the end of the sentence.

Example:

Karger and Stoesz (2010) indicated that,

> Poverty is a fluid . . . process for most Americans. The University of
>
> Michigan's Panel Study of Income Dynamics . . . followed 5,000 families
>
> for almost 10 years (1969 – 1978) and found that 2 percent of families
>
> were persistently poor throughout the entire period. (p. 112)

Brackets for Changes or Adding Words

At times, you must change or add a word or two to quoted material so that the reader can make sense of the quote in its new context.

- When you add a word or two or your own, put them between brackets: [ ]

    Example:

    > Jones (2012) asked what "knowledge, skills, and values [were] necessary
    >
    > for culturally competent service provision" (p. 3).

Note: On most keyboards, brackets are located to the right of the "P" key.

Quotation Marks and Punctuation Placement

When using quotation marks, make sure to display them correctly in conjunction with other punctuation marks, such as *commas*, *periods*, *semicolons*, and *colons*. (The style of punctuation described below is called *closed style*. For information on *open style*, see page 368.)

Here are a few rules to remember:

- *Commas* and *periods* (including ellipses marks) are placed inside quotation marks.

    Example: When I read the case file, "Brown et.al.," I immediately

    called my supervisor. In her message back to me, she

    stated, "Call me immediately."

- *Semicolons* and *colons* are placed on the outside of quotation marks.

    Example: The judge instructed, "Leave the courtroom immediately"; we all responded accordingly.

- Footnotes are placed directly on the outside of quotation marks (no space added).

    Example: According to the Infectious Disease Clinics (2008), the

                         virus can spread quickly: "Insects, birds and some

                         species of animal are carriers . . . across the continent."[2]

- The placement of *question marks* (and *exclamation points*) depends on the meaning. That is, does the quotation itself pose a question, or is the quotation within a sentence that poses the question.

    Example: Did Browning really say, "less is more"?
                         Was it Elizabeth who said, "What are our options?"

Note: Often quotations are introduced by placing a comma directly after the word that introduces the quote.

Recap

A key element of citation is detail: the more that you practice, the better your skills become.

Now that you know the basics of APA citation style, you can readily use online journal databases that provide APA citation formats. You can find a wealth of information online, including sites that format references in APA style and do it free of charge. In addition, free tutorials are available online, including those prepared by the APA:

http://www.apastyle.org/learn/tutorials/basics-tutorial.aspx

The more you work with APA style, the easier it becomes.

Writing Workshop

APA Formatting

Instructions:

Write a paper summarizing why it is important to adapt formatting for readers; also summarize key elements of APA formatting style. If you wish, compare and contrast APA style with other styles.

Format your paper in APA style, and include the following parts:

- Title page
- Abstract
- Introduction
- Body (at least 2 pages)
- Reference Page

Use at least 2 levels of headings.

Note: As an alternative to the above, select a paper that you have previously written and revise it using APA format and citation style. Also, write your instructor a process message explaining the kinds of changes you made from the first draft to the last one.

References

APA. (2009). *Concise rules of APA style.* Washington, DC: Author.

APA. (2010). *Publication manual of the American Psychological Association* (6th ed.). Washington, DC: Author.

Cummins, L. K., Byers, K. V., & Pedrick, L. (2011). *Policy practice for social workers: New strategies for a new era.* Indianapolis, IN: Allyn & Bacon.

Lundsford, A., & Connors, R. (2001). *The new St. Martin's handbook.* Boston, MA: Bedford/St. Martin's Press.

Purdue University. (2013). Online Writing Lab (OWL). Retrieved from http://owl.english.purdue.edu/owl/

Stevens, A. (2009). *Some guidelines from the publication manual of the American Psychological Association.* Gary, Indiana: Indiana University Northwest.

Andrea G. Tamburro, MSW, EdD, Contributed to this chapter.

PART 2: PROCESS AND STRUCTURE

At times, process and structure can seem at odds with each other; for example, when you write, you may lose your ideas as you try to get them on page correctly. In part, here is how to solve this problem:

- First, manage the writing process effectively: learn to compose freely.
- Second, diligently build your editing and revising skills.

While you compose, you are creating: you are putting original thoughts on paper. While you edit and revise, you are analyzing, evaluating, and re-working structure on many levels; but you are also gaining new insight into your topic.

Composing is a process, and Chapter 7 gives you tools for managing the writing process. However, do not underestimate the discipline it takes to apply what you learn. Composing is the most difficult part of writing because you are *thinking on paper*, and each new insight takes energy and effort.

Revising is also a process. You start your journey to build editing skills by working on the *sentence core*, the power base of every sentence. The sentence core teaches you structure, opening the door for understanding grammar for writing and for applying principles of editing and revising.

You will further your understanding of the sentence core and structure in Part 3, Mechanics of Writing. Once you understand structure, issues of style, such as using the active voice, applying parallel structure, and being concise become easy. These principles are covered in Part 4, Grammar for Writing, and Part 5, Editing for Clarity.

Here is what you will learn in Part 2, Process and Structure:

Chapter 7, **Writing as Process**: you learn how to manage the writing process, separating composing from editing. You also learn about pre-writing and revising as well as about audience, purpose, and voice.

Chapter 8, Dynamic Sentences: you learn how to control the sentence core, the starting point for gaining control of structure. Structure provides the context for understanding verbs, pronouns, and modifiers; understanding the sentence core also sets the stage for learning principles of editing, such as active voice, pronoun viewpoint, and parallel structure.

Chapter 9, Cohesive Paragraphs and Transitions: you learn how to develop cohesive, coherent paragraphs. Effective paragraphs contribute to reader-friendly writing.

By the time you finish this book, you may find that you are an incurable editor; but that will happen only if you apply what you are learning to your own writing. As you work through each chapter, write on a daily basis; writing in a journal loosens up your composing skills. However, to develop your thinking skills, you need to use writing to solve problems.

7

Writing as Process

When you write, are you focused more on the *product* or the *process*?

1. Do you try to figure things out in your head *before* putting words on the page?
2. Do you stop to correct grammar and punctuation *as you compose*?
3. Do your ideas dissolve before you get them down?
4. Do you send out your writing without proofreading or editing it?

If you answered *yes* to any of the above, you may think that you have *writer's block*. However, writer's block is the inability to produce new work, and none of the above relate to writer's block: they all relate to *editor's block*, which is far more common. Editor's block results in part from being overly concerned with product at the expense of process.

- *Editor's Block Type A:* You edit as you compose, and your ideas get jammed in your head or dissolve before they reach the page.

- *Editor's Block Type B:* You do not proofread or edit your work because you feel anxious about mistakes or are unsure of what to correct.

You can overcome *Editor's Block Type A* by separating composing from editing, which is discussed next. You will overcome *Editor's Block Type B* by improving your editing skills, which each chapter of this book addresses.

Focusing on the *writing process* rather than *final product* assists you in achieving an important aim of writing, which is *to learn*. Writing develops your thinking skills, partly because writing itself is a problem-solving activity. As you write, you gain insight that leads to deeper levels of understanding. Writing forces you to clarify your thinking.

Even so, when writing is difficult for you, none of that matters. You want to get your writing tasks finished as quickly as possible so that you can bring your suffering to an end. That way of thinking leads to the *first and final draft* approach to writing: you force yourself to get your words down right as you compose. As you try to get your words down right, your ideas evaporate before they hit the page. Being stuck is frustrating.

The fact is, trying to make too many decisions all at the same time is one reason why you get stuck. First and final draft writing is a habit that results from anxiety about the final product, a habit that also makes writing much more difficult than it needs to be. Therefore, here is the most important principle to learn about the writing process:

Do *not* compose and edit at the same time.

To compose freely, you must not only understand the writing process but also embrace the process. Dropping the first and final draft mentality is a huge first step, even if you think the first and final draft approach works for you. You see, even if you achieve good grades, the first and final draft approach robs you of long-term learning.

In this chapter, you learn composing techniques and tools as well as more about each phase of the writing process. Then in the following chapters, you learn how to make effective editing decisions to improve your final product.

So let us get started learning how to manage the process so that you gain control of your writing.

Process to Product

The best papers look as if they were easy to write: the words flow and the ideas link together logically. Yet behind every beautiful, finished piece of writing lies uncertainty and hard work. Even the best writers question themselves and their ability as they write. While writing *Grapes of Wrath*, John Steinbeck wrote in his journal,

I'm not a writer, I've been fooling myself and other people. I wish I were.
My work is not good, I think—I'm desperately upset about it. Have no
discipline any more . . . (as cited in Hathaway, 1991, p. 48)

Writing—or any creative activity for that matter—involves facing the unknown. Uncertainty never feels good. Therefore, one challenge all writers have is immersing themselves in uncertainty as they work toward deeper understanding.

Once you start writing, you gain deeper insight into your topic, even when you are not consciously thinking about it. Writing forces you to make progress, even when it feels painful: putting critical thoughts on paper takes energy and courage because you are forced to think clearly.

Writing is a creative process, so you cannot depend on formulas to produce good writing. However, embracing the process allows you to take your attention off of the product and instead to focus your energies to get the best results.

The writing process consists of distinct phases, for example:

- *Composing:* creating, inventing, exploring, solving problems
- *Proofreading:* correcting grammar, punctuation, and spelling
- *Editing:* improving the quality and structure of sentences
- *Revising:* changing, rearranging, and reinventing

Though the above phases are not sequential, they are cyclical. Thus, when you write, move back and forth between compositing activities and editing activities, but stay focused on one type of activity or the other.

Think of composing as a right-brain activity and editing as a left-brain activity. When you compose, you are drawing from your creative side; when you edit, you are drawing on your analytical skills. That is one reason why you can quickly get stuck when you edit as you compose.

Until you are able to compose freely, writing is much more difficult for you than it needs to be. When you stop editing as you compose, and composing still feels excruciatingly difficult, you may not yet understand your topic. When that is the case, focus on *the thinking behind the writing.* In fact, you may be confusing the difficulty of writing with the difficulty of clearly understanding your topic.

So let us add one more phase to the writing process: *pre-writing.* You see, the writing process actually begins *before* you start to compose.

Pre-Writing and Composing

Have you ever started writing and found yourself stuck? Trying to compose before you are ready contributes to *writer's block.*

Writing is a process because learning is a process. By focusing on pre-writing activities, you develop your understanding of your topic in a more gentle, natural way and have a better chance for good results. So if you find yourself avoiding a writing task, do some pre-writing activities:

- *Pre-writing:* reading, thinking, discussing, summarizing

Reading is a form of meditation or reflection, and some of your best ideas bubble up as you read. Activities such as walking or discussing your project with a friend also allow you to reflect on your topic. Reflective thinking gives you insights when you least expect them; so when you feel blocked, change activities but stay engaged.

As you read and discuss, jot down insights and questions and put concepts in your own words. Keep a notebook or note cards handy so that you can collect your insights as you experience them.

However, do not make the mistake of thinking that you need to understand your topic completely before you start writing:

Write to learn.

Write yourself clear-headed: as you write, your understanding becomes clearer. Go back and forth between pre-writing and composing: when you feel stuck, read more and then discuss your ideas with a peer. After you read and take notes, summarize what you have learned *in your own words*. (Cut and paste plagiarism destroys careers and confidence.)

Set a time to write, and then show up and trust the process:

Start early and write often,
even when you do not feel like writing.

As soon as you take action, you will feel better and have something to show for your efforts. Getting your ideas on the page, even when your thinking is still unclear, is a hurdle you must overcome. You need to get your rough draft thinking on the page before your best insights appear.

Write about what you know first. Start with the body, developing your core ideas. The body will lead you to your conclusion. Once you have written your conclusion, you will have a clear idea about how to write your introduction, posing the questions you have already answered.

At some point, you must come to terms with your purpose for writing. You see, without clarifying your purpose, you cannot be sure that you understand your mission.

Here are two mistakes writers make:

1. Trying to understand their purpose fully *before* they start writing.

2. Thinking their project is complete *without* defining their purpose.

Whether you define your purpose before you start writing or whether you jump right into a task to see where it leads depends partly on your learning style. For example:

- *Global learners* tend to be spontaneous, jumping right into a task to see where it will lead.

- *Analytic learners* plan and organize, focusing on the details.

Can you tell by the above descriptions which type of learner you are? If not, you can go to the Internet to research *learning styles*. Knowing your learning style validates your unique approach and aids you in making effective choices, especially about the planning elements of writing.

Though global learners might want to jump right in and start writing, analytical learners are likely to prefer putting down more details before they start writing. So let us look at some elements of planning next.

Problem, Purpose, and Plan

Once you understand your purpose, your purpose will drive the writing process. However, when you start a project, you may try to develop your response at the peril of not understanding the question at the root of the problem. You see, on some level, all writing involves *solving a problem*, even though the problem may not always be obvious.

> *What is the question? If there is no question, then there is no answer.*
>
> —Gertrude Stein

Focus on understanding the problem, and eventually your purpose will become clear. By articulating your purpose, you not only understand your mission more clearly, you can then also convey it to your audience more effectively.

To define your purpose, start by defining your problem:

- What is my core question?

Next, turn your question into a **thesis statement**:

- A thesis statement is a one- or two-sentence summary of the problem along with a general overview of the writer's response.

Though you covered how to write a thesis statement in Chapter 1, "Academic Writing," here is a brief review.

Let us say your task is to write about pollution and the environment. Start by stating the problem as a question:

Thesis Question: How does pollution affect the environment?

Then turn your question into statement:

Pollution affects the environment by . . .

Finally, once you understand some of the broader implications of your question, draft a statement that reflects your broad response:

Thesis Statement: Pollution affects the environment by destroying specific aspects of it, such as nature and wildlife.

As you write about your purpose, avoid using the word *purpose*. For example, your first draft might include a statement such as the following:

The purpose of this paper is to discuss how pollution affects the environment.

When you revise your purpose statement, remove the word *purpose*:

Pollution destroys the environment, especially wildlife and natural habitats.

Next, let's look more closely into planning tools. Though analytic learners might prefer to write an outline first, global learners are more inclined to use less structured planning tools such as the ones discussed below.

Planning Tools

The planning tools discussed here will assist you in getting your ideas on the page as you prepare to compose. For example, a tool such as mind mapping focuses your attention and draws upon your critical and creative thinking. Though analytic learners might prefer to write an outline first, global learners are more inclined to use less structured planning tools such as the ones discussed below.

If you do not now think of yourself as being creative, ask yourself if you are good at solving problems. Creativity entails solving problems. *Creativity is listening to the obvious and responding effectively.* Focus on solving the problem, and your writing will flow.

Mind Maps   This form of brainstorming, also called *clustering*, allows you to get your ideas down in a quick, spontaneous way. First, choose your topic. Next, write your topic in the middle of the page, circling it. Finally, free associate ideas, as in the mind map that follows, which is in response to the question, "What is difficult about writing?"

Figure 7.1. Mind Map: What is difficult about writing?

Spend three minutes creating a mind map on your topic before you start composing.

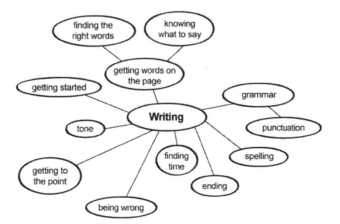

Mind mapping is an alternative to writing a formal outline. Use mind mapping to get your ideas on the page before they dissolve. Also use mind mapping to plan your day or an important phone call. *Select a topic and work on it for 3 minutes.*

Scratch Outlines   Rather than using the cluster technique of mind mapping, simply make a list of your ideas. Keep a notepad close at hand so that you collect your insights as they come to you.

Page Maps   Put the key points from your scratch outline or mind map along the side of a blank page. Then fill in the details by using each key point as the topic for a focused-writing activity.

This technique helps eliminate one of the biggest fears of any writing task: starting with a blank page. For example, imagine that you did a mind map on *finding a job*; the following could be your side headings:

Figure 7.2. Page Map: Finding a Job

Once you complete your mind map, use the information to create a page map.

Finding a Job
Introduction
    Thesis Statement:
    Finding a job requires skill and know-how.
Networking
    Associations
    Local Organizations
    Online
Portfolio
    Résumés
    Letters of Reference
    Work Samples
Pay and Benefits
    Medical and Dental
    Tuition Reimbursement
    Training

Once you have your page map, write about what you know first. When you get stuck, do more research.

Fishbone Diagrams   A fishbone diagram is also known as a *root-cause diagram* because it forces you to probe deeply into a problem. First, identify the problem. Next, identify major components of your problem. For each component, ask *why* five times.

For example, if you had difficulty completing a writing task, you could first turn your problem into a statement and then work through it by asking the question *why* five times.

Problem statement: I am having difficulty with this writing task.

Why?   I am having trouble getting started.

Why?   I am feeling as if it is out of my control.

Why?   I don't understand the topic well enough.

Why?   I haven't done my research.

Why?   I haven't taken the time to find resources.

Once you have gained insight into your problem, here is an additional step to add to your fishbone diagram process:

Next Step: Do research today from 3 to 4 p.m.

Journalist's Questions   Journalists focus on the *who, what, when, where, why*, and *how* of an event. When you find yourself stuck, use these questions to tease out the dynamics of your problem.

- **Who?**   Who is involved or affected? What are their attitudes and beliefs?

- **What?**   What problems need to be resolved? What are the desired outcomes? Which details are important, which irrelevant?

- **When?**   When did the event happen? What is the timeline? Is the time frame relevant?

- **Where?**   Is a specific location involved? Is the location significant? What is unique about the location?

- **How?**   How did the events occur or the situation evolve? Who did what?

- **Why?**   Why did this happen? Why is this important? Why is my solution the best?

In addition to using these questions to identify purpose, you may also adapt these questions to plan your task:

- **Who?**   Who is my reader? What does my reader expect?

- **What?**   What am I trying to achieve? What outcomes can I expect?

- **When?**   What is my time frame? When is this project due? What internal due dates do I need to set?

- **How?**   How will I complete this task? How can others assist me?

- **Why?**   Why is this issue important?

See beyond your own point of view by examining the problem from various angles; also consider your reader's viewpoint. If you are arguing a point or trying to persuade your audience, include the opposing argument and then show how your points are superior.

Composing Tools

Once you have done some planning, you are ready to start composing. When you compose, focus on getting your ideas down in a quick and spontaneous way. In other words, do not try to screen your thoughts or edit your words until after you have drafted your ideas.

Freewriting

Pick up a pen and start writing: get your words on the page in a free-flow, stream-of- consciousness way. As you freewrite, you build your ability to compose freely while blocking out your compulsion to correct your writing.

If you have never tried freewriting, simply set the clock for 10 minutes and start writing. Since writing is a problem-solving activity, you may find yourself actively working on solving problems that now drain your energy. Freewriting helps clear your head, allowing you to focus and renew your energy.

Focused Writing

Choose a topic and write about only that topic for about 10 to 15 minutes or 3 pages.

Focused writing can help you make good use of small amounts of time that would otherwise be lost. Focused writing can also help you jump-start a project that you have been avoiding.

If you have difficulty composing, do more research. Read about your topic and take notes. Jot down your insights and write about your current understanding.

By developing your thinking behind your writing using a process-oriented approach, you can avoid some of the excruciatingly difficult moments. The key is writing about your topic as you learn about it.

As you know, proofreading and editing are separate and critical steps in the writing process.

Proofreading and Editing

As you now know, many people suffer as much from editor's block as they do from writer's block: they do not know what to look for to improve the quality of their writing, so they hold their breath, turn in their work, and hope for the best.

The only real solution to editor's block is to develop proofreading and editing skills. Proofreading and editing are distinct activities:

- When you *proofread*, you are correcting grammar, punctuation, and spelling (but you are not changing the wording).

- When you *edit*, you are upgrading the quality of writing by improving its readability.

The best time to proofread a document is after you have edited it. Since editing is about making changes, you defeat your purpose if you proofread your writing to perfection before your words are in final form. Often a deadline will put a natural end to editing—but if you do not leave enough time to proofread after you edit, your document is likely to contain errors.

Here are some **proofreading tips**:

1. Establish proofreading as the final part of your writing process.

2. Set an internal deadline before your project is due so that you have time to correct your work.

3. Read your document sentence by sentence to make sure each is correct, clear, and complete.

4. Print out a copy of your final draft—you will see errors on a hard copy that you will not see on the computer screen.

5. Keep a log of the types of errors you consistently make along with examples of how to correct them.

Here are some **editing tips:**

1. Throughout your writing process, go back and forth between composing and editing or revising.

2. Remove or re-write sentences that do not make sense.

3. Edit important documents with a peer.

4. Have someone read your paper out loud to you.

5. Leave as much time as you can between your final draft and your final edit, also allowing sufficient time to revise your document.

6. As you go through each chapter in this book, develop an editing checklist.

While proofreading and editing ensure that a document is correct and written in a reader-friendly style, revising brings your work to its highest level of quality. After you review the proofreader's marks, you take a look at what is involved when you revise your writing.

Revising

Revising is a *re-visioning* process. Revising requires that you see your material with fresh eyes and an open mind. You are ready to revise once you know your topic at a deeper level than when you first started writing about it.

Change is inherent in the thinking process, and answers change as your thinking evolves. As you revise, you are likely to find that you must shed some of your original thinking, which can be painful. You are also likely to find that you must shed some of your well-constructed sentences and paragraphs, which can also be difficult.

To revise, you must step back and evaluate your document and its purpose. Here are some qualities of the **revising process**:

- *Re-visioning.* Has your vision shifted? Does your purpose statement or thesis still reflect the essence of your document? What are your main points?

- *Questioning.* Are there gaps in your thinking? Have you developed your thinking beyond first responses or superficial ones? Are you overly attached to an answer that may not be complete? Are you trying to make answers fit where they do not fit?

- *Identifying Critical Issues*. Can your reader easily identify your main points? Have you presented critical information first? Do you need to reorganize information or eliminate empty information?

- *Rewriting*. Do you need to rewrite some parts because you have reached a new perspective?

First drafts are the most difficult because the content is unfamiliar. Once the topic becomes familiar, ideas flow and writing becomes easier.

Writing, specifically revising, is a *recursive activity*: *recursive* means that it is a process that can repeat itself indefinitely. Each time you go into a piece of writing to revise it, your new vision reflects your deeper understanding. And, at some point, you also need to say to yourself, "This piece is finished—it's time to move on!"

Voice and Audience

Voice is an elusive element of writing that speaks to a reader, engaging the person as well as the intellect. Voice is the connective tissue of all types of writing, not just creative or personal writing, but professional writing as well. Whenever writing does not engage readers, they have difficulty connecting with the topic at hand.

Developing your voice is as important as understanding your audience. In fact, the first step in adapting to your audience is writing in a reader-friendly style. Simple, clear, concise writing meets the needs of any audience more effectively than does complicated, artificial writing. Therefore, before you worry too much about your audience, focus on developing your voice, your style.

If your writing is more complicated than your speech, keep the following in mind:

If you would not say it that way, do not write it that way.

Right now, you may be going out of your way to make your writing sound more formal, using words such as *utilization* instead of *use*. Or perhaps you use canned phrases such as *per your request*. Would you ever sit across the table with someone at lunch and say, "Per our previous discussion" or "Thank you in advance"?

Readers do not connect with writing unless it is alive and in the moment. To change your writing style, let go of artificial, canned constructions and instead begin to say what you mean in a clear, direct voice. As you write more, this kind of simple writing will come naturally to you. By the way, to avoid using *per*, simply say, *as we discussed*. And a simple *thank you* is sufficient; *in advance* can sound presumptuous, detracting from the good sentiment that you intended.

Getting past the stage of complicated writing may seem challenging at first. The only solution is to write freely and frequently until you bring your writing to a higher level of skill and comfort.

However, complicated writing may not be your issue. Could it be that your writing sounds too informal and your grammar needs repair? If that is the case,

> *Just because you would say it that way*
> *does not mean that you should write it that way.*

At face value, this saying seems to contradict the previous. However, different writers have different issues. Regardless of the issue that interferes with your writing, your solution is the same: write freely and frequently.

Finding your voice is not a one-time event. *Voice* is a process in which you reconnect with yourself, your topic, and your readers every time you sit down to write. Connecting with yourself and others is what makes writing challenging and also what turns writing into a powerful learning tool. As you gain insight, you grow personally and have the opportunity to make important changes.

 If you have not yet found your voice, stay committed to the process. As discussed, the first step involves writing until you feel as comfortable writing as you do speaking. The next step is learning how to connect with any topic until you learn it well enough to write freely about it. The final step entails editing and revising your writing until it meets the needs of your audience.

On the path to finding your voice, ask yourself:

- Who is my audience? What do my readers need to know?

- What are my insights and key points?

- What can I teach my readers so that they gain value?

Writing in a journal daily is one step in the process of finding your voice: you are writing not only about topics that are close to your heart but also about topics that you know by heart, which allows you to compose freely. As you write honestly about a topic, you have the opportunity to develop yourself more fully, if that is one of your objectives. When you compose, do not worry about your voice. Once you are able to write freely, your voice will appear. First get your ideas, your insights, your reflections on the page.

Others may still not hear your voice until after you edit your work. Right now, your voice may be buried under unnecessary and complicated words and the passive voice. Writing from an effective and consistent point of view may also feel out of reach. As you learn to edit, you also learn how to cut and reshape your words so that they connect with your readers.

After a while, you will know whether or not you are speaking from your voice as you compose. Even then, you need to edit out the clutter so that your voice comes through strong and clear. You see, finding your voice may be about composing, but clarifying your voice is more about *editing*. Adapting your writing for your audience is as much about editing as it is about composing. Does that surprise you?

Critical Voices

As you write, you may find that you are critical of yourself. Be aware that you may be hyper-sensitive when it comes to expressing your creativity. When you criticize yourself, you drain your energy and motivation.

Shut down your critics.

Shutting down your inner critic is more difficult than dealing with criticism from others. In fact, the worst part of criticism from others is that it triggers self-criticism, those automatic negative thoughts that drain your energy and self-confidence.

When you feel especially critical of yourself, write about it. Writing about your fears and your feelings processes them so that you do not get stuck feeling helpless. Write until you talk yourself back into feeling strong and secure.

By showing your writing to others when you feel confident, you are more likely to accept their feedback graciously. If your objective is to learn how to improve, you are likely to gain knowledge that spurs you on. However, if your objective is to impress someone, you are likely to be disappointed. Hence, just as you want to shut down your critics, also take your expectations out of your writing.

When your expectations of what other people think are high, their words are more likely to sound negative or critical. You will have reached an important point in your skill development when you can turn negative-sounding comments into feedback that spurs you on to higher levels.

An unconscious fear of criticism is worse than criticism itself. That is because once you hear the actual words, you can regroup and emerge stronger. In contrast, fear is paralyzing, and the only way to combat fear is to take action. Start writing, even if you are writing about your own fears.

Fear of criticism goes hand in hand with an expectation of perfection. When you are disappointed about not being perfect, you are setting yourself up:

Perfect writing does not exist.

Perfection exists only in the mind, so do not beat yourself up for being human. Instead, expect mistakes, knowing they are the doorway to growth. Each time you embrace a mistake, you have an opportunity to do more than correct the error, you have an opportunity to build your own character.

There are no secrets to success. It is the result of preparation,
hard work, and learning from failure. –Colin Powell

Once you learn to embrace your mistakes as learning opportunities, not simply accept them, you will have learned a critical life lesson as well.

In Chapter 8, "Dynamic Sentences," you focus on *sentence core*, which is the most important element of editing—in fact, the sentence core is the powerhouse of every sentence that you write.

Before going to the next chapter, do the activities at the end of this chapter.

Recap

Learning how to edit helps you make effective writing decisions with more confidence and less effort. However, the only way to become a better writer is to write more, using writing as a problem-solving tool.

Remember, the more you write, the better your skills become, with or without a teacher or writing coach.

Here are some of the key points stressed in this chapter:

➢ Compose freely without looking for the right word or the right wording.

➢ Respond to writing anxiety by working on your task.

➢ Go back and forth between composing and editing as you work through your project.

➢ Allow time to revise your work by setting an internal deadline that is earlier than your external deadline (your actual due date).

➢ Proofread your document as your last step.

➢ Reach your audience by simplifying your writing.

- ➤ Shut down all critics, including yourself, so that you stay energized and focused.

- ➤ Use pre-writing and planning tools such as mind mapping, scratch outlines, focused writing, and page maps.

- ➤ Follow the plan outlined in this book—no excuses and no shortcuts.

As you write, you are tapping into your creativity and gaining insight. You are also building critical thinking skills and making more effective writing decisions so that you improve your career opportunities.

Writing Workshop

Activity 1: What Is Difficult About Writing?

Write a short paper discussing your history as a writer.

1. What is it about writing that challenges you? What causes you to want to give up and walk away?

2. What do you think about your ability to write? What kinds of experiences have shaped your feelings about writing?

3. Have you ever received feedback that made you question your ability to succeed?

4. Finally, what is good about writing? What do you like about writing? How can writing help you grow?

Start by mind mapping the question or by completing a scratch outline. Next do a focused writing: sit down and write. Do not edit your writing as you compose—just get your ideas on the page.

Writing about your experiences opens the process so that you can make substantial progress. By honestly revisiting some experiences, you can let go of them as well as the unproductive ways of thinking that hold you back.

As an ancient saying tells us,

If you hold it in, it will destroy you; if you let it out, it will free you.

Activity 2: Journaling

Writing daily in a journal is a potent form of self-reflection.

The clarity that journaling brings can lead to freedom from the past, giving you more options in the present and in the future. That is because writing is a discovery process that aids you in understanding your own story more deeply. In fact, many people write their memoirs by journaling about one experience at a time. As you journal, you gain insight into who you are, what motivates you, and how to make important changes.

When you journal, do not correct your grammar, punctuation, or spelling: *just write!* Start your journal, and follow the 2 x 4 method: 2 pages, 4 times a week.

1. Get a notebook so that you stay organized.

2. Write for 10 minutes or 2 pages, pouring whatever is on your mind or in your heat onto the pages of your journal.

Journaling helps you find your voice as you gain the experience of using writing as a problem-solving tool. See the example of a journal that follows.

Figure 7.3. Sample Journal

Write 2 pages in your journal at least 4 times a week, and you will make progress.

> The holidays are just getting started, and I'm looking forward to celebrating with my family. I'm writing this journal in the cafeteria while I wait for my friends to meet me. It's kind of weird; I mean at the beginning of the semester, I hated writing journals and never knew what to write about. Now I can't say that I love to write journals, but it's not as hard to write about things anymore. The ideas just come to me now. In the beginning, I would sit for 10 or 20 minutes just trying to think of something to write about. Now it's like 5 seconds and I say to myself, "Oh yeah, that will be easy to write about."
>
> Sometimes I write about how I am feeling, and other times I write about what I am learning in my classes or what is going on in my life. Although it still feels weird sitting here in the cafeteria with everyone around me, I don't really care all that much. I can sit here and write about whatever I want, and that feels good.

Skills Workshop

Pre-Assessment

Instructions: Go to **www.thewriterstoolkit.com** to take the skills assessment.

1. In the upper left corner, click on the *Skills Assessment* tab.

2. Print a copy of the assessment.

3. Spend a maximum of 15 minutes completing the assessment.

4. Give a copy of the completed assessment to your instructor.

The assessment contains the following 3 parts:

Part A: Grammar

Part B: Punctuation

Part C: Word Usage

It is not about the test: It is about what you learn. Once you take the pre-assessment, do not review it until you complete the book. If you turn back and forth between the test and the new principles that you are learning, your final score will not be a valid assessment of your improvement. Trust the process: you will improve!

Skill Profile

How did you score?

For each incorrect answer, deduct 2 points.

Pretest 1: Grammar Skills   _____ incorrect (20 possible)   _____

Pretest 2: Punctuation Skills   _____ incorrect (20 possible)   _____

Pretest 3: Word Usage Skills   _____ incorrect (10 possible)   _____

Total Points: _____

References

Hathaway, N. (1991). Unleash your creativity. New York, NY: *New Woman*.

Indiana University. Writing Tutorial Services. Retrieved June 2009 from

http://<www.indiana.edu/~wts/pamphlets/thesis_statement.shtml>

8

Dynamic Sentences

Effectively-written sentences come alive to the reader, provoking understanding, insight, and at times even action. Thus, when you think of sentence structure, open yourself to the exciting possibilities that become real: once you can control sentence structure, you are able to bring your readers to a higher level of meaning and action.

Dynamic sentences result from effective editing, and this chapter provides a foundation for editing. You start your process by reviewing principles of reader-friendly sentences, the key to effective writing.

As you review sentence elements such as subjects and verbs, you also learn how to turn fragments into complete sentences and how to correct run-on sentences.

Each principle builds upon the next, so don't take shortcuts: start from the beginning and expect some surprises.

What Is a Sentence?

Think for a moment: *What is a sentence?* You write sentences every day, but can you define what a sentence is?

On the line below, define what a sentence is *or* jot down the words or ideas about sentences that pop into your mind:

_____

Once you can define what a sentence is off of the top of your head, you will have reached the critical starting point of understanding grammar for writing. Understanding sentence structure enables you to fix common yet serious writing errors such as sentence fragments and run-on sentences. So enjoy the review.

Here is the definition of a sentence:

> A *sentence* consists of a <u>subject</u> and a <u>verb</u> and expresses a <u>complete thought</u>.

Even if your definition does not match the above definition exactly, it can still be correct. For example:

- Some people use the word *noun* instead of *subject*.
- Some use the word *predicate* instead of *verb*.
- Some use the phrase *can stand on its own*, rather than *complete thought*.

Another term for sentence is **independent clause**. The word *clause* refers to *a group of words that has a subject and verb*. When a clause cannot stand on its own, it is a **dependent clause**.

Here is a recap:

- *Independent Clause:* a group of words that has a subject and a verb and expresses a complete thought; an independent clause is a complete sentence.
- *Dependent Clause*: a group of words that has a subject and a verb but does not express a complete thought; a dependent clause cannot stand on its own.

When a sentence consists of an independent clause and a dependent clause, the independent clause is the **main clause**.

What Is the Sentence Core?

Together the subject and verb form the **sentence core**. The sentence core is the critical link between grammar and writing style because it is the hub or powerhouse of every sentence. As a result, being able to control the core improves your grammar as well as your writing style.

Here are few points about subjects and verbs:

- In sentences, the subject almost always precedes the verb.
- The verb determines the subject of the sentence.
- The verb also determines the object, if there is one.

Since the first step in analyzing sentences is identifying the core, let us look at basic sentence structure. Statements are generally structured as follows:

S   V   O

subject – verb – object

In the following examples, the <u>verbs</u> are underlined twice; the <u>subjects</u>, once; and the **objects** are in bold typeface, for example:

<u>Marcus</u> <u><u>attended</u></u> the **conference**.

S   V   O

While all sentences have a subject and verb, not all sentences have an object:

The <u>train</u> <u><u>arrived</u></u>.

S   V

For questions, the subject and verb are partially inverted and a helper is needed:

<u><u>Did</u></u> the <u>train</u> <u><u>arrive</u></u>?

V   S   V

<u><u>Has</u></u> <u>Marcus</u> <u><u>attended</u></u> the **conference**?

V   S   V   O

It is easier to identify the subject and verb of a question if you first invert it back to a statement; for example:

<u><u>Did</u></u> the <u>train</u> <u><u>arrive</u></u>?   The <u>train</u> <u><u>did</u></u> <u><u>arrive</u></u>.

In practice exercises, identify the verb first and then its subject:

1. The verb is usually easier to identify than the subject.

2. The verb of a sentence determines its subject.

After you identify the verb, work *backward* in the sentence to find its subject.

Now let us look at subjects in more detail. To start, are you aware that the *grammatical subject* of a sentence may not be its *real subject*?

What Is a Subject?

Ideally, the subject of a sentence drives the action of the verb and answers the question of who or what performs the action of the verb.

As Gordon (1993) explains in *The Deluxe Transitive Vampire*, "the subject is that part of a sentence about which something is divulged; it is what the sentence's other words are gossiping about" (p. 3).

The subject of a sentence usually comes in the form of a **noun** or **pronoun** or **noun phrase:**

- A *noun* is a person, place, or thing, but it can also be an intangible item that cannot be seen or felt, such as *joy* or *wind* or *integrity*.

- A *pronoun* is a word that can be used in place of a noun, such as *I, you, he, she, it, we, they, who,* and *someone,* among others.

- A *phrase* is a group of related words that does not have a subject and predicate and cannot stand alone; a noun phrase consists of a noun and modifiers.

Though knowing how to identify whether a subject is a noun or pronoun or phrase is valuable, another type of analysis is even more important. For example, did you realize that the *real subject* of a sentence could be different from its *grammatical subject*?

When you can identify the difference between the real subject and the grammatical subject, you will gain more control of your writing style.

What Is a Grammatical Subject?

Every sentence has a **grammatical subject**, defined as *the simple subject that precedes the verb in a statement*. The grammatical subject is simply referred to as *the subject*. Being able to recognize the grammatical subject is important; however, it is not always stated in the sentence.

A **complete subject** consists of the **simple subject** and all the words that modify it. For writing purposes, the simple subject is important for a few reasons, but primarily because a subject must agree with its verb. In the following, the simple subject of each sentence is underlined once:

The new <u>manager</u> will chair the committee.

All <u>members</u> of the task force are in the conference room.

They are working diligently.

Her honesty is admirable.

When the grammatical subject is not stated, it becomes an **implied subject**. Implied subjects come in the form of *you understood* or *I understood.*

Here is a recap:

- A *grammatical subject* precedes its verb in a statement.

- When the grammatical subject is not present in the sentence, it becomes an *implied subject.*

- Implied subjects come in the form of *you understood* or *I understood.*

- *You understood* is displayed as follows: (You)

- *I understood* is displayed as follows: (I)

In each of the following examples, the implied subject is in parentheses and the verb is double underlined:

(You) Please take your seat in the front of the room.

(You) Feel free to call me if you have a question.

(I) Thank you for your assistance.

The subjects discussed so far—grammatical subjects that are complete, simple, and implied—all relate to structure. The type of subject that more directly relates to writing style is the *real subject.*

What Is a Real Subject?

The real subject of a sentence and the grammatical subject are sometimes the same, but sometimes different. Since the real subject is a critical element of writing style, it merits attention.

You may be feeling a little confused right now because you were not aware that the *grammatical subject* (the subject that precedes the verb) of a sentence was not necessarily its *real subject*. In fact, the term *real subject* may be unfamiliar:

- The real subject is the *who* or *what* that performs the action of the verb: the real subject drives the action.

Here is an example of a sentence in which the real subject and grammatical subject are one and the same:

Billy <u>threw</u> the ball.

In the following sentence, the grammatical subject is *ball*; the real subject is *Billy*, the person performing the action. However, *Billy* is in the object position.

The <u>ball</u> <u>was thrown</u> by Billy.

When the person or thing performing the action is not the grammatical subject, a sentence is considered **passive**. When the person or thing performing the action is the grammatical subject, the sentence is considered **active** (for more information, see Chapter 15, "Active Voice").

Here is a recap:

- The *grammatical subject* precedes the verb.

- The *real subject* drives the action of the verb.

When the real subject and the grammatical subject are the same, sentences are also more likely to be clear, concise, and reader friendly.

You gain more practice with real subjects in Chapter 15, "Active Voice." Now here are a few details about verbs, but just enough to help you recognize them.

What Is a Verb?

The verb is the central force of every sentence, determining the subject and the object, if there is one.

In English, the verb is also the central way to indicate time. In other words, the verb tense tells you whether an event *happened* yesterday, *is happening* now, or *will happen* tomorrow. In fact, the verb is the only part of speech that changes time—that is why verbs have tenses.

Here is some basic information about verbs:

- All verbs have a **base form**; *to* plus the base form of a verb is its **infinitive**: *to go, to see, to be.*

- All verbs have a **gerund form**: a *gerund* consists of *ing* plus the base form of the verb: *going, walking, being.*

- Verbs often string together, most often showing up in pairs, as in *will go* or *does know*.

- Common helping verbs are *to be* (is, are, was, were), *to have* (has, have, had), and *to do* (do, did, done).

Here are some hints to help you recognize the verb of a sentence:

1. Look for a word that expresses action, such as *speak, implement,* or *recognize.*

2. Look for a word that tells time and in doing so changes form, such as *speak, spoke, spoken,* and so on.

3. Look for the words *not* and *will*:

   a. You will generally find a verb after the word *will,* such as *will implement, will speak, will recognize, will find,* and so on.

   b. You will generally find a verb before and after the word *not,* such as *did* not *go, has* not *recognized,* and *has* not *spoken.* (The word *not* does not function as a verb but instead modifies a verb and negates it.)

Here are a few more examples:

Expressing Action:

   Michael *finishes* his projects on time.

   The committee *meets* every Friday.

   I *complete* the inventory monthly.

Changing Time:

   Michael *finished* his projects on time.

   The committee *met* every Friday.

   I *will complete* the inventory.

Preceding/Following *Not* or *Will*:

   Michael *will finish* his projects on time.

   The committee *did* not *meet* every Friday.

   I *will* not *complete* the inventory.

In the following, the verb of each sentence is underlined twice, the subject once:

Alexander watched the PowerPoint presentation.

My new manager will apply the policy to everyone in our department.

The meeting is not scheduled for May 29.

He discovers errors in our reports every week.

At times, a verb will need a helper, which is also known as an **auxiliary**. When you see a *helper verb*, look for another verb to follow it. Here are common helping verbs and their various forms:

Infinitive	Verb Forms
to be	is, are, was, were, being
to have	have, has, had, having
to do	do, did, done, doing

In the following examples, verbs are underlined twice and subjects once:

Marc had offered to prepare the agenda.

The meeting was cancelled.

The change did not affect our schedules.

Take a few minutes to complete the exercise below.

PRACTICE 8.1

Sentence Core

Instructions: Identify the sentence core in the following sentences: identify the verb first and underline it twice, then underline the subject once.

1. Social workers take a strengths perspective.

2. I thanked them for their support.

3. Thank you for asking that question.

4. Our new program will begin in one month.

5. Examine the client's request before approving the program.

Note: See page 403 for the key to the above exercise.

What Is a Compound Subject?

A compound subject consists or two or more words or phrases. In the following examples, verbs are underlined twice, subjects once:

> Alice and Joyce attended the conference.

> Your brother and sister can assist you with the solving the problem.

> The committee and its chairperson will decide the direction of the group.

At times, compound subjects are redundant, for example:

> My thoughts and ideas are clearer today than they were yesterday.

> The issues and concerns were discussed at the last meeting.

Why not simply say:

> My thoughts are clearer today than they were yesterday.

> The issues were discussed at the last meeting.

Edit your writing closely so that you cut redundant subjects.

PRACTICE 8.2

Redundant Subjects

Instructions: First identify the sentence core by underlining the verb twice and the subject once; then cut the redundant subject.

Weak: My plan and strategy for the campaign caught their interest.

Revised: My strategy for the campaign caught their interest.

1. My friends and associates tell me that being positive is an asset.
2. The details and specifics about the project were fascinating.
3. Visitors and guests should sign in at the front desk.
4. My goals and objectives reflect my dreams.
5. The results and outcomes reflect our success.

Note: See page 403 for the key to the above exercise.

What Is a Compound Verb?

A compound verb consists of two or more main verbs along with their helpers, as in the following:

> My <u>associate</u> <u>had</u> <u>called</u> and <u>asked</u> me for a favor.

> Hard <u>work</u> <u>causes</u> me to apply myself and <u>focuses</u> my attention.

> <u>Jogging</u> <u>improves</u> my health, <u>motivates</u> me, and <u>encourages</u> me to eat less.

As subjects can be redundant at times, so can verbs:

> <u>I</u> <u>read</u> and <u>analyzed</u> the report.

> The <u>assistant</u> <u>listened</u> to their responses and <u>recorded</u> them.

Why not simply say:

> <u>I</u> <u>analyzed</u> the report.

> The <u>assistant</u> <u>recorded</u> their responses.

Thus, whenever you use compound verbs, check for redundancy. Of course, a sentence can have a compound subject and a compound verb, for example:

> <u>Margie</u> and <u>Seth</u> <u>opened</u> the invitation and <u>expressed</u> their surprise.

PRACTICE 8.3

Compound Verbs

Instructions: First, identify the sentence core by underlining the verb twice and the subject once; next, cut verbs that are redundant.

Weak: <u>Mary</u> <u>identified</u> and <u>requested</u> the rooms for the conference.

Revised: <u>Mary</u> <u>requested</u> the rooms for the conference.

1. Milton's decision uncovers and reveals his true motives.
2. Mark's actions surprised me and caught me off guard.
3. We started the project and worked on it for two hours.
4. I understand and appreciate your commitment to our mission.
5. Melanie greeted us and welcomed us to the new resource center.

Note: See page 403 for the key to the above exercise.

What Is a Compound Sentence?

A compound sentence contains two main clauses. In the following examples, verbs are underlined twice, subjects once:

> <u>Joe</u> <u>called</u> about facilitating the discussion, and <u>he</u> <u>expressed</u> an interest.

> The new <u>ad</u> <u>will</u> <u>run</u> for two weeks, but then <u>we</u> <u>will</u> <u>need</u> a new one.

> My <u>manager</u> <u>asked</u> me to include the details, so <u>I</u> <u>presented</u> the entire report.

When writing a compound sentence, make sure that you are not randomly connecting ideas, for example:

> Joe called about the opening in social services, and we need to run an ad.

What is the above sentence leading to? How are these two ideas linked? Disjointed ideas are fine if you are speaking with someone face to face; however, when you write, limit your sentences to *one controlling idea.*

In fact, the ideas in the above sentence might not be disjointed. One idea may be related to the other, but the relationship between the ideas is not shown because of the way that the sentence is written. What if the above sentence were written as follows:

> Because we have an opening in social services, Joe suggested that we run an ad.

When you learn about conjunctions later in this chapter and in the next, you will see how to use conjunctions to show relationships among ideas.

What Is a Phrase?

A phrase is a group of related words that does not have a subject *and* predicate and thus cannot stand alone. Here are two important types of phrases and their definitions:

- *Infinitive phrase:* an infinitive along with its object or complement and modifiers. (An infinitive is the word *to* plus the base form of a verb, as in *to go, to walk*, and *to speak.*)

- *Gerund phrase:* a gerund along with its object or complement and modifiers. (A gerund is formed by adding *ing* to the base form of a verb, as in *going, walking*, and *speaking.*)

Infinitive phrases:	**Gerund phrases:**
to go to the store	going to the store
to buy what you need	buying what you need
to attend class daily	attending class daily
to inform the staff	informing the staff

In addition to gerund and infinitive phrases, you are probably somewhat familiar with prepositional phrases. Here is a brief reminder of how to identify a prepositional phrase:

- *Prepositional phrase:* a preposition along with a noun and its modifiers. Some common prepositions are *between, from, to, on, under, with, by,* and *along.*

Prepositional phrases:

on the table	*behind* the desk
to the store	*by* the bookcase
after the meeting	*between* the two of us

Though prepositional phrases can give writers challenges, the most challenging types of phrases for writers are *gerund* and *infinitive* phrases.

For example, writers need to use gerund and infinitive phrases consistently within a sentence or in a list. In the examples below, notice how the inconsistent phrases become reader friendly when they are presented as gerund or infinitive phrases:

Inconsistent list:

1. Maintenance of client list.
2. Expense accounts calculated.
3. Travel arrangements made.

Gerund Phrases:

1. *Maintaining* client lists.
2. *Calculating* expense accounts.
3. *Making* travel arrangements.

Infinitive Phrases:

1. *To Maintain* client lists.

2. *To Calculate* expense accounts.

3. *To Make* travel arrangements.

By removing *to* from the above list of infinitive phrases, each item would start with an active verb.

When you list items, remain consistent in form to ensure that you achieve *parallel construction*: representing words and phrases in the same grammatical form. (See Chapter 16, "Parallel Structure.")

PRACTICE 8.4

Instructions: Use gerund or infinitive phrases to make the following lists parallel.

List 1:

1. Office supplies need to be ordered

2. Appointment scheduling

3. Certificate renewal

List 2:

1. Coordination of schedules

2. Supplies distributed

3. Phoning clients

List 3:

1. Staff training

2. The development of policy

3. Profit and loss reconciliation

Note: See pages 403 for the key to the above exercise.

What Is a Dependent Clause?

A *dependent clause* is a group of words that has a subject and verb but does not express a complete thought; a dependent clause cannot stand on its own.

One common type of dependent clause is a *subordinate clause*. This type of dependent clause begins with a **subordinating conjunction**; to understand dependent clauses, first understand the role that subordinating conjunctions play.

- *Subordinating conjunctions* show relationships between ideas and, in the process, make one idea dependent on the other; subordinating conjunctions appear as single words or short phrases.

Here is a list of common subordinating conjunctions:

after	because	since	until
although	before	so that	when
as	even though	though	whereas
as soon as	if	unless	while

The above list is not a complete list; you can test whether a word or phrase is a subordinating conjunction by placing it at the beginning of a complete sentence. If the complete sentence no longer sounds complete, the word is probably a subordinating conjunction (SC). For example:

Complete sentence:	Bob walked to the store.
SC added:	*If* Bob walked to the store . . . *what then?*

Complete sentence:	The office manager arrived late.
SC added:	*Since* the office manager arrived late . . . *what then?*

Complete sentence:	The sale begins tomorrow.
SC added:	*Even though* the sale begins tomorrow . . . *what then?*

Subordinating conjunctions do what their name implies: *to subordinate* means *to make less than*. In the examples above, you have seen that when you place a subordinating conjunction at the beginning of a complete sentence, the sentence becomes a dependent clause.

Here is another set of examples:

Complete sentence: The attendant gave me a receipt.

Dependent clause: *When* the attendant gave me a receipt . . . *what then?*

Complete sentence: Our car is in the parking lot.

Dependent clause: *Although* our car is in the parking lot . . . *what then?*

Complete sentence: Their committee meets on Friday.

Dependent clause: *After* their committee meets on Friday . . . *what then?*

Putting a period at the end of a dependent clause creates a **fragment**; a fragment is a common error, but a serious one.

Write two sentences below, and then go back and place a subordinating conjunction at the beginning of each of your sentences, as shown in the previous set of examples.

1. _____

2. _____

Do you see how a subordinating conjunction can turn a complete sentence into a fragment? A fragment is a serious grammatical error.

How Do You Correct a Fragment?

A *fragment* is an incomplete statement that is punctuated as if it were a complete sentence. Most often, fragments come in the form of gerund phrases, infinitive phrases, or dependent clauses. The following are some examples of fragments broken down by type:

Gerund Phrases: *Walking* slowly to the beach on a sunny day

Following a list of directions precisely as given

Infinitive Phrases: *To walk* slowly to the beach on a sunny day

To follow a list of directions precisely as given

Dependent clauses: *When* I walk slowly to the beach on a sunny day

After Bob followed the list of directions that you gave him

Notice that neither a gerund nor an infinitive *phrase* contains a subject and a verb. However, when a gerund or an infinitive phrase is long, it can give the illusion that it is a complete sentence.

How you correct a fragment depends on the type of fragment you are dealing with; however, often a simple solution can correct this serious grammatical error.

To correct fragments consisting of gerund and infinitive phrases, use the phrase as the <u>subject</u>, add a <u>verb</u>, and then finish your thought, as follows:

> <u>Walking slowly to the beach on a sunny day</u> <u>makes</u> most people feel good.
>
> <u>To walk slowly to the beach on a sunny day</u> <u>is</u> highly recommended.

Another way to correct a fragment that consists of a gerund or infinitive phrase would be to use the fragment as the **object** of your sentence, adding a <u>subject</u> and a <u>verb</u>, as follows:

> George's favorite <u>activity</u> <u>is</u> **walking slowly to the beach on a sunny day**.
>
> <u>I</u> <u>prefer</u> **to walk slowly to the beach on a sunny day**.

Here is now to correct a fragment resulting from a dependent clause:

1. Use the dependent clause before a main clause to introduce the main clause,

2. Use the dependent clause after a main clause as a finishing thought, or

3. Remove the subordinating conjunction at the beginning of the clause.

In the sentences below, each dependent clause is italicized:

> *When I walk slowly to the beach on a sunny day*, my mind always wanders.
>
> I left work early *because I finished the list of directions precisely as given*.

When the subordinating conjunction is removed, a dependent clause may become a complete sentence; for example:

> ~~When~~ I walk slowly to the beach on a sunny day.
>
> ~~Because~~ I finished the list of directions precisely as given.

Practice turning fragments into sentences by doing the exercise below.

PRACTICE 8.5

Revising Fragments

Instructions: Use your creativity to turn the following fragments into complete sentences.

Incorrect: Finding enough time to complete the report.

Revised: Finding enough time to complete the report was a challenge.

Revised: My challenge was finding enough time to complete the report.

1. Making the right decision at the right time.
2. Because he finished the project earlier than anyone expected.
3. After I made the decision to reclaim my spot on the team.
4. To show interest in a project that no longer has merit.
5. Going slower than planned but staying under budget.

Note: See page 404 for the key to the above exercise.

Now here is a review why the sentence core is important for structure and style.

Why Is the Sentence Core Important?

The sentence core consists of the subject and verb: together the subject and verb convey meaning. One without the other, and meaning is incomplete. In fact, readers become confused if the sentence core is presented ineffectively.

As you read the following example, notice your reaction:

> My associate Jane Culver, who has worked with me on several projects in the last few months and who has a great deal of expertise in the field of writing as well as consulting, will be our keynote speaker.

Does the above sound wordy and confusing? Now read the following:

> My associate Jane Culver will be our keynote speaker. By the way, Jane has worked with me on several projects in the last few months and has a great deal of expertise in the field of writing as well as consulting.

Is the second example easier to understand? The difference between the two is that the second example broke the information into smaller chunks and used the sentence core effectively:

Jane Culver <u>will be</u> . . .   Jane <u>has worked</u> . . .

In general, the closer the subject and verb are to each other, the easier it is for a reader to understand meaning. Here are some editing tips on how to present the sentence core effectively:

1. Keep the subject and verb close to each other.

2. Keep the sentence core close to the beginning of the sentence.

To further enhance the sentence core, focus on using **real subjects** and **strong verbs**. While most verbs are action verbs, the following verbs are considered weak verbs: *make*, *give*, and *take* as well as the *to be* verbs: *is*, *are*, *was*, and *were*; for example:

Weak: Al *will give* you the information about the change.

Revised: Al *will inform* you about the change.

Weak: *Take* that into consideration when you apply.

Revised: *Consider* that when you apply.

Subjects can also be weak. For example, avoid using *it* or *there* as a subject:

Weak: It is time for change.

Revised: The time for change is now.

Weak: There are many decisions pending.

Revised: Many decisions are pending.

Consider the above points as an introduction to the sentence core. When you work on Chapter 10, "Comma Rules," you once again work with the sentence core. When you work on Chapter 15, "Active Voice," you focus on developing a strong sentence core.

Do the following exercise to gain control of the sentence core.

PRACTICE 8.6

Real Subjects and Strong Verbs

Instructions: Edit the following sentences by changing the sentence core so that it consists of a real subject and strong verb.

Weak: It was a decision that Mr. James regrets.

Revised: <u>Mr. James</u> <u>regrets</u> the decision.

1. There are five orders that need to be filled by customer service.
2. It is an electrical problem on the fifth floor that caused the outage.
3. Randy will make a revision of the document today.
4. There is a new report that arrived earlier today.
5. You can make a decision tomorrow.

Note: See page 404 for the key to the above exercise.

Does Sentence Length Affect Readability?

Have you ever read a sentence that you had difficulty understanding? If so, was it an unusually long sentence? The average reader retains information more readily when a sentence contains fewer than 25 words. Here is an editing tip that you can apply at once to improve your writing:

Limit your sentences to 25 words or fewer.

For example:

Sentences that are much longer than 25 words have a tendency to confuse readers because by the time that they get to the end of a long sentence, many readers have already forgotten what the beginning of the sentence was about and need to go back to the beginning and reread it again, which can be very tedious. (57 words) *What do you think?*

Writing shorter sentences gives you more control. When sentences are long, writing decisions become more difficult; and writers more easily make mistakes with grammar and punctuation. Simple, clear, and concise writing is reader-friendly writing. So use the following as your guideline: *Less is more.*

When you write sentences that are long or complicated, count the number of words. If a sentence is longer than 25 words, cut words or break the information into shorter sentences. At times, you will need to do both.

What Is Information Flow?

Information flow is about how you order information for your reader. To start, information is broken into two types: familiar ideas and unfamiliar ideas.

When a sentence starts with a familiar idea as a lead-in to an unfamiliar idea, readers have an easier time making connections. Think of familiar information as *old information*, and think of unfamiliar information as *new information*.

- *Old information* consists of familiar ideas that provide context and anchor the reader in understanding.

- *New information* consists of unfamiliar ideas that extend the reader's understanding.

For example, suppose you are describing the topic of your next paper. As you compose, you may start with the new information.

New to *Old*: Changes in consumer spending habits during an economic downturn will be *the topic of my next paper*.

When you edit, switch the order so that the sentence begins with the familiar, old information, which would be *the topic of my next paper* or simply, *my next paper*, for example:

***Old* to New:** *My next paper* will discuss changes in consumer spending habits during an economic downturn.

By beginning the sentence with the familiar concept (*my next paper*), you ease your readers by providing context for the unfamiliar information. Here is another example in which *our first team meeting* is familiar information:

New to *Old*: A set of ground rules and a membership survey needs to be developed at *our first team meeting*.

***Old* to New:** At *our first team meeting*, we need to develop a set of ground rules and a membership survey.

In the next chapter, you will learn more about information flow.

PRACTICE 8.7

Information Flow

Instructions: In the following sentences, adjust the information flow so that the old information precedes the new information.

New to Old: An abrupt change in consumer spending habits is one reason why the economy has shifted.

***Old* to New:** *One reason that the economy has shifted* is that consumers have changed their spending habits.

1. Too many unnecessary and costly items are not being bought by consumers at this time.
2. Buying good used items at a reduced price is how many consumers are choosing to spend their money.
3. The rapidly increasing cost of gasoline has contributed to a change in consumer attitudes.
4. Outsourcing jobs to third-world countries is a topic you might consider for your next paper.
5. Please consider the cost as well as the time required to make the revisions as you complete your report.

Note: See page 404 for the key to the above exercise.

Before going on to Chapter 9, "Cohesive Paragraphs and Transitions," get extra practice by working on the writing workshop at the end of this chapter.

Recap

This chapter has focused on sentence structure and the sentence core. The sentence core is where structure and style cross paths: gain control of the sentence core, and you gain control of your writing.

➤ To identify the sentence core, identify the verb first and then work backward to find its subject.

➤ To identify a verb, look for a word that expresses action and that changes form when it changes time (past, present, or future).

- Subjects can be implied or understood, such as *I understood* (I) or *You understood* (You): (I) <u>Thank</u> you for your help or (You) <u>Take</u> your time.

- Write sentences in which the grammatical subject and real subject are the same.

- Avoid starting sentences with *it is* or *there are*; instead write sentences that have a real subject and a strong verb.

- When you write a sentence that has a compound subject or verb, check for redundancy.

Writing Workshop

Activity A. Journal

Instructions: What are your dreams and goals?

What do you want out of life and why? Dream a little, but be realistic. You are working hard to improve your skills—what is it that motivates you to do your best?

What changes would you like to see in your life in *six months* from now? . . . *one year? . . . five years?*

Spend about 10 to 15 minutes freewriting, then complete Activity B below.

Activity B. Writing Practice

Instructions: Identify a specific goal and develop an action plan.

Do you have a goal that you want to achieve? For example, would you like to lose weight, improve your diet, get rid of clutter, get organized, improve your finances, or enhance your relationships?

1. Describe your goal in detail.
2. Identify specific steps you plan to take to achieve your goal.
3. Add a time frame to each step. By adding a date to each step in your process, you are creating an *action plan.*

Reference

Gordon, K. (1993). *The deluxe transitive vampire*. New York, NY: Pantheon Books.

9

Cohesive Paragraphs and Transitions

Paragraphs play a vital role in making ideas easily accessible to readers by breaking information into manageable chunks. In fact, readers dread seeing one long paragraph that seems to go on forever. If you have not yet focused on how you create paragraph breaks, now you can.

While you cannot depend on a recipe to write a paragraph, you can rely on a few guidelines. For example, a paragraph can be as short as a sentence or two or as long as seven or eight sentences. However, not all paragraphs are equal. For instance, when you make paragraphing decisions for a paper or essay, you have different considerations from when you make paragraphing decisions for an e-mail. (One difference is that e-mail is more conversational and paragraphs tend to be short.)

If you do not now insert paragraph breaks naturally as you compose, put them in when you edit and revise. Read your writing out loud or have someone read it to you. When you hear a new topic, start a new paragraph.

Once you have enough experience writing, you will make paragraph breaks as a natural part of composing. When you edit, you will structure the content to make your paragraphs *cohesive* and *coherent*.

Review the following principles to learn how to edit and revise paragraphs effectively and also to develop flow and make transitions.

Cohesive and Coherent Paragraphs

Two important qualities of effective paragraphs are cohesiveness and coherency.

- *Cohesive* paragraphs develop only *one main idea* or *topic*, demonstrating a *connectedness* among ideas that support that topic. Adequate details support the main idea so that the reader understands the main point.

- *Coherent* paragraphs develop the main idea through a *logical flow of ideas*: one point leads to another.

As you compose, get your ideas on the page without concerning yourself about paragraphing, otherwise you are likely to lose your thoughts.

The first step in editing a paragraph so that it is cohesive is to identify its **topic sentence**. The next step is ensuring that each sentence in the paragraph develops the topic, creating a **topic string**.

- A *topic sentence* gives an overview of the paragraph; a topic sentence is broad and general.

- A *topic string* is a series of sentences that develop the main idea of the topic sentence. Each sentence extends the controlling idea, giving specifics that illustrate the main idea of the topic sentence.

As you compose, do not be concerned about writing a topic sentence or building a topic string. However, do not be surprised if one of the last sentences that you write ends up being the best candidate for the topic sentence.

Here is a step-by-step process for editing paragraphs:

1. Identify your topic sentence. Select the sentence that best captures the broader, more general topic that the rest of the paragraph develops through specifics.

2. Bring your topic sentence to the beginning of the paragraph as the first sentence.

3. Screen each the remainder of sentences in the paragraph to make sure that it develops some element of the topic sentence.

4. Cut sentences that do not fit, or use them to start a new paragraph.

Many writers are able to insert paragraph breaks as they compose. However, if you do not naturally make paragraph breaks as you compose, work on them when you edit. Eventually, you will hear when a new topic springs from your writing.

Read the draft paragraph that follows, which seems to ramble because it changes topics. As you read the paragraph, ask yourself the following questions:

- What is the main topic? Which sentence expresses the main topic best?

- Which sentences seem off topic?

- Which sentences seem to belong in a different paragraph?

Draft:

I believe editing is important, and I even knew an editor once. But I never knew how to edit before, and I was always confused about how to improve my writing. Before I didn't take the time to edit, now I do because I know how to make corrections and how to how to revise a document. Editing is an important part of the writing process. When you edit, correct errors in grammar and punctuation and try to improve the flow of the writing. Editing also involves putting the purpose up front and then cutting what doesn't belong. When I read papers that are not edited well, I can tell because the writer jumps from one topic to another. Editing can turn a mediocre paper into a good one. Poorly written documents also seem to ramble on and on without paragraph breaks, so add paragraph breaks where they are needed. Take time to edit, and you will see an improvement in your final document.

Edited Version 1

The following version focuses on how to edit but leaves out the writer's own experience:

Editing is an important part of the writing process. When you edit, correct errors in grammar and punctuation and improve the flow of the writing. Put purpose up front and then cut what doesn't belong. Also, add paragraph breaks where they are needed. If you take time to edit, you will see an improvement in your final document.

Edited Version 2

Version 2 takes the writer's point of view. Notice how the voice shifts to the *I* viewpoint:

Editing is important. Before I didn't take the time to edit, but now I do because I know how to correct and revise a document. When I edit, I correct errors in grammar and punctuation and try to improve the flow of the writing. I also put the purpose up front and then cut what doesn't belong. When I take time to edit, I see an improvement in my final document.

For a paragraph to be coherent, ideas must flow logically. In other words, writing should not seem chaotic and full of disjointed ideas. However, as you compose, disjointed ideas seem to make sense. To correct disjointed writing, step away from your work for a while so that you can evaluate your writing objectively.

If you are writing on a computer, the way that your writing sounds when you read it on the screen is different from the way that it will sound when you read it from hard copy.

Here are some steps to take to revise your paragraphs:

- *Print out a copy.* Writing sometimes reads differently in hard copy from the way it reads on the screen.

- *Have a peer read it.* Ask for specific changes that you can make to upgrade the quality of your writing.

- *Keep an open mind.* Others will see things that you cannot; expand your perspective by trying new ideas, even if they feel uncomfortable at first. You can always toss them out after you have given them a chance to expand your thinking.

In academic writing, use at least four sentences. One topic sentence and at least three sentences to explain, expand, and support the topic sentence. Principles of information flow can also assist you in understanding how to adjust your writing so that it is reader friendly.

Information Flow

As you learned in the last chapter, information flow orders ideas so that readers have an easier time connecting how one idea relates to another.

- *Old Information* is familiar information that provides a context for your reader.

- *New Information* is unfamiliar information that extends the reader's understanding.

Information flow can create smooth transitions between ideas that would otherwise sound disjointed. However, information flow is not complete without one more category of information, and that is *irrelevant information*. Here is the third and final category of information flow:

- *Empty Information*: information that is irrelevant to the topic at hand.

Here are three versions of a paragraph about *listening* (which is considered the old information). As you read the first paragraph, identify the empty, irrelevant information.

Can you identify the empty information in the paragraph below?

> *Listening* is an important part of communicating. *If you take the time to listen* to them, most people will tell you about their lives. *As you listen*, ask questions, and most people will reveal more about themselves. I once had a job in retail sales, and a big part of the job was *listening*. I didn't do well when I first started because *I wasn't a good listener. Once you become a better listener*, you will understand people, even if they think differently from the way that you think.

Here is how the paragraph sounds without the empty information:

> *Listening* is an important part of communicating. *If you take the time to listen*, most people will tell you about their lives. *As you listen*, ask questions, and most people will reveal more about themselves. *Once you become a better listener*, you will understand people, even if they think differently from the way that you think.

Once the irrelevant, empty information is removed, the paragraph flows more effectively. However, below is the same paragraph, but this time the information flow is reversed: new information appears at the beginning of each sentence and the consistent, old topic *listening* appears at end:

> An important part of communicating is *listening*. Most people will take the time to tell you about their lives *if you listen*. Ask questions, and most people will reveal more about themselves *as long as you take the time to listen*. You will understand people, even if they think differently from the way that you think, *once you become a better listener*.

Does the above paragraph lose its flow and sound choppy? By putting new information first, does the reader need to work harder to find meaning?

As you compose, you may naturally put new information on the page first and then connect it to your topic (or old information). As you edit, revise the flow of sentences that start with new information by presenting old information first.

Here is the same paragraph one more time, but this time putting the topic sentence at the end:

> If you take the time to listen to them, most people will tell you about their lives. As you listen, ask questions, and most people will reveal more about themselves. Once you become a better listener, you will understand people, even if they think differently from the way that you do. Listening is an important part of communicating.

Can you see how the topic sentence provides the context for the paragraph and how putting it first aids the reader in understanding?

Apply the principles of information flow in the practice below.

PRACTICE 9.1

Paragraphs and Information Flow

Instructions: In the following paragraph, adjust the information flow by:

1. Identifying the topic sentence and bringing it to the beginning of the paragraph.

2. Adjusting information flow so that sentences begin with old information and end with new information.

3. Cutting empty information.

> Writing can be hard and frustrating because sometimes I can't decide on what to write or what to say. Allow yourself to write freely and make mistakes as you compose. Good writing is about composing and editing. Identify the mistakes that you have made and correct them when you edit. A paper should have a beginning, a middle, and an end. Good writing becomes easy to produce once you understand how to manage the writing process.

Note: See page 404 for a suggested revision; answers may vary.

Paragraphs and Viewpoint

Another component of an effective paragraph is consistent viewpoint, which partly depends on the way that you use pronouns. Though you will work with pronouns in detail in Chapter 13, "Pronouns," here is an introduction to *pronoun viewpoint* or *point of view*.

A viewpoint can be described as *the eyes through which writing is being portrayed*. Pronoun viewpoint, or point of view, can emanate from first, second, or third person, singular or plural.

	Singular	**Plural**
First or person:	I	We
Second person:	You	You
Third person:	He, She, It	They
	One	One

The third person viewpoint *it/they* could represent the topic about which you are writing. For example, if you were writing a summary about nutrition, you would not necessarily speak from your own point of view, for example:

> Good nutrition leads to good health. Highly nutritional foods include fruits and vegetables as well as legumes and grains. These foods are high in vitamins and fiber, which is good for the digestive system.

Once you establish a point of view for a particular piece of writing, remain consistent with that point of view within individual sentences and paragraphs and even entire documents.

The following sentences highlight how to stay consistent with viewpoint:

First person singular viewpoint:

> Listening is a skill which *I* would like to improve. When *I* listen, *I* sometimes hear things that change *my* life.

Shifting viewpoint:

Incorrect: Listening is a skill which *we* should all improve. When *I* listen, *you* sometimes hear things that change *your* life.

Corrected: Listening is a skill which *we* should all improve. When *we* listen, *we* sometimes hear things that change *our* lives.

Corrected: Listening is a skill which ***all*** can improve. When ***people*** listen, ***they*** sometimes hear things that change ***their*** lives.

Here is a sentence written from each of the various viewpoints:

When ***I*** write, ***I*** must pay attention to every detail.

When ***you*** write, ***you*** must pay attention to every detail.

When a ***person*** writes, ***he/she*** must pay attention to every detail.

When ***we*** write, ***we*** must pay attention to every detail.

When ***people*** write, ***they*** must pay attention to every detail.

When ***one*** writes, ***one*** must pay attention to every detail.

For the pronoun *one*, the only appropriate antecedent is *one*; in other words, *he* and *she* are not antecedents for *one*.

PRACTICE 9.2

Pronoun Point of View and Consistency

Instructions: Edit the following short paragraphs by correcting for pronoun consistency.

1. I usually work late on Thursdays because you can get a lot done at the end of the week. When you work late, I usually see other people working late also. Having your boss notice that you are putting in extra time always makes me feel good.

2. Good nutrition leads to good health. When we eat well, you are likely to feel better. People do not find it easy to eat in a healthful way, though. I usually prefer to eat fast food at the end of the day when you are tired.

Note: See page 405 for the key to the above exercise.

Transitional Sentences

Transitional sentences and paragraphs are also elements of information flow, making broad connections between old information and new information.

Transitional sentences provide logical connections between paragraphs. The transitional sentence glances forward and links the topic of one paragraph with the main idea of the next, for example:

> In the next section, our analysis demonstrates the strengths and weaknesses of the model that we applied in our study.

> Next we discuss how good communication leads to success.

> Although production waste has economic implications, waste also has an impact on the environment.

Transitional sentences prepare the reader to understand the content of the next paragraph by seeding its purpose and making new key ideas familiar.

Transitional Paragraphs

In addition to transitional sentences, **transitional paragraphs** assist readers by achieving the following:

- Summarizing the key ideas of the current section.

- Indicating how the major theme of the document will be developed in the next section.

Here is a transitional paragraph that summarizes the key ideas of a current section:

> This chapter discusses several of Deming's famous 14 points, known as the Deming Management Method. As they relate to workforce diversity and managing change, the following topics are discussed: poorly implemented management systems, disrespectful and fearful work environments, interdepartmental antagonism, and weak leadership.

Here is a transitional paragraph that glances forward to a next section:

> The educational reform process enabled the faculty to make effective curriculum changes. The evolving curriculum also brought faculty closer to achieving the aims of general education within the stated mission, which is discussed in the next section.

Next, you will examine how to use conjunctions to make transitions.

Connectors as Transitions

As you have seen, old to new information flow helps create smooth transitions between ideas. Another way to create smooth transitions is to use conjunctions.

Do you recall the Sesame Street song, *Conjunction Junction*: "Conjunction Junction, what's your function?" If you remember the song, you may begin to smile as the tune sets in. Here are the three types of conjunctions:

- Coordinating

- Subordinating

- Adverbial

On face value, conjunctions do not seem to play an important role in writing. However, along with subjects and verbs, conjunctions play a critical role in grammar, punctuation, and writing style:

- Conjunctions show relationships and bridge ideas, adding smooth transitions to choppy writing.

- Conjunctions pull the reader's thinking along with the writer's intention.

As you use conjunctions more effectively, your writing style also improves. By pulling the reader's thinking along with yours, you help the reader connect ideas and draw conclusions. Conjunctions focus the reader on key points, making writing clearer and easier to understand.

In addition, conjunctions play a key role in punctuation by signaling where to place commas and semicolons. By learning about conjunctions now, your work in the next chapter with commas will be that much easier.

Understand how conjunctions *function*, and you will be a big step closer to using them effectively in your writing. Though the terms themselves might put you off, realize that it only takes a bit of practice to use the terms *coordinating*, *subordinating*, and *adverbial* with ease.

Coordinating Conjunctions

Coordinating conjunctions connect equal grammatical parts. There are only seven of them, and they are as follows:

and   but   or   for   nor   so   yet

Together they spell the acronym F A N B O Y S: *for, and, nor, but, or, yet, so.* The most commonly used coordinating conjunctions are *and, but,* and *or.* The *equal grammatical parts* that conjunctions connect are *sentences, words,* and *phrases,* which Chapter 10, "Comma Rules," covers in more detail.

Though using a coordinating conjunction as the first word of a sentence is acceptable, it is not preferred and should be used sparingly. But when you do start a sentence with a coordinating conjunction, you are likely to get the reader's attention. In general, the adverbial conjunction *however* is a good substitute for the coordinating conjunction *but.*

Subordinating Conjunctions

As you learned in Chapter 8, "Dynamic Sentences," putting a subordinating conjunction at the beginning of a complete sentence turns the sentence into a dependent clause.

Subordinating conjunctions show relationships between ideas and, in the process, make one idea dependent on the other; they appear as single words or short phrases. Here is a list of some common subordinating conjunctions:

after	because	since	until
although	before	so that	when
as	even though	though	whereas
as soon as	if	unless	while

In addition to subordinating conjunctions, adverbial conjunctions contribute to a reader-friendly writing style.

Adverbial Conjunctions

Adverbial conjunctions bridge ideas, and they are known as *transition* words.

Here are some examples of common adverbial conjunctions:

as a result	for example	in conclusion	otherwise
finally	hence	in general	therefore
generally	however	in other words	thus

Adverbial conjunctions help pull the reader's thinking along with the writer's intention. Use an adverbial conjunction at the beginning of a sentence to *introduce* it, in the middle of a sentence to *interrupt* the flow of thought, or between two sentences as a *bridge*.

Here are examples of adverbial conjunctions and the roles they play:

Introducing:	*Therefore*, I will not be able to attend the conference.
Interrupting:	The Jones Corporation, *however*, is not our vendor of choice.
Bridging:	George will attend the conference in my place; *as a result,* I will be able to assist you on the new project.

Here are some adverbial conjunctions and the kinds of transitions that they make:

Compare or contrast:	however, in contrast, on the other hand, on the contrary, conversely, nevertheless, otherwise,
Summarize:	in summary, in conclusion, as a result, thus, therefore, hence
Illustrate:	for example, for instance, hence, in general, thus, mostly
Add information:	in addition, additionally, also, furthermore, moreover, too
Show results:	fortunately, unfortunately, consequently, as usual, of course
Sequence or show time:	first, second, third, finally, meanwhile, in the meantime, to begin with
Conclude:	finally, in summary, in conclusion

As a reader, use these transition words and phrases to identify key points. As a writer, use these transition words in a conscious way to pull your reader's thinking along with yours.

Besides being bridges and connectors, conjunctions are also comma signals. In the next two chapters, you will see how conjunctions signal where to place a comma or a semicolon.

PRACTICE 9.3

Conjunctions as Connectors

Instructions: Revise the following paragraph by adding conjunctions, thereby improving its flow. *Note*: See page 405 for the key to this exercise.

> The construction for the 9th floor conference room was extended two more weeks. We were not informed until Friday. Our meetings for the following week needed to be reassigned to different rooms. None were available. Jane Simmons agreed to let us use her office. Several serious conflicts were avoided.

As you work on Chapter 10, "Comma Rules," apply what you learned about the sentence core and conjunctions. First, however, complete the exercises at the end of this chapter.

Recap

In this chapter, you have worked on paragraphing; you have also reviewed the three types of conjunctions and how they function as connectors and transition words.

➢ Paragraphs break up information into manageable chunks for the reader.

➢ Every paragraph contains a topic sentence, which is then developed into a topic string.

➢ Cohesive paragraphs focus on one topic.

➢ Coherent paragraphs have a logical flow of ideas, which you create as you edit and revise your work.

➢ A consistent viewpoint helps ensure that a paragraph is coherent as well as grammatically correct.

➤ Conjunctions build bridges between ideas and provide cues about a writer's key points.

➤ As a review, here are the three types of conjunctions and examples:

Coordinating conjunctions:	and, but, or, for, nor, so, yet
Subordinating conjunctions:	if, since, although, because, before, after, while
Adverbial conjunctions:	however, therefore, for example, consequently

In the next chapter, you learn about the role that conjunctions play in comma usage.

Writing Workshop

Activity A: What is on your mind?

Instructions: Start this activity by completing the following sentences.

My passion in life . . .
If I were you . . .
I wish that I were able to . . .
When my best friend says . . .
If I could have any job in the world . . .
The best advice anyone ever gave me . . .
The favorite room in my house . . .
When I was a child . . .

Next, select two or three of your sentences to use as the topic sentence for a paragraph. Use topic sentence as a starting point, developing a topic string that radiates from it.

Finally, revise each paragraph so that it is cohesive and coherent. Pay special attention to using a consistent viewpoint and using effective connectors.

Activity B. Journal

Instructions: Are you journaling on a regular basis? Write two pages at least four times a week, and your skills will become stronger. As you journal, *compose freely.*

PART 3: MECHANICS OF WRITING

Punctuation is the glue that holds language together. Punctuation provides clarity, adding energy and flow by packaging words into logical bundles that make sense. In fact, punctuation communicates with the reader in subtle ways.

Some of the mechanics of writing, such as commas and semicolons, are key to understanding structure. That is because these two punctuation marks help define structure, and working on them reinforces what a sentence is. As a result, once you understand how to use commas and semicolons, you can eliminate fragments and run-ons from your writing.

An element of APA style is using commas and semicolons correctly, and the comma and semicolon rules presented here agree with APA usage. Here is what you will learn in Part 3, Mechanics of Writing:

Chapter 10, Comma Rules: you learn how to place commas based on rules rather than *pauses*. This chapter reinforces your understanding of the sentence core. Also, by having a consistent set of comma rules, you begin to base writing decisions on principles rather than guesses.

Chapter 11, Semicolon Rules: you learn how to use semicolons, which solidifies your understanding of the difference between a sentence and a fragment. This chapter is brief but important; you will further develop your understanding of the sentence core.

With practice, you will use commas and semicolons correctly and, in the process, gain a sense of confidence. Then later in Part 6, More Mechanics, you learn about colons, dashes, ellipses, quotation marks, hyphens, and more. Feel free to skip ahead and read about those marks after you have finished these next two chapters.

Each time you learn solid principles on which to base your writing decisions, you are taking the guessing out of how to produce quality writing. As your skills improve, so should your confidence. Now go have fun as you learn about commas.

10

Comma Rules

What is your main reason for placing a comma in a sentence? Think for a moment. What word popped into your mind?

If you suddenly thought of the word *pause*, you are not alone. That is what most people say. Another common response is *take a breath*. Does it surprise you to learn that neither of these responses provides a valid reason to use a comma?

As a result of placing commas on the basis of pauses, have you ever read the same sentence several times—each time pausing at different places? The *pause approach* turns punctuating into a guessing game, even though guessing should never be involved.

Part of the problem lies in the fact that there is some truth to the *pause rule*. As you have seen, grammar creates natural breaks in structure, and those breaks generally occur between clauses. Now that you have worked on independent and dependent clauses, identifying those natural breaks should seem easy for you, but do not rely on them.

Instead, let go of everything that you thought that you knew about commas. Start fresh, keeping the following in mind:

When in doubt, leave the comma out.

In other words, if you do not know the rule that corresponds with a comma, do not use the comma. If you do the work, this method of learning commas is foolproof. Here is a strategy to tackle this chapter:

1. Go through this entire chapter quickly—within one or two sittings—and do the exercises.

2. Then for the next few days every time that you use a comma, state the rule that corresponds with its use.

3. If you do not know the rule, do not use the comma.

Though comma rules vary slightly from source to source, the rules presented here are consistent with other sources, including APA guidelines. However, this approach instructs you on how to use commas without going into detail about the exceptions, so it may seem less detailed than some other sources.

If you find yourself writing a complicated sentence, simplify your sentence by breaking down the information into more than one sentence. Simplicity is key to reader-friendly writing, which the effective use of commas helps you achieve.

Rule 1: The Sentence Core Rules (SCR)

Do not separate a subject and verb with only one comma.

Though this rule does not indicate where you need to place a comma, this rule keeps you from making serious errors, for example:

Incorrect: The director of my <u>program</u>, <u>stated</u> that I needed one more class.

Corrected: The director of my <u>program</u> <u>stated</u> that I needed one more class.

Whenever you put one comma between a subject and verb, take out the comma *or* see if you need to add a second comma!

Now let us review the remainder of the 12 comma rules, all of which give you guidance on where you should place commas.

Rule 2: Conjunction (CONJ)

Put a comma before a coordinating conjunction (such as and, but, or, for, nor, so, *and* yet) *when it connects two independent clauses.*

By far, the two most common coordinating conjunctions are *and* and *but*. Though some writers automatically put a comma before *and*, a comma is *not* always needed. Therefore, pay special attention about how you use punctuation with these coordinating conjunctions.

As you read the examples below, identify each independent clause. The subject of each clause is underlined once, and the verb twice (making the sentence core apparent at a glance):

<u>Bill</u> <u>stayed</u> late, *and* <u>he</u> <u>worked</u> on the proposal.

The <u>book</u> <u>was</u> <u>left</u> at the front desk, *but* <u>George</u> <u>did</u> not <u>pick</u> it up.

Be careful *not* to add a comma before a coordinating conjunction when only the second part of a *compound verb* follows it, for example:

Incorrect: Bob <u>worked</u> on the proposal, *and* <u>sent</u> it to my supervisor.

Corrected: Bob <u>worked</u> on the proposal *and* <u>sent</u> it to my supervisor.

However, place a comma before a coordinating conjunction when an independent clause precedes it and follows it, for example:

Incorrect: The <u>idea</u> to implement the project <u>was</u> good *so* <u>we</u> <u>plan</u> to start next week.

Corrected: The <u>idea</u> to implement the project <u>was</u> good, *so* <u>we</u> <u>plan</u> to start next week.

The sentence above marked incorrect is an example of a **run-on sentence**: *two or more sentences coming together without sufficient punctuation.*

After working on the practice that follows, you will learn another comma rule that is also based on the use of coordinating conjunctions, Rule 3: Comma Series.

PRACTICE 10.1

Rule 2: Conjunction (CONJ)

Instructions: Place commas where needed in the following sentences. For each main clause, underline the subject once and the verb twice, for example:

Incorrect: Jodie assisted with the last project so Christopher will help us with this one.

Corrected: <u>Jodie</u> <u>assisted</u> with the last project, so <u>Christopher</u> <u>will</u> <u>help</u> us with this one. (CONJ)

1. Mark Mallory is the new case manager and he starts on Monday.

2. Mark will be an inspiration to our staff and an excellent spokesperson for our agency.

3. You can leave him a message but he will not be able to reply until next week.

4. The office in St. Louis also has a new case manager and her name is Gia Rivera.

5. You can mail your information now and expect a reply within the next week.

Note: See page 405 for the key to the above exercise.

Rule 3: Series (SER)

Put a comma between items in a series.

A series consists of at least three items, and you may have learned that the comma before the conjunction is not required. That is true. Although the comma before the conjunction *and* is not required, it is preferred, for example:

> I <u>brought</u> potatoes, peas, *and* carrots to the pot luck.

> The <u>estate</u> <u>was</u> <u>left</u> to Robert, Rose, Charles, *and* Sophie.

> My favorite activities are walking, doing yoga, *and* swimming.

In the first example, how would you prepare the "potatoes, peas, and carrots": separately or mixed? What if the comma were missing after *peas*, as in "potatoes, peas and carrots"? Would you prepare them separately or mixed?

In the second example, would the estate necessarily be split the same way if the comma after *Charles* were missing? For example:

> The estate was left to Robert, Rose, Charles *and* Sophie.

In fact, the above sentence is open for debate. Some could argue that the estate should be split only three ways, with Charles and Sophie splitting a third. For clarity, separate each entity (or separate individual) with a comma.

Another mistake that writers make is place a comma before *and* when it connects *only two items*, especially when the items are long phrases (shown in italics below):

Incorrect:	The <u>assistant</u> <u>provided</u> *a series of examples*, and *a good recap of the meeting*.
Corrected:	The <u>assistant</u> <u>provided</u> *a series of examples* and a *good recap of the meeting*.

After you complete the practice below, work on Rule 4: Introductory.

PRACTICE 10.2

Rule 3: Series (SER)

Instructions: Place commas where needed in the following sentences. For each main clause, underline the subject once and the verb twice, for example:

Incorrect:	Jerry asked for squash peas and carrots.
Corrected:	<u>Jerry</u> <u>asked</u> for squash, peas, and carrots. (SER)

1. We were assigned Conference Rooms A and B on the first floor.

2. Make sure that you bring your laptop cell phone and client list to the meeting.

3. You should arrange the meeting call your supervisor and submit your housing assessment.

4. Mitchell Helen and Sally conducted the workshop on anger management.

5. They gave a workshop for Elaine Arlene Donald and Joanne on preparing housing packets for the elderly.

Note: See page 405 for the key to the above exercise.

REVIEW POINT   Here are the three types of conjunctions that play a role in punctuation, along with a few examples of each:

Coordinating conjunctions:	and, but, or, nor, so, yet
Subordinating conjunctions:	if, after, while, when, as, although, because, as soon as
Adverbial conjunctions:	however, therefore, thus, for example, in conclusion

Conjunctions also play a role in creating a reader-friendly writing style because they cue the reader to the meaning you are conveying.

Rule 4: Introductory (INTRO)

Put a comma after a word, phrase, or dependent clause that introduces an independent clause.

Since this rule is a bit complicated, review each of the various parts: *word*, *phrase*, and *dependent clause*.

- *Word:* in general, *word* refers to an adverbial conjunction such as *therefore*, *however*, and *consequently*, among others.

  However, I <u>was</u> not able to attend the conference.

  Therefore, <u>we</u> <u>will convene</u> the meeting in Boston.

- *Phrase:* in general, *phrase* refers to a prepositional phrase, a gerund phrase, or an infinitive phrase.

  During that time, he spoke about the plan in detail.

  Leaving my bags at the airport, I took a taxi into the city.

  To arrive earlier, Michael rearranged his entire schedule.

- *Dependent clause:* a dependent clause begins with a subordinating conjunction, such as *since*, *because*, *although*, *while*, *if*, and so on.

  Although my <u>calendar</u> <u>is</u> full, <u>we</u> <u>can meet</u> this Friday.

  Before <u>you</u> <u>arrive</u> at my office, (<u>you</u>) <u>call</u> my assistant.

  Until <u>I</u> <u>am</u> available, <u>you</u> <u>can work</u> in an extra office.

Placing a comma after a subordinating conjunction is a common mistake, for example:

Incorrect: *Although*, the information is timely, we cannot use it.

Corrected: *Although* the information is timely, we cannot use it.

Do *not* place the comma after the subordinating conjunction: place the comma after the dependent clause!

After you complete the practice that follows, you learn about commas that come in sets, as with Rule 5: Nonrestrictive.

PRACTICE 10.3

Rule 4: Introductory (INTRO)

Instructions: Place commas where needed in the following sentences. For each main clause, underline the subject once and the verb twice:

Incorrect: Although Mary flew to Boston she arrived a day late.

Corrected: Although <u>Mary</u> <u>flew</u> to Boston, <u>she</u> <u>arrived</u> late. (INTRO)

1. Because the letter arrived late we were not able to respond on time.

2. However we were given an extension.

3. Although the extra time helped us we still felt pressured for time.

4. To get another extension George called their office.

5. Fortunately the director was agreeable to our request.

Note: See page 406 for the key to the above exercise.

Rule 5: Nonrestrictive (NR)

Use commas to set off explanations that are nonessential to the meaning of the sentence.

To applying this rule correctly, you must first understand the difference between *restrictive* and *nonrestrictive*.

- *Restrictive information* is *essential* and should not be set off with commas.

- *Nonrestrictive information* is *not essential* and can be set off with commas.

Whenever you set off information between two commas, you are implying that the information can be removed without disturbing the structure or meaning of the sentence. Nonrestrictive elements often come in the form of *who* or *which* clauses.

The two examples below illustrate this rule (*who* clauses are italicized):

<u>Alice</u> <u>Walker</u>, *who is a prestigious author*, <u>will</u> <u>be</u> the keynote speaker.

The <u>woman</u> *who is a prestigious author* <u>will</u> <u>be</u> the keynote speaker.

In the first example above, you would still know who the keynote speaker would be even if the *who* clause were removed:

Alice <u>Walker</u> <u>will</u> <u>be</u> the keynote speaker.

However, in the second example, the meaning of the sentence would be unclear if the *who* clause were removed:

The <u>woman</u> <u>will</u> <u>be</u> the keynote speaker. *Which woman?*

In fact, all commas that come in sets imply that the information set off by the commas can be removed; so here is another reminder of how to use commas with *essential* and *nonessential* elements:

- *Essential information* is restrictive and should *not* be set off with commas.

- *Nonessential information* is nonrestrictive and can be set off with commas.

Complete the following practice to reinforce your understanding.

PRACTICE 10.4

Rule 5: Nonrestrictive (NR)

Instructions: Place commas where needed in the following sentences. For each main clause, underline the subject once and the verb twice. The essential and nonessential clauses are shown in italics, for example:

Incorrect: The artist, *who designed our brochure,* lives in New Orleans.

Corrected: The <u>artist</u> *who designed our brochure* <u>lives</u> in New Orleans. (no commas needed)

1. Our manager *who specializes in project grants* will assist you with this issue.

2. Tomas Phillips *who works only on weekends* will call you soon.

3. The therapist *who researched this case* is not available.

4. Nick Richards *who is in a meeting until 3 p.m.* can answer your question.

5. Your new contract *which we mailed yesterday* should arrive by Friday.

Note: See page 406 for the key to the above exercise.

Rule 6: Parenthetical (PAR)

Use commas to set off a word or expression that interrupts the flow of a sentence.

This rule applies to *adverbial conjunctions* or other *short phrases* interjected into a sentence. By interrupting the flow of the sentence, a parenthetical expression places stress on the words immediately preceding it or following it.

Parenthetical expressions should be set off with commas because they are nonessential and can be removed, as in the following three examples.

Mr. Connors, *however*, arrived after the opening ceremony.

You can, *therefore*, place your order after 5 p.m. today.

The project, *in my opinion*, needs improvement.

Can you see how each adverbial conjunction (shown in italics) could be removed, leaving the sentence complete and clear in meaning?

A common mistake occurs when a writer uses a semicolon in place of one of the commas, for example:

Incorrect: Ms. Philippe; in fact, approved the request last week.

Corrected: Ms. Philippe, in fact, approved the request last week.

When a semicolon precedes an adverbial conjunction, generally two sentences are involved: the adverbial conjunction functions as a bridge or a transition rather than an interrupter. (See Chapter 11, "Semicolons.")

Another common mistake occurs when a writer uses only one comma rather than a set of commas, for example:

Incorrect: Our outreach team, therefore will assist you at your convenience.

Corrected: Our outreach team, therefore, will assist you at your convenience.

Incorrect: Mr. Jones, however will plan this year's event.

Corrected: Mr. Jones, however, will plan this year's event.

In terms of structure, adverbial conjunctions are often nonessential elements. However, these conjunctions play an important role in writing style by giving clues to meaning and helping readers identify key points.

PRACTICE 10.5

Rule 6: Parenthetical (PAR)

Instructions: Place commas where needed in the following sentences. For each main clause, underline the subject once and the verb twice.

Incorrect: Our contract however did not include fee for services.

Corrected: Our <u>contract</u>, however, <u>did</u> not <u>include</u> fee for services. (PAR)

1.   Clinical Services I believe can best assist you with this issue.

2.   T. J. therefore will work this weekend in my place.

3.   Our invoice unfortunately was submitted incorrectly.

4.   The new contract in my opinion meets specifications.

5.   Brown Company of course recommended us to a vendor.

Note: See page 406 for the key to the above exercise.

WRITING TIP   *A Note about Style*: Comma Parenthetical (PAR) shows you the correct way to punctuate a sentence when an adverbial conjunction occurs in the middle of a sentence, for example:

Our outreach team, *therefore*, will assist you.

However, you can often make your sentence more reader friendly by moving the adverbial conjunction to the beginning of the sentence, for example:

Therefore, our outreach team will assist you.

Adverbial conjunctions play an established role in writing. However, writers often interject introductory comments such as "I believe" or "I think," for example:

I think the answer will become clear as we move forward.

Remove these types of unnecessary expressions, for example:

The answer will become clear as we move forward.

Can you see how these changes make a sentence flow more effectively?

Rule 7: Direct Address (DA)

Use commas to set off the name or title of a person addressed directly.

Often the name of the person being addressed directly appears at the beginning of the sentence; however, the person's name can also appear in the middle or at the end of the sentence, as shown below:

> *Donald*, <u>you</u> <u>can</u> <u>arrange</u> the meeting in Dallas or Fort Worth.

> <u>I</u> <u>gave</u> the invitation to everyone in the department, *Marge*.

> Your <u>instructions</u>, *Professor*, <u>were</u> clear and to the point.

In each of the above examples, notice that the name of the person being addressed is *not* the subject of the sentence.

The sentences below also contain a direct address, but the subject of each sentence is implied. As you read each sentence, ask yourself *who* is performing the action of the verb.

> <u>Thank</u> you, *Astrid*, for speaking on my behalf.

> <u>Feel</u> free to call my office at your convenience, *David*.

> *Traci*, please <u>assist</u> me with the spring conference.

In the first sentence above, the implied subject is *I understood*; in the second and third, the implied subject is *you understood*:

> *I* <u>thank</u> you, Astrid, for speaking on my behalf.

> *You* <u>feel</u> free to call my office at your convenience, David.

> Traci, *you* please <u>assist</u> me with the spring conference.

You will find that in sentences that contain a direct address, the subject is often implied.

After you complete the practice below, work on Rule 8: Appositive.

PRACTICE 10.6

Rule 7: Direct Address (DA)

Instructions: Place commas where needed in the following sentences. For each main clause, underline the subject once and the verb twice:

| **Incorrect:** | Johnny you should study that problem in more depth. |
| **Corrected:** | Johnny, <u>you</u> <u>should</u> <u>study</u> that problem in more depth. (DA) |

1. Give your report to the auditor by Friday Marcel.

2. Jason do you have tickets for the game?

3. Doctor I would like to know the results of my tests.

4. Would you like to attend the banquet Alice?

5. Thank you for inviting me George.

Note: See page 406 for the key to the above exercise.

Rule 8: Appositive (AP)

Use commas to set off the restatement of a noun or pronoun.

With an appositive, an equivalency exists between the noun and its descriptor. In the examples below, the appositives are show in italics:

> <u>Carolyn</u>, *my co-worker from Atlanta*, <u>requested</u> the date.

> <u>Mr. Johns</u>, *the building commissioner*, <u>refused</u> to give us a permit.

To check if the descriptor is an appositive, ask yourself questions that would indicate if an equivalency exists, such as the following:

> *Who is Carolyn?* My co-worker from Atlanta.

> *Who is my co-worker from Atlanta?* Carolyn.

> *Who is Mr. Johns?* The building commissioner.

> *Who is the building commissioner?* Mr. Johns.

When an appositive occurs in the middle of a sentence, using only one comma not only creates a mistake but also changes the meaning of the sentence. Notice how the following sentences differ in meaning:

| **Incorrect:** | <u>Josef</u>, my former <u>boss</u> <u>gave</u> me the information. |
| **Corrected:** | <u>Josef</u>, my former boss, <u>gave</u> me the information. |

In the first sentence above, the subject shifts to *boss* because of Rule 1 which states, "Do not separate a subject and verb with only one comma." Leaving out the comma after *Josef* changes the meaning of the sentence: without the comma, grammar dictates that *boss* would become the subject rather than *Josef*.

This rule applies to appositives that are not restrictive, but some appositives are restrictive. A restrictive appositive is not set off with commas because the appositive is essential for clear meaning.

For example, let us say that you have a brother named Charles, and he is joining you for dinner; the appositive would be *nonrestrictive*:

Appositive: My brother, Charles, will join us for dinner.

If you had only one brother, you could take *Charles* out of the sentence, and the reader would still know who you were talking about. However, what if you had five brothers? If you took *Charles* out of the sentence, would the reader know which brother would join you for dinner? By using commas to set off *Charles*, the above sentence translates to:

My brother will join us for dinner.

Thus, for a *restrictive appositive*, omit the commas:

Restrictive Appositive: My brother Charles will join us for dinner.

Do not set off a *restrictive appositive* with commas, as illustrated by the sentence above. However, focus on identifying nonrestrictive appositives until you clearly understand this principle: nonrestrictive appositives are far more common, and they are set off with commas.

Complete the practice below before going on to Rule 9: Addresses and Dates.

PRACTICE 10.7

Rule 8: Appositive (AP)

Instructions: Place commas where needed in the following sentences. For extra practice, underline the subject once and the verb twice in each main clause, for example:

Incorrect: Elaine my cousin taught social work classes.

Corrected: <u>Elaine</u>, my cousin, <u>taught</u> social work classes. (AP)

1. Jacob Seinfeld our associate director decided to hire Williams.

2. My lab partner Carol Glasco applied for a job here.

3. Jim Martinez the registrar approved your request.

4. The department chair Dr. George Schmidt did not receive your transcript.

5. The director asked Clair my sister to join us for dinner.

Note: See page 407 for the key to the above exercise.

Rule 9: Addresses and Dates (AD)

Use commas to set off the parts of addresses and dates.

The term *set off* means that commas are placed on both sides of the part of the address or date to show separation. For example, notice how commas surround *Massachusetts* and *California* as well as *August 15*:

Boston, Massachusetts, is the best city to host the conference.

Sally has worked in Long Beach, California, for the past five years.

On Wednesday, August 15, my friends celebrated the *Ferragosta*.

Does it surprise you to learn that a comma is required *after* the state name when a city and state are written together? If so, you are not alone; the following mistake is common:

Incorrect: Dallas, Texas is a great city to start a new business.

Corrected: Dallas, Texas, is a great city to start a new business.

The same is true for dates; the second comma in the set is often left off incorrectly, as follows:

Incorrect: Jerome listed August 15, 2009 as his start date.

Corrected: Jerome listed August 15, 2009, as his start date.

Another type of error occurs when a writer puts a comma between the month and the day, for example:

Incorrect: September, 4, 2010 was the date on the application.

Corrected: September 4, 2010, was the date on the application.

Never put a comma between the month and the day, as shown in the above *incorrect* example.

After completing the practice that follows, work on Rule 10: Words Omitted.

PRACTICE 10.8

Rule 9: Addresses and Dates (AD)

Instructions: Place commas where needed in the following sentences. For extra practice, underline the subject once and the verb twice in each main clause, for example:

Incorrect: The conference is planned for August 19 2012 in Denver Colorado.

Corrected: The <u>conference</u> <u>is</u> <u>planned</u> for August 19, 2012, in Denver, Colorado. (AD)

1.   Send your application by Friday December 15 to my assistant.
2.   San Antonio Texas has a River Walk and Conference Center.
3.   Would you prefer to meet in Myrtle Minnesota or Des Moines Iowa?
4.   Springfield Massachusetts continues to be my selection.
5.   We arrived in Chicago Illinois on May 22 2011 to prepare for the event.

Note: See page 407 for the key to the above exercise.

Rule 10: Word Omitted (WO)

Use a comma in place of a word or words that play a structural role in a sentence.

This type of comma occurs infrequently. Most of the time, the word that has been omitted is either *that* or *and*.

The problem is *that* the current situation is quite grim.

The problem is, the current situation is quite grim.

Mr. Adams presented the long *and* boring report to the board.

Mr. Adams presented the long, boring report to the board.

After the practice below, work on Rule 11: Direct Quotation.

PRACTICE 10.9

Rule 10: Word Omitted (WO)

Instructions: Place commas where needed in the following sentences. Underline the subject once and the verb twice for each main clause:

Incorrect: My suggestion is you should contain the situation now.

Corrected: My <u>suggestion</u> <u>is</u>, you should contain the situation now. (WO)

Corrected: My <u>suggestion</u> <u>is</u> *that* you should contain the situation now. (WO)

1. The president shared two intriguing confidential reports.
2. The photo shoot is on Tuesday at 5 p.m. on Wednesday at 6 p.m.
3. The problem is some of the results are not yet known.
4. Leave the materials with Alicia at the Westin with Marcia at the Hilton.
5. Silvia presented a short exciting PowerPoint on Italy.

Note: See page 407 for the key to the above exercise.

Rule 11: Direct Quotation (DQ)

Use commas to set off a direct quotation within a sentence.

A direct quotation is a person's exact words. In comparison, an indirect quotation does not give a speaker's exact words and would *not* be set off with commas.

Direct Quotation: Gabrielle said, "I have a 9 o'clock appointment," and then left abruptly.

Indirect Quotation: Gabrielle said that she had a 9 o'clock appointment and then left abruptly.

Direct Quotation: Dr. Gorman asked, "Is the environment experiencing global warming at a faster rate than previously predicted?"

Indirect Quotation: Dr. Gorman asked whether the environment is experiencing global warming at a faster rate than previously predicted.

An exception to this rule relates to short quotations: a short quotation built into the flow of a sentence does not need to be set off with commas.

Short Quotations: Marian shouted "Help!" as she slid on the ice.

My boss told me "Do not sweat the small stuff" before he let me go.

The advice "Give the project your best this time" sounded patronizing rather than encouraging.

With direct quotations, whether set off with commas or blending with the flow of the sentence, capitalize the first word of the quotation. Since using punctuation with quotation marks can be confusing, apply the following closed punctuation guidelines.

Punctuation placement with quotation marks:

- Place commas and periods on the *inside* of quotation marks.

- Place semicolons and colons on the *outside* of quotation marks.

- Place exclamation marks and question marks based on meaning: these marks can go on the *inside* or *outside* of quotation marks.

For example:

Mr. Jones said, "Your performance exceeds requirements," and I could not be happier.

Refer to the item in your inbox marked, "September Meeting Cancelled."

I had not read Chapter 5, "Persuasive Communication"; therefore, I could not respond correctly.

Did Mark say, "Arrive promptly at 10 a.m."?

Mark said, "Arrive promptly at 10 a.m.!"

Regardless of where the punctuation mark is placed, never double punctuate at the end of a sentence.

You will learn about each of the above points in detail when you work on Chapter 22, "Quotation Marks, Apostrophes, and Hyphens."

Complete the following practice before moving to your last comma rule, Rule 12: Contrasting Expression or Afterthought.

PRACTICE 10.10

Rule 11: Direct Quotation (DQ)

Instructions: Place commas where needed in the following sentences. For each main clause, underline the subject once and the verb twice.

Incorrect:	Jeffery insisted go back to the beginning before you decide to give up!
Corrected:	Jeffery insisted, "Go back to the beginning before you decide to give up!" (DQ)

1. Patrick shouted get back before we had a chance to see the falling debris.

2. According to Tyler all children can learn if they find an interest in what is taught.

3. My father warned me when you choose an insurance company, find one with good customer service.

4. Sharon encouraged me by yelling go for the gold as I was starting the race.

5. Lenny said to me good luck on your exam before I left this morning.

Note: See page 407 for the key to the above exercise.

Rule 12: Contrasting Expression or Afterthought (CEA)

Use a comma to separate a contrasting expression or afterthought from the main clause.

A contrasting expression or afterthought adds an interesting twist to writing style. The expression following a CEA comma grabs the reader's attention, for example:

Go ahead and put the property on the market, if you can.

I asked for the information so that I could help Bill make the sale, not take it from him.

My cousin Buddy, not my brother Chuck, drove me to the airport.

In fact, omitting the CEA comma is not a serious error; however, using the CEA comma makes your comments stand out and gives your writing a conversational flow.

After you complete the Practice below, complete the worksheets at the end of this chapter so that you get the practice that you need.

PRACTICE 10.11

Rule 12: Contrasting Expression or Afterthought (CEA)

Instructions: Place commas where needed in the following sentences. For extra practice, underline the subject once and the verb twice in each main clause, for example:

Incorrect: Elaine attended Southern State University not Northern State.

Corrected: <u>Elaine</u> <u>attended</u> Southern State University, not Northern State. (CEA)

1.   You will find the manuscript in John's office not in Bob's.

2.   Marcus secured the contract but only after negotiating for hours.

3.   Chair the budget committee if you prefer.

4.   Lester rather than Dan received the award.

5.   Work to achieve your dreams not to run away from your fears.

Note: See page 407 for the key to the above exercise.

Recap

Have you stopped placing commas on the basis on pauses? If so, the quality of your writing along with your confidence improves each time that you use a comma consciously and correctly.

If you have not completed all of the exercises in the chapter, go back and work on them now. For best results, follow the directions exactly as prescribed. Though analyzing comma use in this way may seem challenging at first, you will improve your skills.

For additional practice, go to, **www.thewriterstoolkit.com**.

Writing Workshop

Activity A. Writing Practice

Instructions: Write a short paper entitled, *What Is Learning?*

We become what we learn.
—John Dewey

- Do you agree?

- What effect does learning have on your life?

- Do you value what you learn? What kinds of learning do you value most?

- What are the different types of learning? Is emotional learning different from intellectual learning?

- How do you feel when you have an insight about something important?

- When you are motivated, do you work harder to learn?

If you can, discuss the topic and these questions with a peer before you start writing.

Activity B. Journal

Mistakes are an integral part of the learning process. Journal about a mistake that you recently made. Write about what you learned and the insights that you had reflecting upon your mistake.

- Were you able to turn the situation around?

- Could you have reacted differently?

- Do you try to get things perfect?

- What are pros and cons of being a perfectionist?

Skills Workshop

For additional practice, go to **www.thewriterstoolkit.com**.

By getting extra practice, you will bring your skills to a higher level of expertise. Analyzing comma use may seem challenging in the beginning. However, this approach ensures that you will learn how to use commas effectively, which is a benefit throughout your writing career.

Comma Rules

Rule 1: The Sentence Core Rules (SCR)
Do not separate a subject and verb with only one comma.

Rule 2: Conjunction (CONJ)
Use a comma to separate two independent clauses when they are joined by a coordinating conjunction (and, but, or, nor, for, so, yet).

Rule 3: Series (SER)
Use a comma to separate three or more items in a series.

Rule 4: Introductory (INTRO)
Place a comma after a word, phrase, or dependent clause that introduces an independent clause.

Rule 5: Nonrestrictive (NR)
Use commas to set off nonessential (nonrestrictive) words and phrases.

Rule 6: Parenthetical (PAR)
Use commas to set off a word or expression that interrupts the flow of a sentence.

Rule 7: Direct Address (DA)
Use commas to set off the name or title of a person addressed directly.

Rule 8: Appositive (AP)
Use commas to set off the restatement of a noun or pronoun.

Rule 9: Addresses and Dates (AD)
Use commas to set off the parts of addresses and dates.

Rule 10: Word Omitted (WO)
Use a comma for the omission of a word or words that play a structural role in a sentence.

Rule 11: Direct Quotation (DQ)
Use commas to set off direct quotations within a sentence.

Rule 12: Contrasting Expression or Afterthought (CEA)
Use a comma to separate a contrasting expression or afterthought.

11

Semicolon Rules

Most people find commas a necessity, sprinkling them throughout their writing even when unsure about how to use them correctly. It does not work that way with semicolons, however. Many people develop an aversion to using semicolons, hoping to avoid them for life!

The truth is, you *can* avoid using semicolons. However, if you do not use semicolons, you are sometimes likely to put a comma where a semicolon belongs, creating a serious grammatical error. While semicolons are not similar to commas, they are similar to periods: semicolons, like periods, create major breaks in structure, for example:

- A semicolon is a full stop that is not terminal.
- A period is a full stop that is terminal.

A period brings the sentence to an end, but a semicolon does not. Most of the time, the following rule of thumb for using semicolons works:

A semicolon can be used in place of a period.

Therefore, when using a period would be incorrect, you probably should not use a semicolon either.

Since you never *need* to use a semicolon, why use one? Because, though you may not yet realize it, punctuation speaks to your reader in subtle, yet powerful ways.

Here are two things to consider about the semicolon:

1. The semicolon whispers to your reader that two sentences share a key idea.
2. The semicolon alerts readers to slight shades of meaning, helping readers see connections and draw relationships.

In addition, once you use your first semicolon correctly, you are likely to feel more confident about your writing.

In addition, the more serious you become about writing, the more you will enjoy using the less common punctuation marks, such as the semicolon as well as the colon, dash, and ellipsis marks (see Chapter 20). These less common marks give you choices and options; but more importantly, they give your voice a fingerprint and add momentum to your message.

Here are the three basic semicolon rules:

1. *Semicolon No Conjunction:* use a semicolon to separate two independent clauses that are joined without a conjunction.

2. *Semicolon Transition:* use a semicolon before and a comma after an adverbial conjunction that acts as a bridge or transition between two independent clauses.

3. *Semicolon Because of Comma:* when a clause needs major and minor separations, use semicolons for major breaks and commas for minor breaks.

Before working on each of the semicolon rules, write two sentences, each of which contains a semicolon. Then check back to see if you used the semicolon correctly after you work through the semicolon rules in this chapter.

1. _____

2. _____

Rule 1: Semicolon No Conjunction (NC)

Use a semicolon to separate two independent clauses that are joined without a conjunction.

This semicolon rule closely relates to the comma conjunction (CONJ) rule, which states "place a comma before a coordinating conjunction when it connects two independent clauses." When a conjunction is not present, separate the two independent clauses with a period or a semicolon, for example:

Comma Conjunction: <u>Al</u> <u>went</u> to the store, *but* <u>he</u> <u>forgot</u> to buy bread. (CONJ)

Semicolon No Conjunction: <u>Al</u> <u>went</u> to the store; <u>he</u> <u>forgot</u> to buy bread. (NC)

Period: <u>Al</u> <u>went</u> to the store. <u>He</u> <u>forgot</u> to buy bread.

Notice how each sentence has a slightly different effect based on how it is punctuated. Do you see how choppy the writing sounds in the example above which uses a period, thereby breaking up the sentences?

In general, avoid writing short, choppy sentences. One way to achieve that goal is to use a semicolon instead of a period. The semicolon no conjunction (NC) rule is best applied when two sentences are closely related, especially when one or both sentences are short.

The examples and practice exercises in this book are designed to help you gain a better understanding of structure. Understanding structure provides a foundation that will help you improve your editing skills as well as your writing style.

Before moving to the next semicolon rule, do the exercise below so that you gain practice applying what you have just learned.

PRACTICE 11.1

Rule 1: Semicolon No Conjunction (NC)

Instructions: Place semicolons where needed in the following sentences. For each main clause, underline the subject once and the verb twice, for example:

Incorrect: Addison arrived at 8 o'clock, she forgot the agenda.

Corrected: Addison arrived at 8 o'clock; she forgot the agenda. (NC)

1.   Keri will not approve our final report she needs more documentation.

2.   Ask Bryan for the report he said that he completed it yesterday.

3.   Arrive on time to tomorrow's meeting bring both of your reports.

4.   A laptop was left in the conference room Johnny claimed it as his.

5.   Recognize your mistakes offer apologies as needed.

Note: See page 408 for the key to the above exercise.

Rule 2: Semicolon Transition (TRANS)

Use a semicolon before and a comma after an adverbial conjunction when it acts as a transition between two independent clauses.

This semicolon rule corresponds to the comma parenthetical (PAR) rule. With a comma parenthetical, an adverbial conjunction (shown in italics) interrupts one independent clause, for example:

Comma PAR: Bob, *however*, will determine the fees.

Instead, the semicolon transition rule involves two complete sentences with an adverbial conjunction providing a bridge or transition between the two:

Semicolon TRANS: Bob will determine the fees; *however*, he is open to suggestions.

For those who avoided semicolons prior to working on this chapter, here is how you might have punctuated the above sentence:

Incorrect: Bob will determine the fees, *however*, he is open to suggestions.

In the above example, by placing a comma where a semicolon (or a period) would belong, your result is a run-on sentence. This kind of error is common yet serious.

Whenever you see an adverbial conjunction in the middle of a sentence, read through the sentence at least twice to ensure that your punctuation is correct.

Here are more examples of the semicolon transition rule (with the adverbial conjunctions shown in italics):

Lidia wrote the grant; *therefore*, she should be on the committee.

The grant was accepted; *as a result*, we will receive funding.

You should call their office; *however*, (you) do not leave a message.

Now that you have reviewed this rule, can you see how, at times, that you may have used a comma when you should have used a semicolon?

PRACTICE 11.2

Rule 2: Semicolon Transition (TRANS)

Instructions: Place commas and semicolons where needed in the following sentences. For each main clause, underline the subject once and the verb twice, for example:

Incorrect: Feranda left, however, she forgot her case notes.

Corrected: Feranda left; however, she forgot her case notes. (TRANS)

1.   Carol suggested the topic fortunately Carlos agreed.

2.   The case management team offered assistance however their time was limited.

3.   Ken compiled the data therefore Mary crunched it.

4.   The numbers turned out well as a result our new budget was accepted.

5.   Roger ran in the marathon unfortunately he was unable to finish.

Note: See page 408 for the key to the above exercise.

Rule 3: Semicolon Because of Comma (BC)

When a clause needs major and minor separations, use semicolons for major breaks and commas for minor breaks.

This semicolon rule differs from the other two rules because it does not involve a full stop; in other words, this rule does not follow the *semicolon in place of period* rule of thumb that you learned earlier.

In addition, the semicolon because of comma (BC) rule occurs less frequently than the other types of semicolons; that is because most sentences do not call for both major and minor breaks. Even though you will not use this semicolon rule as often as the others, this rule is nonetheless necessary at times.

Apply this rule when listing a series of city and state names, for example:

Semicolon BC: Joni will travel to Dallas, Texas; Buffalo, New York; and Boston, Massachusetts.

Since the state names need commas around them, reading the previous sentence *without* semicolons would be confusing; for example:

Incorrect: Joni will travel to Dallas, Texas, Buffalo, New York, and Boston, Massachusetts.

Also apply this rule when listing a series of names and titles:

Semicolon BC: The committee members are Jeremy Smith, director of finance; Marjorie Lou Kirk, assistant vice president; Carson Michaels, accountant; and Malory Willowbrook, broker.

A more complicated example would include major and minor clauses within a sentence:

Semicolon BC: Millicent asked for a raise; and since she was a new employee, I deferred to Jackson's opinion.

Semicolon BC: Dr. Jones suggested the procedure; but I was unable to help, so he asked Dr. Bender.

PRACTICE 11.3

Rule 3: Semicolon Because of Commas (BC)

Instructions: Place commas and semicolons where needed in the following sentences. In each main clause, underline the subject once and the verb twice.

Incorrect: Gladys has lived in Boise, Idaho, Biloxi, Mississippi, and Tallahassee, Florida.

Corrected: Gladys has lived in Boise, Idaho; Biloxi, Mississippi; and Tallahassee, Florida. (BC)

1. Please include Rupert Adams CEO Madeline Story COO and Mark Coleman executive president.

2. By next week I will have traveled to St. Louis Missouri Chicago Illinois and Burlington Iowa.

3. Mike applied for jobs in Honolulu Hawaii Sacramento California and Santa Fe New Mexico.

4. Your application was received yesterday but when I reviewed it information was missing.

5. You can resubmit your application today and since my office will review it you can call me tomorrow for the results.

Note: See page 408 for the key to the above exercise.

Writing Style: Punctuation and Flow

Using punctuation *correctly* is one element of writing. Another element is applying punctuation *effectively*: punctuation packages your words, developing a rhythm that affects the style and tone of your writing.

Writing generally does not flow well when it consists of short, choppy sentences. However, at times short, choppy sentences create a desired dramatic effect, as in the following:

Conan arrived late today. He resigned.

When you want to reduce the choppy effect that short sentences can create, semicolons can often add flow to your writing, but not always. Consider the following example:

Jay priced the condo lower; he needs to relocate.

In the previous example, connecting the independent clauses with a semicolon does not necessarily reduce the choppy effect. The reader needs a transitional word to build a bridge between the cause and the effect.

Here are some ways to solve the problem through the use of conjunctions:

Jay priced the condo lower *since* he needs to relocate.

Jay priced the condo lower *because* he needs to relocate.

Jay priced the condo lower; *unfortunately*, he needs to relocate.

In each example above, the conjunction smoothed out the flow of the writing. By giving the reader a transitional word, the reader can more readily draw a connection between the meaning of the two clauses.

Recap

Punctuation is one more tool to help you connect with your reader and get your message across. Work with punctuation until you understand how it helps you to express your voice: experiment with punctuation and conjunctions until you gain a sense of how to use them effectively.

Semicolon Rules

Rule 1: Semicolon No Conjunction (NC)

Use a semicolon to separate two independent clauses that are joined without a conjunction.

Rule 2: Semicolon Transition (TRANS)

Use a semicolon before *and a comma* after *an adverbial conjunction when it acts as a transition between two independent clauses.*

Rule 3: Semicolon Because of Comma (BC)

When a clause needs major and minor separations, use a semicolon for major breaks and a comma for minor breaks.

Writing Workshop

Activity A. Writing Practice

Instructions: Identify a topic that interests you then find an academic journal (in hard copy or on the Internet).

1. What is the overall purpose of the article or its thesis?

2. What audience does the article target?

3. Is the tone emotional or persuasive? Please explain.

4. Identify two or three key points that the article makes.

5. Write a paragraph to summarize each key point.

6. What did you learn from the article that you will apply?

For a more formal start to your essay, give the author's first and last name, the title of the article, and then the purpose of the article, as shown below:

> In his article *Write for Results*, Smith (2009) argues that writing
>
> is the most critical skill for career success today.

Use APA citation style. See Chapter 6, "APA Citation Style," for basic guidelines on formatting and citing in APA style.

Activity B. Journal

Instructions: Write a page or two describing the color green.

What does *green* remind you of? Explore the feelings that the color green evokes, for example:

"The color green reminds me of summer and trees as well as money and my favorite shirt. When I think of green, I feel fresh and full of energy. . . ."

- Spend about 3 minutes doing a mind map.
- Spend 10 to 15 minutes doing a focused writing.

Your final draft should be a minimum of one page long.

Skills Workshop

Punctuation is the key to editing skills because punctuation teaches you structure.

- For extra practice with semicolons, go to **www.thewriterstoolkit.com**.

PART 4: GRAMMAR FOR WRITING

Chapter 12: Verbs

Chapter 13: Pronouns

Chapter 14: Modifiers

Grammar defines the structure of a language. As you have learned, the sentence core plays a critical role in grammar and writing. Now in Part 3 you work on using elements of the sentence core correctly: verbs and pronouns.

The formal grammar of a language does not change much, even over long periods of time. However, every formal language has several informal, micro varieties.

For example, languages such as Spanish, French, and Italian have many different varieties. The Spanish that is spoken in Spain differs from the Spanish that is spoken in Mexico or South America. The French that is spoken in Paris differs from the French that is spoken in the south of France. In Italy, every region has its own *dialetto*, and each dialect is considered a valid, though informal, variety of Italian.

The same is true of English—many different types of English are spoken. People from various English-speaking countries speak different varieties of English, and even people from the same country speak different varieties of English.

You can break down language use even further by noticing the different dialects that people speak within the same city or even within the same household. In fact, most people who speak English are fluent in more than one variety.

Varieties of a language vary in the following categories:

1. Grammar

2. Word Usage

3. Pronunciation

Do you speak differently when you are at school from when you are at home or with friends? Right now, you may not be fully aware of how you **switch codes**, which means change language patterns. However, if you focus on how you speak, you may find yourself making subtle shifts or using certain words in one situation that you would never use in another.

The chapters in this part explore how the grammar of Standard English, which is also called Edited English, differs from other varieties of English. The first step in understanding language usage is understanding language in context.

English and Its Varieties

In school, you are used to working with **Standard English** or **Edited English**. Your textbooks are written in Edited English, which corresponds closely to the way Standard English is spoken.

Standard English is the language that is spoken formally and used by most of the media. Just turn on the 6 o'clock news, and you will hear the newscaster speaking formal Standard English; however, listen to an interview with the man on the street, and you are likely to hear **local language**, a **micro-language** of Standard English.

A local language is an informal language pattern. In fact, each of us speaks one form of local language or another—no one speaks or writes formal English perfectly: *it ain't even possible!*

Here is what you need to know:

- *Edited English* or *Standard English* is known as formal English, and it facilitates communication in multi-cultural environments.

- *Local language* is known as informal language, and it is the language of choice with family and friends.

How do you know the difference between Standard English and local language? Rather than focusing on an official definition, think about what you already know.

- What does it sound like when someone is speaking *proper*?

- What does it sound like when someone is speaking *country*?

Does this way of describing formal and informal language patterns give you insight into how you use language in your day-to-day activities? Language is alive, and each language pattern has unique benefits. The more you understand about using language in *context*, the more confident you will be in every situation.

Your goal now is to tune in to the difference between these two types of English. Since local language develops naturally, there is no need to work on it. However, most people need to work on their formal English, so that is what you will be doing when you work on verbs, pronouns, and modifiers in the following chapters.

Language Use and Context

To some degree, everyone is **bidialectal**, which means being proficient in different varieties of the same language.

By working on formal English—and keeping it separate from your local language—your *bi-dialectal* abilities will become even more defined than they are now. Your goal is to switch codes based on the context, shifting from one language system to another with awareness and confidence. For instance, if you were on a job interview, using formal English would be the most effective choice, if that particular job called for it. However, when you are with your friends or family, local language is the natural choice.

Global Communication and Formal English

Global communication is multi-cultural communication: people from different backgrounds and different countries come together to speak the same language. Knowing the difference between formal and informal language patterns becomes important with global communication.

People from non-English-speaking countries who study formal English also have their own brand of local English. For example, some people from India speak a local language called *Hinglish*, which is a combination of Hindu and English. A combination of Spanish and English is called *Spanglish*.

Local varieties, or dialects, in the United States include Appalachian, Boston English, Black Vernacular English, Cajun, Chicano, and Hawaiian Pidgin, among many others. In fact, every major city has its own form of local language. In Chicago and Boston, people use the term *yous guys*; in the South, people use *y'all*; in and around Ohio, people use *you'ins*; and in Texas, you will hear the term *all y'all*. The formal equivalent for all of these terms is *you*.

Just think how confusing communication would be in global settings if everyone spoke their own local English rather than formal English. More time would be spent trying to understand the meaning of the words than getting the job done.

The global environment that exists in most public arenas has brought a new urgency for proficiency in using Edited English. However, do not let formal English interfere with how you speak when you are in casual settings: local language plays a key role in your relationships with friends and family. If you start to speak formally in places where formal language does not fit, your relationships may suffer.

Workshop Activity

Instructions: With a partner, discuss the differences in language that you hear all around you every day.

1. Make a list of words and phrases from local language and then translate them into Edited English.

2. Make a list of terms that you use in text messages, and translate them into Edited English. Is text messaging more similar to local language or Edited English? Please explain.

Note: As you complete the exercises in this chapter, use your local language as a springboard to improve your formal English skills, building a wall between the two language systems.

12

Verbs

Verbs are sources of power and energy, bringing ideas to life. Though vital, verbs can seem complicated. Fortunately, by learning only a few basic principles, you can use verbs effectively and confidently.

Here is what you will work on in this chapter:

- Regular and Irregular Verbs in Past Time

- Present Tense Third Person Singular: the *–S* Form

- Consistency of Verb Tense

- Active Voice

- Parallel Structure

- Subjunctive Mood

This chapter starts by reviewing verb parts, such as **past tense forms** and **past participle forms**, which cause writers unique problems.

After you do the basic work with verbs, you are introduced to topics that improve the quality and flow of your writing: the **active voice** and **parallel structure**. Though this chapter introduces these topics, in Part 5 an entire chapter is devoted to each (Chapter 15, "Active Voice," and Chapter 16, "Parallel Structure.")

Finally, this chapter covers the **subjunctive mood**. The subjunctive mood makes writing and speech sound more sophisticated for those times when you are in formal settings.

To refresh your memory, review the list of action verbs on the next page.

Action Verbs

Use strong verbs to add power to your writing.

accelerate	edit	instruct	proceed
accept	empower	interpret	produce
adapt	encourage	introduce	promote
aid	energize	invent	propose
amplify	enhance	judge	provide
analyze	enlist	justify	rank
apply	establish	launch	rate
arrange	estimate	lead	rearrange
assemble	evaluate	learn	recognize
assist	examine	listen	reconcile
awaken	expand	maintain	reconstruct
break down	explain	modify	reinforce
build	extend	mold	relate
challenge	focus	monitor	reorganize
change	formulate	motivate	report
choose	fortify	negotiate	restore
compile	generalize	observe	review
complete	generate	operate	revise
compose	guide	orchestrate	rewrite
compute	heal	organize	score
construct	help	orient	seek
consult	hypothesize	originate	serve
convert	ignite	outline	simplify
coordinate	illustrate	participate	solve
counsel	implement	perform	stimulate
create	incorporate	persuade	summarize
demonstrate	increase	pinpoint	support
describe	influence	plan	synthesize
design	initiate	point out	teach
develop	inspect	prepare	train
devise	inspire	present	use
devote	install	preserve	widen
direct	institute	process	write

Verbs in Past Time

Though some of this basic information about verbs was covered in Chapter 8, "Dynamic Sentences," it is important enough to merit a review.

1. All verbs have a base form: *to* plus a base form of a verb is called an *infinitive*; for example: *to see, to do, to be, to walk.*

2. All verbs have a *past tense* form and a *past participle* form:

    - A past tense form does *not* take a *helper verb* (also called an *auxiliary verb*).

    - A past participle form must be used with a helper verb.

Base	**Past Tense**	**Past Participle**
walk	walked	*have* walked
do	did	*have* done

3. Common helper verbs are *to have* and *to be*, as follows:

Have:	has, have, had
Be:	is, are, was, were

Based on the way past tense is formed, verbs are broken down into two broad categories: *regular verbs* and *irregular verbs*. After you complete the exercise below, you will first work with regular verbs and then move on to irregular verbs.

PRACTICE 12.1

Instructions: Before you go any further in this chapter, find out which irregular verbs are troublesome for you.

1. With a partner, fill in the *Irregular Verb Inventory* on page 223.
2. Which verbs do you and your partner need to work on?
3. Select a topic that you and your partner are both interested in, and together write a paragraph in past time.

Regular Verbs in Past Time

The vast majority of verbs are regular, which means that the past tense and past participle forms are both created by adding –ed to the base form, for example:

Base	Past Tense	Past Participle
walk	walked	*have* walked
file	filed	*has* filed
comment	commented	*had* commented
argue	argued	*have* argued

Here are some examples of how errors are made with past tense verbs in Edited English:

Incorrect: We *walk* to the store yesterday after class.
Corrected: We *walked* to the store yesterday after class.

Incorrect: The committee *argue* all afternoon.
Corrected: The committee *argued* all afternoon.

Incorrect: After we *had serve* the meal, we gave awards.
Corrected: After we *had served* the meal, we gave awards.

If you leave off the –ed ending with past time regular verbs in your writing, in all likelihood you also leave off the –ed ending in your speech.

Notice your speech patterns: do you speak differently with your friends from the way that you speak in more formal environments, such as a classroom? If so, practice pronouncing the –ed ending so that you become as fluent with *school talk* as you are with local language. Repetitive practice is a key in changing language patterns.

Here are more examples using verbs that have an –ed ending in Edited English:

Incorrect: The assistant *help* me with my application.
Corrected: The assistant *helped* me with my application.

Incorrect: Mark had *refer* to the incident when we spoke last week.
Corrected: Mark had *referred* to the incident when we spoke last week.

Work on the following exercise to gain practice using verbs in past time.

PRACTICE 12.2

Regular Verbs in Past Time

Instructions: Correct the following sentences by using the Edited English past tense form of the verb.

Incorrect: My friend assist me with the class project.

Corrected: My friend *assisted* me with the class project.

1.   The coach misplace the roster before the game began.

2.   My counselor suggest that I submit my résumé.

3.   Bart receive the award for most valuable player.

4.   Last week no one on our team want the schedule to change.

5.   When Jonika suggest that we meet after school, everyone was pleased.

Note: See page 408 for the key to the above exercise.

Irregular Verbs in Past Time

Irregular verbs are used differently in local language in two important ways from how they are used in Edited English.

First, in local language, an irregular past tense form is sometimes used with a helper, as in the examples that follow.

Local Language:	**Edited English:**
Lida *has wrote* the paper.	Lida *has written* the paper.
Bob *has spoke* to the director.	Bob *has spoken* to the director.
Alisha *has saw* that movie.	Alisha *has seen* that movie.

Second, in local language, an irregular past participle is sometimes used without a helper, as follows:

Local Language:	Edited English:
Lucas *seen* the paper.	Lucas *has seen* the paper.
Marc *spoken* to the director.	Marc *has spoken* to the director.
Alisha *done* good work.	Alisha *has done* good work.

As you can see, irregular verbs create different problems for writers than regular verbs do. To use irregular verbs correctly in Edited English:

1. Know the Edited English past tense of each irregular verb.

2. When using the past tense form, do *not* use a helper or auxiliary verb.

3. When using the past participle, use a helper.

Before completing Practice 12.3, Irregular Verbs in Past Time, one more troublesome verb merits review, and that is the *lend*. (Make sure that you select your choice *before* you read the explanation below.)

Which of the following sounds correct to you?

Choice 1:   Jason loaned me his car.

Choice 2:   Jason lent me his car.

The verb *lend* is irregular; its past tense form and past participle form are the same: *lent*. However, the word *loan* is a noun. As a noun, *loan* has neither action nor past tense forms. The correct choice above is Choice 2.

Using the noun *loan* as a verb is common, but it is local language; for formal situations, use *lend*.

PRACTICE 12.3

Irregular Verbs in Past Time

Instructions: Correct the following sentences by using the Edited English past tense form of the verb.

Incorrect: George has went to the meeting.

Corrected: George has *gone* to the meeting.

1. We already seen that movie last week.
2. The professor said that you had wrote a good paper.
3. I brang my lunch today, so you don't need to loan me money.
4. Bob loaned me $5 so that I could go to the game.
5. The assistant has took all the papers to the office.

Note: See page 409 for the key to the above exercise.

The –S Form: Third Person Singular

In Edited English, all third person singular verbs in simple present tense end in an *s*. By referring to third person singular verbs as the –*s* form, you remain aware of their unique spelling.

Here are some examples:

Incorrect: Bob **don't** give the information to anyone.

Corrected: Bob **does not** (doesn't) give the information to anyone.

Incorrect: Martha **have** the right attitude about her job.

Corrected: Martha **has** the right attitude about her job.

Incorrect: My teacher **say** that the paper is due on Friday.

Corrected: My teacher **says** that the paper is due on Friday.

Work on the exercise that follows to get practice using the –*s* form.

PRACTICE 12.4

The −S Form

Instructions: Correct the following sentences by using the −s form.

Incorrect: When Lenny have a question, he ask for advice.

Corrected: When Lenny *has* a question, he *asks* for advice.

1. The coach say that we need to practice for one more hour.

2. Our team finish in first place every year.

3. Taylor have chosen the players for both teams.

4. The coach have enough good players already.

5. If the group listen carefully, they will learn the information.

Note: See page 409 for the key to the above exercise.

Verb Tense and Consistency

When you are writing, do not shift verb tense unnecessarily. In other words, stay in present tense *or* past tense unless the meaning of the sentence demands that you change tenses.

Incorrect: Arthur says that the game started on time.

Corrected: Arthur said that the game started on time.

Incorrect: After we went to the store, then we go to the movies.

Corrected: After we went to the store, then we went to the movies.

Complete the following exercise to get practice using verb tense consistently.

PRACTICE 12.5

Verb Tense and Consistency

Instructions: Correct the following sentences so that the tense remains consistent.

Incorrect: My friend tells me that she had lunch already.

Corrected: My friend *told* me that she *had* lunch already.

1.   The note is not clear and needed to be changed.

2.   My boss says that I arrived late to work every day this week

3.   The new computers arrive today, so then I had to install them.

4.   Yesterday my counselor tells me I needed to take an extra elective.

5.   Last week my teacher tells me that I had to redo the paper.

Note: See page 409 for the key to the above exercise.

Active Voice

The active voice keeps writing clear and engaging. To understand how to revise a passive sentence to active voice, let us start with a passive sentence:

Passive: The ball was thrown by Billy.

First, identify the main verb, which is *sent*. Next, identify the *real subject*. The real subject is the person or thing performing the action of the verb. In a passive sentence, the real subject is different from the grammatical subject, which precedes the verb in a statement.

In the passive example above, *who threw the ball? Billy did.*

Active: Billy threw the ball.

Here are the steps to change a sentence from passive to active voice:

1.   Identify the main verb of the sentence.

2.   Identify the real subject by asking, *who performed the action of the verb?*

3.   Place the real subject at the beginning of the sentence.

4.   Follow the real subject with the verb, making adjustments for agreement.

5.   Complete the sentence with the rest of the information.

Using the above steps, here is how to revise the following sentence from passive voice to active voice:

The team captain was replaced by the coach.

1. What is the main verb?   replaced
2. Who was doing the replacing?   the coach
3. Begin the sentence with the real subject: The coach . . .
4. Follow the real subject with the verb: The coach replaced . . .
5. Complete the sentence: The coach replaced the team captain.

Here is the structure for the *passive voice*:

Subject	**Verb**	**Object**
	was done	
What	is being done	*by whom.*
	will be done	

Here is the structure for the *active voice:*

Subject	**Verb**	**Object**
	did	
Who	does	*what.*
	will do	

Do you see how much more complicated passive voice is than active voice?

Can you see why active voice makes writing more direct, clear, and concise?

PRACTICE 12.6

Active Voice

Instructions: Change the following sentences from passive to active voice.

Passive Voice: The meeting had been planned by Suzie.

Active Voice: Suzie had planned the meeting.

1. The assignment was given by my math instructor.
2. The car was purchased for me by my Uncle John.
3. The new soccer jersey was chosen by the entire team.
4. An annual art exhibit will be planned by the Art Council.
5. Your invoice should be paid by the beginning of the month.

Note: See page 409 for the key to the above exercise.

Parallel Structure

Parallel structure means putting similar sentence elements, such as words and phrases, in the same grammatical form. Parallel structure adds balance, which helps writing flow well.

Parallel structure often involves infinitives and gerunds. As you will recall, an infinitive consists of *to* plus the base form of the verb, as in *to see*, *to go*, or *to keep*. A gerund consists of the base form of the verb plus *ing*, as in *seeing*, *going*, or *keeping*. (For more information on gerunds and infinitives, see pages 136 to 137; on gerund and infinitive phrases, see pages 141 to 143.)

Even though the words *go*, *see*, and *keep* are verbs, they function as nouns when they are in their infinitive or gerund form. When you list items in a sentence, be consistent: use gerunds *or* infinitives.

Inconsistent structure: My favorite activities are *to jog*, *swimming*, and *going to the park and golfing*.

Parallel structure: My favorite activities are *jogging*, *swimming*, and *golfing*.

Likewise, when you create a list, apply parallel structure to the way you list your items.

Here is an inconsistent list:

Goals for tomorrow:

1. Buy new tennis outfit.

2. Making an appointment with tennis coach.

3. Time for doing homework must be planned in.

To make this list parallel, start each item with a gerund or an infinitive:

Gerunds:

1. Buying new outfit.

2. Making an appointment with tennis coach.

3. Planning time for homework.

Infinitives:

1. (To) Buy new tennis outfit.

2. (To) Make an appointment with tennis coach.

3. (To) Plan time for homework.

Note that using an infinitive without the word *to* is the same as using a verb in the *imperative mood* (see page 211). You will go over this topic and other elements of parallel structure in Chapter 16, "Parallel Structure

Besides gerunds and infinitives, also make sure that your sentences do not shift from active voice to passive voice, as shown in the examples that follow.

Unnecessary Shift: Bob received his brother's old car because a new car was bought by his brother.

Parallel Structure: Bob received his brother's old car because his brother bought a new car.

Work on the following exercise to practice applying parallel structure.

PRACTICE 12.7

Parallel Structure

Instructions: Edit the following sentences for parallel structure.

Incorrect: Our assignment included reading, to write a paper, and it was necessary to give a presentation as well.

Corrected: Our assignment included *reading*, *writing*, and *giving* a presentation.

1. My professor asked me to submit a new paper and handing it in on Friday was required.

2. My friends and I plan to visit a cathedral and seeing the ancient ruins in Rome.

3. Everyone focused on showing good team spirit and to win the game.

4. Your attitude will go a long way toward achieving success and get what you want in life.

5. I received the new soccer jerseys, and now they must be passed out.

Note: See page 409 for the key to the above exercise.

Mood

In addition to tense, verbs also express *mood*: mood expresses the writer's attitude toward a subject. Here are the possible moods that verbs can convey:

- Indicative: straight-forward, matter of fact

- Imperative: exclamatory, expressing requests or commands

- Subjunctive: possibility, contrary to fact

The *indicative mood* is the most common mood; and most writing, including this text, is written in the indicative mood.

   Less common is the *imperative mood*, but the imperative mood is easy to recognize when it is used in exclamations; for example, *Stop! Don't go there!* Since the imperative mood is expressed only in the second person (you), it is the perfect voice for writing instructions. (For information on using the imperative to write lists, see page 277.)

The most challenging mood to use correctly is the subjunctive mood. The subjunctive mood expresses improbability, and an improbability often comes in the form of a *wish* or *a possibility*. The subjunctive mood is also used with certain requests, demands, recommendations, and set phrases.

- For the *past subjunctive*, *to be* is always expressed as *were*. For example: If I *were* you . . . I wish I *were* . . . and so on.

- For the *present subjunctive*, the verb is expressed in the *infinitive* form. For example: It is critical that John *attend* the program.

When the subjunctive mood is used, language sounds sophisticated and formal. Therefore, by developing expertise in using the subjunctive mood, you have the option of using it when you are in formal settings.

Past Subjunctive

Statements following the words *wish* and *if* are possibilities and would be written in the past subjunctive. In a past subjunctive statement, the verb *to be* is always represented as *were*.

Local Language:	**Edited English:**
I *wish* I *was* the captain.	I *wish* I *were* the captain.
Barb *wishes* she *was* captain.	Barb *wishes* she *were* captain.
Bob *wishes* it *was* true.	Bob *wishes* it *were* true.

When a sentence begins with the word *if*, often the statement that follows is a *condition* rather than a statement of fact. Express such conditional statements in subjunctive mood.

Incorrect: If he *was* certain, we would buy the product.
If she *was* here, she would understand.
If I *was* you, I would go to the game.

Corrected: If he *were* certain, we would buy the product.
If she *were* here, she would understand.
If I *were* you, I would go to the game.

Practice using subjunctive mood until you feel comfortable using it so that you have the option of using it in formal situations.

Present Subjunctive

The present subjunctive occurs in *that clauses* expressing wishes, commands, requests, or recommendations. The present subjunctive is expressed by the infinitive form of the verb, regardless of the person or number of the subject.

> The coach said that it is imperative (that) you be on time.
>
> It is essential (that) your brother assist you with the project.
>
> Malcolm suggested (that) the team be invited to the opening.
>
> The counselor requested (that) Mark submit his paperwork.

The word *that* is essential when the words *said* or *reported* precede it, thereby showing that a direct quote does not follow. However, the word *that* is implied even when removed.

PRACTICE 12.8

Subjunctive Mood

Instructions: In the following subjunctive sentences, circle the correct form of the verb. (The correct answer is shown in bold below.)

Incorrect: The instructions require that the package (is, be) sent via UPS.

Corrected: The instructions require that the package (is, **be**) sent via UPS.

1. The president insisted that Melba (attends, attend) the reception.
2. Jacob wishes that he (was, were) on this year's team.
3. If Dan (was, were) your team captain, would you support him?
4. My mother said that it is imperative that my sister (complete, completes) her college education.
5. If I (was, were) you, I would run for office.

Note: See page 410 for the key to the above exercise.

Recap

Verbs can be complicated, but a few basic principles solve most writing problems. Practice until you feel confident: repetition is key to achieving success with any type of skill development.

➢ Do not use a helper verb with past tense forms, but do use a helper with past participle forms.

➢ Apply the –s form for all third person singular verbs.

➢ Within a sentence, do not shift verb tense unnecessarily.

➢ Use active voice to produce writing that is clear and concise.

➢ Apply parallel structure to produce writing that flows well.

➢ Use subjunctive mood to express possibility, but not fact.

➢ For past subjunctive, use *were* for the verb *to be*; for present subjunctive, represent verbs in their infinitive form.

Writing Workshop

Activity A. Writing Practice

Compose a brief description of yourself using the prompts below. Each response should be at least five sentences, but you can write as much as you would like beyond the minimum. This activity gives you an opportunity to apply your newly refreshed knowledge of verb tense.

"I Was, I Am, I Will Be, I Wish I Were"

1. At one time in my life, I was . . .

2. At this time in my life, I am . . .

3. In five years I will be . . .

4. I wish I were . . .

Activity B. Journal

Choose one special or memorable experience from your life, and write about it.

What incident pops into your mind? Why is it significant? How old were you? What did you learn from it?

Writing about significant incidents in your life is an excellent form of self-reflection . . . and an excellent way to start your memoir.

Skills Workshop

Irregular Verb Inventory

Instructions: Fill in the past tense and past participle forms below. Use a helper verb, such as to be (is, are, was, were) or to have (*has, have,* or *had*) with each past participle. *Note:* See page 134 for the key to the Irregular Verb Inventory.

Base Form	Past Tense	Past Participle
arise	arose	*have* arisen
become	became	*has* become
break	broke	*was* broken
bring		
buy		
choose		
do		
drink		
drive		
eat		
fly		
forget		
freeze		
get		
forget		
go		
know		
lend		
prove		
say		
see		
set		
sink		
sit		
show		
speak		
stand		
take		
throw		
write		

IRREGULAR VERB CHART

Base Form	Past Tense	Past Participle
arise	arose	arisen
become	became	become
break	broke	broken
bring	brought	brought
buy	bought	bought
choose	chose	chosen
dive	dived, dove	dived
do	did	done
draw	drew	drawn
drink	drank	drunk
drive	drove	driven
eat	ate	eaten
fall	fell	fallen
find	found	found
fly	flew	flown
forget	forgot	forgotten
freeze	froze	frozen
get	got	got, gotten
give	gave	given
go	went	gone
grow	grew	grown
know	knew	known
lend	lent	lent
lose	lost	lost
prove	proved	proved, proven
ride	rode	ridden
say	said	said
see	saw	seen
set	set	set
sink	sank	sunk
sit	sat	sat
show	showed	showed, shown
speak	spoke	spoken
stand	stood	stood
swim	swam	swum
take	took	taken
throw	threw	thrown
wear	wore	worn
write	wrote	written

Standard Verb Tenses

SIMPLE TENSE		DESCRIPTION
Past	spoke	an action that ended in the past
Present	speak	an action that exists or is repeated
Future	will speak	an action that will happen in the future

PROGRESSIVE TENSE

Past	was speaking	an action that was happening in the past
Present	am/is/are speaking	an action that is happening now
Future	will be speaking	an action that will happen in the future

PERFECT TENSE

Past (Distant Past)	*had* spoken	an action that ended before another action in the past
Present (Recent Past)	*has/have* spoken	an action that started in the past and was recently completed or is still ongoing
Future	will have spoken	an action that will end before another future action or time

PERFECT PROGRESSIVE TENSE

Past	had been speaking	an action that happened in the past over time before another past action or time
Present	has/have been speaking	an action occurring over time that started in the past and continues into the present
Future	will have been speaking	an action in the future occurring over time before another future action or time

COACHING TIP

Shift Your Focus to the *You* Point of View

The *you* viewpoint puts the focus on your client. However, when you compose, your words need to flow freely; so even if you start every sentence with *I*, that's all right. Compose for yourself, then edit for your reader.

When you edit, shift your thinking to your reader by shifting from the *I* viewpoint to the *you* viewpoint.

***I* Viewpoint:**	*I* am writing to let you know that *I* would like to invite you to our next meeting.
***You* Viewpoint:**	Would *you* be interested in attending our next meeting?

By speaking directly to your reader through the *you* viewpoint, you engage your reader and tune in to your reader's needs. Here are more examples:

***I* Viewpoint:**	*I* am interested in the position in social work. *I* would like to know what you think about the change. *I* would like to encourage you to apply for the position.
***You* Viewpoint:**	(*You*) Please tell me about the position in social work. What do *you* think about the change? *You* should apply for the new position.

At times, the subject of a sentence is implied or understood, as in the first *you* viewpoint example above. The *you understood* subject is represented as *(you)*.

13

Pronouns

Most people are not aware of the mistakes that they make with pronouns, so keep an open mind as you go through this chapter. You see, you may be making common mistakes with pronouns but not be aware of it. For example, is it "between you and *I*" or "between you and *me*"? Should you give the report to "John and *myself*" or to "John and *me*"?

In case you need a refresher, a *pronoun* is a word that is used in place of a noun or another pronoun; for example, *I, you, he, she, it, we,* and *they* as well as *who, that, which, someone,* among others.

One of the biggest mistakes that people make with pronouns is using a formal-sounding pronoun such as *I* in place of a less-formal sounding pronoun such as *me*. That kind of mistake is called a *hyper-correction*.

Hyper-correction is common. Unsure speakers pick up incorrect pronoun use almost the way they would pick up a virus, changing their speech so that it sounds right. If you want to use pronouns correctly, base your decisions on how they *function* in a sentence and not how others use them; then you will have sound and principle on your side.

To start, pronouns are classified by *case:* the four cases of personal pronouns are *subjective, objective, possessive,* and *reflexive*. In this chapter, you first review how pronouns function based on case and then how to use them consistently. In addition to working with other types of pronouns, such as *relative* and *indefinite pronouns*, you review *pronoun viewpoint* and APA guidelines for using pronouns effectively in academic writing.

Learning a few basic principles about pronouns will give you control and confidence in the way that you use them. Your goal is to use pronouns consistently within sentences and paragraphs.

For a quick refresher of personal pronouns, review the following chart.

	Subjective	Objective	Possessive	Reflexive
Singular				
1st Person	I	me	my, mine	myself
2nd Person	you	you	your, yours	yourself
3rd Person	he	him	his	himself
	she	her	hers	herself
	it	it	its	itself
Plural				
1st Person	we	us	our, ours	ourselves
2nd Person	you	you	your, yours	yourselves
3rd Person	they	them	their, theirs	themselves

Here is a summary of the role that each case plays in a sentence:

- *Subjective* case pronouns function as *subjects* of verbs, and thus a subjective case pronoun is used as the subject of a sentence.

- *Objective* case pronouns function as *objects*, usually of verbs or prepositions.

- *Possessive* case pronouns *show possession* of nouns or other pronouns.

- *Reflexive* case pronouns reflect back to subjective case pronouns; reflexive case pronouns are also known as *intensive case pronouns*.

Subjects Versus Objects

Your first step in gaining control of pronouns lies in using subjective case and objective case pronouns correctly.

At the core of pronoun use, here is the question you need to answer:

Does the pronoun function as a subject *or as an* object?

Here is why many writers make mistakes with subjective case and objective case pronouns:

1. Subjective case pronouns sound more formal than objective case pronouns. An unsure speaker will use *I* or *he* as an object, when *me* or *him* would be correct.

2. When a pronoun is part of a pair, incorrect pronoun use can sound correct.

Here are some examples:

Incorrect:	Bill asked Mike and *I* to assist him.
Correct:	Bill asked Mike and *me* to assist him.
Incorrect:	George and *me* went to the game last Friday.
Correct:	George and *I* went to the game last Friday.

In place of a subjective case pronoun or an objective case pronoun, some writers incorrectly substitute a reflexive case pronoun.

Incorrect:	George and *myself* went to the game last Friday.
Incorrect:	Bill asked Mike and *myself* to assist him.
Incorrect:	Sue and *yourself* can work on the project.

Instead, use reflexive case pronouns only when they refer to a subjective case pronoun or a noun that is already part of the sentence.

Here are some examples using reflexive case pronouns correctly:

> *I* will do the work *myself.*
>
> *You* can complete the project *yourself*, if you have the time.
>
> *Susan* referred to *herself* as the person in charge of hiring.
>
> The *dog* bit *itself* in the foot, mistaking his foot for a bone!

To use subjective case and objective case pronouns correctly, first identify whether the pronoun functions as a *subject* or as an *object*. If the pronoun stands alone, it is easier to test by sound.

If the pronoun is part of a pair, use the following substitutions:

1. Use *I* if you could substitute *we*:

    Sam and I went to the game: *We* went to the game.

2. Use *me* if you could substitute *us*:

    Sally asked *Juan and me* for help: Sally asked *us* for help.

3. Use *he* or *she* if you could substitute *they*:

    Martin and he finished the project: *they* finished the project.

4. Use *him* or *her* if you could substitute *them*:

    Melissa encouraged *LaTika and her* to go: Melissa encouraged *them*.

Another way would be to simplify your sentence by taking out the other person and then testing for sound. Using examples from above, here is how you would test your pronoun based on sound:

Incorrect: Sam and *me* went to the game.

Simplify: ~~Sam and~~ *me* went to the game.

Correct: Sam and *I* went to the game.

Incorrect: Sally asked Juan and *I* for help.

Simplify: Sally asked ~~Juan and~~ *I* for help.

Correct: Sally asked Juan and *me* for help.

Incorrect: Martin and *him* finished the project.

Simplify: ~~Martin and~~ *him* finished the project.

Correct: Martin and *he* finished the project.

Incorrect: Bill asked Mike and *myself* to assist him.

Simplify: Bill asked ~~Mike and~~ *myself* to assist him.

Correct: Bill asked Mike and *me* to assist him.

PRACTICE 13.1

Subjects and Objects

Instructions: Correct the following sentences for pronoun usage.

Incorrect: When you call the office, ask for myself or Alice.

Corrected: When you call the office, ask for *me* or Alice.

1. If you can't reach anyone else, feel free to call myself.
2. The director told Catie and I to role play again.
3. Fred and her collected for the local food drive.
4. His manager and him have two more reports to complete.
5. That decision was made by Jim and I.

Note: See page 410 for the key to the above exercise.

Pronouns Following *Between* and *Than*

Using pronouns after *between* and *than* can be confusing. The local language versions are so common that they sound correct to more people than the correct usage sounds. Let us start with *between*.

Which of the following sounds correct to you? (Select your choice *before* you read the explanation that follows.)

Choice 1:   Between you and *I*, we have too much work.

Choice 2:   Between you and *me*, we have too much work.

Remember the saying, *What is the object of the preposition?* The word *between* is a preposition, and an object would follow it. When *between* is followed by a pronoun, the correct choice would be an objective case pronoun such as *me* or *him* or *her* or *them*. Therefore, the correct choice is "between you and *me*."

The conjunction *than* causes challenges for speakers and writers alike. Which of the following sounds correct to you?

Choice 1:   Paco is taller than *me*.

Choice 2:   Paco is taller than *I*.

Since the word *than* is a conjunction, a subject *and* a verb would follow it. Oftentimes the verb is implied, which makes an objective case pronoun sound correct even when it is not correct. If you selected the second choice above, you would be correct. The statement actually reads, "Paco is taller than I (am)."

Here is what you need to know:

- Use the objective case after the preposition *between*.

    Incorrect: You can split the project between *Bob* and *I*.

    Corrected: You can split the project between *Bob* and *me*.
    You can split the project between *us*.

    Incorrect: That issue should remain between *yourself* and *I*.

    Corrected: That issue should remain between *you* and *me*.

- Use the subjective case after the conjunction *than* when a subject and implied verb follow it. To be correct without sounding too formal, include the implied verb in your speech and writing.

    Incorrect: Mitchell has more time than *me*.
    Corrected: Mitchell has more time than *I (have)*.

    Incorrect: Erin runs faster than *me*.
    Corrected: Erin faster than *I (run)*.

Once again, using pronouns correctly involves basing usage on principle rather than sound and avoiding the habit of hyper-correcting! In other words, until you can apply the principle, you cannot use the way it sounds as a guide.

PRACTICE 13.2

Pronouns Following *Between* and *Than*

Instructions: Correct the following sentences for pronoun usage.

Incorrect: The discussion was between John and I.

Corrected: The discussion was between John and *me*.

1.   Between you and I, who has more time?

2.   Beatrice sings better than me.

3.   The decision is between Bob and yourself.

4.   The Blue Jays are more competitive than us.

5.   You can split the work between Margaret and I so that it gets done on time.

Note: See page 410 for the key to the above exercise.

Pronoun and Antecedent Agreement

An *antecedent* is a word to which a pronoun refers. In the following example, *teachers* is the antecedent of *they* and *their*.

> All *teachers* said that *they* would submit *their* monthly progress reports on time.

Pronouns must agree in number and gender with their antecedents. Many antecedents are not gender specific, such as *person* or *doctor* or *teacher* or *lawyer*. For a singular antecedent that is gender neutral, use combinations of pronouns to refer it, such as *he/she* or *him/her*. For example, the antecedent *doctor* is gender neutral.

> When a *doctor* performs *his* or *her* duties, *he* or *she* must remain attentive to *his* or *her* patients.

Lack of agreement between pronouns and their antecedents usually occurs within sentences that contain an antecedent that is singular. Here are some examples:

Incorrect: When a *person* writes, *they* need to stay focused.

Corrected: When a *person* writes, *he* or *she* needs to stay focused.

Incorrect: Every *attendee* should make *their* own reservations.

Corrected: Every *attendee* should make *his* or *her* own reservation.

An easier way to correct the above sentences would be to make the antecedent and its corresponding pronouns plural:

Correct: When *people* write, *they* need to stay focused.

Correct: All *attendees* should make *their* own reservations.

To practice correcting pronoun-antecedent agreement, complete the following exercise.

PRACTICE 13.3

Pronoun and Antecedent Agreement

Instructions: Correct the following sentences for pronoun-antecedent agreement.

Incorrect: When an employee calls in sick, they should give a reason.
Corrected: When *employees* call in sick, *they* should give a reason.

1. When a case manager does not relate well to their clients, they need more training.
2. A server is going beyond her job description when they prepare carry-out orders for customers.
3. A pilot has a challenging job because they work long hours under difficult conditions.
4. When a student does not turn in their work, they should expect penalties.
5. A writer needs to submit their work in a timely manner.

Note: See page 410 for the key to the above exercise.

Point of View and Consistency

Besides making sure that your pronouns agree with their antecedents, also make sure that you remain consistent with your point of view. Any of the following viewpoints are acceptable, depending on the piece that you are writing:

	Singular	Plural
First or person:	I	We
Second person:	You	You
Third person:	He, She, It	They

Each point of view has a different effect. If you are writing about your own experience, use the *I* point of view. If you are communicating directly with your reader, use the *you* point of view.

I Viewpoint: When *I* started this project, *I* implied . . .

You Viewpoint: (*You*) Take your time as you read the examples so that *you* can . . .

In business, writers often use the *we viewpoint*, also known as the *editorial we*, to stress that they represent their company, as in the following:

We Viewpoint: *We* at First Trust Bank value your business.

Once you select a point of view, remain consistent with that point of view. *Do not shift point of view within sentences or paragraphs.*

Here are the various points of view:

When *I* speak, *I* must pay attention to *my* audience.
When *you* speak, *you* must pay attention to *your* audience.
When a *person* speaks, *he* or *she* must pay attention to *his* or *her* audience.
When *we* speak, *we* must pay attention to *our* audience.
When *people* speak, *they* must pay attention to *their* audience.

In the above, can you identify the pronoun-antecedent agreement? For example, if you use a singular antecedent such as "person," you must also use singular pronouns such as *he* or *she, him* or *her,* and *his* or *her.* A common mistake that writers make is to use plural pronouns with singular antecedents.

Though the use of *one* as a pronoun is not common in the United States, other English-speaking countries commonly use the *one* point of view, for example:

When *one* speaks, *one* must pay attention to *one's* audience.

Here are some examples of shifting point of view:

Incorrect: *I* like to swim because it's good for *you*.

Corrected: *I* like to swim because it's good for *me*.

Incorrect: *An employee* should follow the rules because
                    you never know when *your* manager is observing *you*.

Corrected: *An employee* should follow the rules because *he* or *she* never
                    knows when *his* or *her* manager is observing *him* or *her*.

Even though the above sentence is correct, notice how tedious it is to present it in third person singular. A better choice would be to make the antecedent plural or to use the *you* viewpoint:

Correct: *Employees* should follow the rules because *they* never know
                    when *their* manager is observing *them*.

Correct: *You* should follow the rules because *you* never know when
                    your manager is observing *you*.

How you adapt your topic for your audience helps determine the point of view you select. Once you select a point of view, the key is using it consistently. Edit individual sentences for consistency, and also edit paragraphs for consistency. At times, even entire documents must maintain consistency.

Another issue with pronouns relates to unclear pronoun and antecedent agreement. To be clear, restate the antecedent rather than use a pronoun, for example:

Incorrect: *Sam and Mike* went to the meeting together so that *he* could
                    present the information himself.

Corrected: *Sam and Mike* went to the meeting together so that *Mike*
                    could present the information himself.

PRACTICE 13.4

Point of View and Consistency

Instructions: Correct pronoun usage in the following sentences.

Incorrect: I appreciate having time off because it relieves your stress.

Corrected: *I* appreciate having time off because it relieves *my* stress.

1.   I enjoy jogging because exercise keeps you fit.

2.   You should follow the guidelines until we finish the project.

3.   As long as you stay motivated, I won't mind finishing the project.

4.   A person should strive to get the best education possible so you can have a satisfying career.

5.   Sue and Mary worked on the project together, and she will present it at the next conference.

Note: See page 410 for the key to the above exercise.

Relative Pronouns: *Who*, *Whom*, and *That*

When writers do not know how to use *whom* correctly, they often misuse the pronouns *who* and *that*. Here is a review of how to use each pronoun correctly.

1.   Use w*ho* as the subject of a clause or a sentence.

Who gave you the report?
Who said that the program starts now?

2.   Use w*hom* as an object of a preposition, a verb, an infinitive, or other verb phrase.

To whom are you referring?
You are referring to whom?

3.   Use *that* when referring to things, not people.

The yellow car is the one that is broken.
Not: Mary is the person *that* spoke first.

4. Use *who* as a subject complement of a linking verb such as *is*, *are*, *was*, or *were*.

Who do you want to be when you grow up?
You want to be *who* when you grow up?

When you are having difficulty choosing among the relative pronouns *who*, *whom*, and *that*, choose **who**.

When in doubt, use *who*.

Here is why:

1. *Whom* is falling out of use: only a small fraction of the population use *whom* correctly.

2. People who use *whom* correctly reserve its use for highly formal situations.

3. Using *whom* incorrectly sounds strange.

To improve your speech as well as your writing, instead focus on pronouncing your words clearly.

Local Language: *Whoja* go to the ballgame with?

Informal English: *Who* did you go to the ballgame with?

Formal English: With *whom* did you go to the ballgame?

Work on the exercise that follows to gain additional practice using *who*, *whom*, and *that*.

PRACTICE 13.5

Relative Pronouns: *Who, Whom,* and *That*

Instructions: In the following sentences, circle the pronoun for correct usage.

Incorrect: Michael is the person (who, that) operates the machinery.

Corrected: Michael is the person (**who**, that) operates the machinery.

1. (Who, Whom) completed the monthly report?

2. (Who, Whom) are you going to the meeting with?

3. Is Jim the person (who, whom) spoke with you?

4. The doctor (that, who, whom) saw you yesterday is not available.

5. Every person (who, that) arrives late will be turned away.

Note: See page 411 for the key to the above exercise.

Relative Pronouns: *That* and *Which*

Though *that* and *which* are somewhat interchangeable, here is how to choose between the two.

- Use *that* with *restrictive* information, which is information that should not be removed if the meaning is to remain clear.

- Use *which* with *nonrestrictive* information, which is information that can be set off with commas and removed.

Here are some examples with a brief explanation following each:

Example 1:   Our house that we bought last summer needs a new roof.

Example 1 gives the impression that more than one house was purchased—it is the house that was bought last summer that needs a new roof.

Example 2:   Our house, which we bought last summer, needs a new roof.

Example 2 indicates that only one house was purchased, and that house was bought last summer.

Example 3:   The report that came out in August reveals our position.

Example 3 indicates that more than one report came out, and the report of interest is the one that came out in August.

Example 4:   The report, which came out in August, reveals our position.

Example 4 indicates that there was only one report, and that one report came out in August.

Indefinite Pronouns

Indefinite pronouns are words that replace nouns without specifying the noun they are replacing. To use an indefinite pronoun correctly, first determine whether it is singular or plural.

Singular Indefinite Pronouns:

another	everybody	each	neither	somebody
anyone	everything	either	nobody	something
anybody	much	every	one	someone
everyone	nothing	no one		

- Singular indefinite pronouns always take a singular verb:

  Every situation *calls* for a different response.

  Neither of the girls *works* here.

  Someone is ready for a promotion.

Plural Indefinite Pronouns:

both, few, many, others, several

- Plural indefinite pronouns always take a plural verb:

  Many (of the participants) *were* unprepared.

  Several (invoices) *arrive* daily.

Indefinite Pronouns, Singular or Plural:

all, none, any, some, more, most

- Indefinite pronouns that can be singular or plural are generally followed by a prepositional phrase that contains a noun. If the noun that the indefinite pronoun refers to is singular, then the pronoun is singular. If the noun is plural, then the pronoun is plural.

Here are examples of indefinite pronouns; make special note of the noun in the prepositional phrase that follows each:

None of the cake *was* eaten.

None of the cookies *were* gone.

All of the paint *has* spilled.

All of the brushes *are* spoiled.

Work on the exercise below; also make a list of the indefinite pronouns that are troublesome for you, and practice using them until you build your skill.

PRACTICE 13.6

Indefinite Pronouns

Instructions: Correct the following sentences for pronoun usage and agreement.

Incorrect: Throw away any of the pens that doesn't work.

Corrected: Throw away any of the pens that *don't* work.

1. Either one of the programs work perfectly.

2. Everyone who finished the project are free to go.

3. None of the employees sends e-mail on Saturday.

4. Some of the assignments needs to be distributed before noon today.

5. Everything run much better when we are all on time.

Note: See page 411 for the key to the above exercise.

APA Style and Pronoun Usage

APA style encourages clear and concise writing and gives directives about using pronouns effectively. Therefore, let us look at the following three pronoun viewpoints and how they fit into your academic writing:

- Third Person Viewpoint
- *I* Viewpoint
- *We* Viewpoint (aka *editorial* we)

By the way, avoid using the *you* viewpoint in academic writing. Though the *you* viewpoint is effective in contexts which call for you to connect directly with your reader, most academic writing requires a formal and objective tone.

Third Person Viewpoint

For academic writing, the third person viewpoint is the most commonly used point of view. When you summarize the work of others or speak about a topic, choose the third person viewpoint, for example:

Third Person: *Barnes argues* that too much time spent on the Internet . . .

The *Internet distracts* learners when . . .

APA style also recommends that writing focus on the research and not the researchers conducting it. Therefore, when you summarize a research article, use the third person point of view. Start by stating the author's name but then shift your focus to the research itself, for example:

> *Barnes* (2010) *argues* that the Internet can divert users from their original objective, causing them to lose time and focus. The research specifically identifies students as being at risk for getting sidetracked from academic tasks. Findings include data about distracted learners who experience more stress than value from experiences in which they lose focus.
>
> The *Internet has* many uses, ranging from personal interests to being an academic research vehicle. Unfortunately, sites such as Facebook actually interfere with student learning and their research on the Internet.

Since most of your academic writing will be in the *third person viewpoint*, learn to speak with consistency in that viewpoint. Otherwise, you may unknowingly make errors that distract your readers and cause you to lose credibility.

At times, however, other viewpoints are not only necessary but desirable.

I Viewpoint

When you describe research that you have conducted, use the *I* viewpoint. However, many writers mistakenly avoid using *I*, ending up with writing that is unnecessarily complicated. Though overusing the *I* viewpoint detracts from the quality of writing, so does using the passive voice when the context calls for using the *I* viewpoint.

For example, the *I* viewpoint is preferred to the passive voice below:

Passive: The research design was implemented to evaluate . . .

I **Viewpoint**:   *I* designed the research to evaluate . . .

Use the *I* viewpoint when you refer to research that you have conducted yourself. When you conduct research with others, use the *we* viewpoint instead. However, once again, keep the focus on the research and not yourself.

We Viewpoint

When you work with others on a project, use the *we* viewpoint (also known as the *editorial* we) when you refer to yourself and your coauthors. For example, the editorial *we* is preferred to referring to yourselves in the third person:

Third Person   The authors received a grant to cover the cost of resources.

We Viewpoint   We received a grant to cover the cost of resources.

Consistency is an important element of viewpoint. Always remain aware of the viewpoint in which you are writing and shift only as planned. Otherwise, you are likely to shift from one point of view to another haphazardly, losing control of the quality of your document.

Since the third person viewpoint is an essential viewpoint of academic writing, complete the exercise below to hone your skills.

PRACTICE 13.7

Instructions: Edit the following paragraph, screening for pronoun consistency.

I enjoy working on team projects because you learn so much from your teammates. A team member needs to be helpful because they never know when they will need assistance from his or her colleagues. When you are on a team, every member needs to carry their weight. That is, teammates who do not do his or her share of the work can be a burden to the team and jeopardize their project.

If a team member stays motivated, you are more valuable to the team. I always strive to do my best because you never know when you will need to count on your team members.

Note: See page 411 for the key to the above exercise.

Recap

To make a correct choice with pronouns, focus on the way that the pronoun functions in the sentence: is the pronoun being used as a subject or as an object?

➢ Subjective case pronouns function as subjects of verbs.

➢ Objective case pronouns function as objects of verbs, objects of prepositions, and objects of infinitives.

➢ Reflexive case pronouns refer back to a subjective case pronoun or noun; for example: *I* will do the work *myself*.

➢ The pronoun *who* functions as a subject; *whom*, as an object.

➢ *Who* refers to people; *that* refers to objects: When in doubt, choose *who*.

➢ Pronouns must agree in number and gender with their antecedents and in number with any items of possession.

➢ For most academic writing, use the third person viewpoint.

➢ Use the *I* viewpoint when you discuss research that you conducted; use the *editorial we* when you discuss research that you have conducted with others.

➢ One key to using pronouns and antecedents consistently is to use plural antecedents.

Writing Workshop

Activity A. Writing Practice

Instructions: Select a topic that you would like to write about. Write two paragraphs: one from your viewpoint (first person singular) and another from the third person viewpoint (singular or plural), for example:

First Person: I enjoy vacations, and I take one in June.

Third Person: A vacation helps people relax and enjoy life.

When you are finished, compare your paragraphs with a partner.

Activity B. Journal

Instructions: In Chapter 8, you identified a goal that you wanted to achieve and wrote about it. Have you made progress toward your goal? What are some steps to get you closer to achieving your goal?

14

Modifiers

A *modifier* is a word or group of words that describes another word or even a complete sentence. Common modifiers include *adjectives* and *adverbs* as well as *infinitive phrases* and *gerund phrases*.

Though a modifier is not a core element of a sentence, a modifier can be an important element. Writers sometimes use modifiers excessively, thinking that the modifier will intensify their meaning; instead, a modifier can have the opposite effect and detract from meaning.

While modifiers add richness and depth when used necessarily and correctly, modifiers are just as often overused or misused. For example, certain categories of modifiers known as *hedges* and *emphatics* create the opposite of their desired effect. In other words, when you say that you are going to a *really, really important meeting*, you would sound more effective by saying that you are going to *an important meeting*. To keep your writing clear and concise, use modifiers sparingly and correctly.

Other issues with modifiers relate to hyper-correcting, such as using *more* or *less* along with the suffix *–er*, as in *more prettier* or *more better*. Another form of hyper-correcting is using double negatives, as in "B. J. *didn't* make *no* sense at yesterday's meeting."

To use a modifier correctly, place the modifier close to the word or words that it modifies. At times, misusing a modifier can be amusing. For example, when someone says, "Bill gave the assignment to our staff that no one wanted," should *the staff* feel offended?

Modifiers have as much to do with speaking as they do with writing. In this chapter, you once again work with local language patterns, translating them into Edited English. You start by working on the basics and then work through the other types of issues that occur with modifiers.

Modifiers: The Basics

The most basic point about modifiers relates to whether the modifier describes a noun or a verb:

- Adjectives modify nouns and pronouns.

- Adverbs (which often end in *ly*) modify verbs, adjectives, and other adverbs.

In the following examples, *good* is an adjective modifying the noun *paper* and *well* is an adverb modifying the verb *did*.

> Everyone in economics turned in a *good* paper.
>
> Everyone in economics did *well*.

Here are some common errors that writers make with adjectives and adverbs:

- Modifying action verbs with adjectives.

  Incorrect: Bill drives *good*.

  Corrected: Bill drives *well*.

- Modifying state of being verbs with adverbs.

  Incorrect: I felt *badly* about the situation.

  Corrected: I felt *bad* about the situation.

- Using *more*, *most*, *less*, or *least* and adding a suffix such as −*er* or −*est* to form a comparative or superlative modifier.

  Incorrect: We were *more busier* yesterday than today.

  Corrected: We were *busier* yesterday than today.

- Misplacing modifiers result when modifiers are placed away from the word or words they modify.

  Incorrect: The *book* was placed on the shelf *with the bent cover*.

  Corrected: The *book with the bent cover* was placed on the shelf.

- Dangling modifiers result when the subject of the phrase does not immediately follow the modifying phrase.

| **Incorrect**: | *Walking into my office*, my coffee spilled on the carpet. |
| | *Who* was walking into the office? *I was.* |

Because gerund phrases and infinitive phrases need a subject, the first noun that follows the phrase is considered the subject of the phrase. In the above Incorrect example, the sentence literally reads that "the coffee is walking into the office."

To correct the dangling modifier above, either turn the phrase into a clause (for example: *as I walked into my office*) or put the subject of the phrase immediately after it (for example: *Walking into my office, I . . .*).

| **Corrected:** | *As I walked into my office*, my coffee spilled on the carpet. |
| **Corrected:** | *Walking into my office, I* spilled coffee on the carpet. |

Modifiers and Verbs

The two broad categories of verbs are *action verbs* and *state-of-being verbs*, which are also called *linking verbs*.

Common linking verbs are forms of *to be* (is, are, was, were), *appear, become, seem*, and at times *smell, taste, feel, sound, look, act*, and *grow*.

- *Action verbs* are modified by **adverbs**:

  The computer <u>runs</u> *well*.

  The presenter <u>spoke</u> *loudly*.

  (You) <u>Drive</u> *safely*.

- *Linking verbs* are modified by **adjectives** because they are subject complements:

  I <u>feel</u> *bad* about the situation.

  The proposal <u>sounds</u> *good*.

  The situation <u>is</u> *bad*.

One of the most common mistakes that speakers make is to say *I feel badly* when they are referring to their own state of being. Instead say, *I feel bad*.

PRACTICE 14.1

Modifiers and Verbs

Instructions: Correct the use of adjectives and adverbs in the following sentences:

Incorrect: When you speak too loud, you may get an unwelcome response.

Corrected: When you speak *too loudly*, you may get an unwelcome response.

1.   Drive slow so that you do not get in an accident.

2.   George feels badly about the situation.

3.   The trainer spoke too loud, and our group was offended.

4.   The music sounds well to all of us.

5.   The entire group felt badly about the change in management.

Note: See page 411 for the key to the above exercise.

Comparative and Superlative Modifiers

When using adjectives or adverbs to compare, use *more, less, most*, or *least* or a suffix such as *−er* or *−est* to show the degree of comparison (but do not use both). Follow these rules:

1.   When you compare *two items*, use the **comparative** form of the modifier. The comparative is formed by adding the suffix *−er* or by adding *more* or *less*.

2.   When comparing *three or more* items, use the **superlative** form of the modifier. The superlative is formed by adding the suffix *−est* or by adding *most* or *least*.

Speakers as well as writers need to be aware of this principle, for example:

Incorrect: Brad is the *most tallest* player on the team.

Corrected: Brad is the *tallest* player on the team.

Incorrect: I am *more hungrier* now than I was an hour ago.

Corrected: I am *hungrier* now than I was an hour ago.

PRACTICE 14.2

Comparative and Superlative Modifiers

Instructions: Correct the use of modifiers in the following sentences.

Incorrect: I felt more hungrier after I ate lunch than before.

Corrected: I felt *hungrier* (or *more hungry*) after I ate lunch than before I ate.

1. Use your editing skills to make this letter more better than it was before.

2. Toni made the most silliest comment at the board meeting on Tuesday.

3. I was the most hungriest person in the room but the last to be served.

4. Of all the people at this college, I live the most farthest from campus.

5. Our committee is more further along on this project than I could have imagined.

Note: See page 411 for the key to the above exercise.

Implied Words in Comparisons

At times statements include incomparable items because implied words are left off. This kind of error often occurs when making comparisons using the conjunction *than*, for example:

Incorrect: Our products are better than our *competitor*.

Corrected: Our products are better than our *competitor's products* (*are*).

Corrected: Our products are better than our *competitor's* (*products*).

Incorrect: This production line runs faster than *anyone else*.

Corrected: This production line runs faster than *any other (production line runs)*

Corrected: This production line runs faster than *anyone else's production line (runs)*.

Notice how incomparable items are made comparable by placing a subject and verb (which is often implied) after the conjunction *than*.

Work on the exercise that follows to gain practice with this principle.

PRACTICE 14.3

Implied Words in Comparisons

Instructions: In the following sentences, correct the use of adjectives and adverbs, for example:

Incorrect: Macy's introduced their line of clothing faster than us.

Corrected: Macy's introduced their line of clothing faster than *we introduced ours*.

1. Roger's office is nicer than our manager.

2. My office has more windows than you.

3. Reggie learned to use the software sooner than me.

4. The executives ordered their lunches before us.

5. However, our desserts were much tastier than them.

Note: See page 412 for the key to the above exercise.

Modifiers and Their Placement

Placing modifiers close to the word or words they modify keeps meaning clear. In fact, placing modifiers separate from the words they modify can create a grammatical error as well as an ambiguous meaning.

When you place modifiers correctly, your writing has better flow and clearer meaning. Here are some examples of misplaced modifiers:

Incorrect: The report was assigned to the Albuquerque office *on policy errors*.

Corrected: The report *on policy errors* was assigned to the Albuquerque office.

Incorrect: The applicant was the best candidate *arriving late to the interview*.

Corrected: The applicant *arriving late to the interview* was the best candidate.

Incorrect: Our merger created chaos for us *with the other company*.

Corrected: Our merger *with the other company* created chaos for us.

Incorrect: The truck pulled into the dock area *with huge dents*.

Corrected: The truck *with huge dents* pulled into the dock area.

Some modifiers, such as gerund and infinitive phrases, take as their subject the nearest noun or pronoun. When an incorrect subject is placed next to the phrase, the result can be amusing.

Here are some examples of dangling modifiers:

Incorrect: Arriving late, the presentation ran over the time limit.
Corrected: Arriving late, the *presenter* ran over her time limit.

Incorrect: Following the instructions, the papers were filed incorrectly.
Corrected: Following the instructions, *I* still filed the papers incorrectly.
Corrected: Although *I followed* the instructions, the papers were filed incorrectly.

Incorrect: Entering the conference room, Bob's notebook fell to the ground.
Corrected: Entering the conference room, *Bob* dropped his notebook.
Corrected: As *Bob entered* the conference room, he dropped his notebook.

Incorrect: To achieve a higher grade, Sue's paper needed to be revised.
Corrected: To achieve a higher grade, Sue needed to revise her paper.

Misplaced modifiers are easy to overlook because, as the speaker or writer, you understand what you are trying to say. As you edit, be on the lookout for these faulty constructions.

PRACTICE 14.4

Modifiers and Their Placement

Instructions: Correct modifier placement in the following sentences.

Incorrect: George will give a presentation at this week's meeting *on how to implement the new community services*.

Corrected: George will give a presentation *on how to implement the new community services* at this week's meeting.

1. The report is due in September on policy change.

2. Major issues must be addressed at the fall meeting relating to dress policy.

3. Filling out the forms, a mistake was made by the applicant.

4. The letter was sent out yesterday giving details about the incident.

5. Answering the phone, my feet slipped right out from under me.

Note: See page 412for the key to the above exercise.

More on Correct Placement

Whereas adjectives are generally placed before or after the word they modify, most adverbs can be placed in various positions depending on the meaning the writer wishes to convey.

However, place adverbs such as *only, nearly, almost, ever, scarcely, merely, too,* and *also* directly before or after the word they modify. When these adverbs are placed a distance from the word or words that they modify, meaning can get distorted. Consider how the position of *only* changes the meaning of the following sentence:

Only I intend to assist you.	*. . . no one else will.*
I intend *only* to assist you.	*. . . and do nothing else.*
I intend to assist *only* you.	*. . . and no one else.*

Be on the lookout when you see any of these adverbs so that you ensure that they are placed directly before or after the word they modify.

PRACTICE 14.5

More on Correct Placement

Instructions: Correct adverb placement in the following sentences.

Incorrect: Bob only was trying to help you.

Corrected: Bob was *only* trying to help you.

1. I only received three copies of the report.

2. Louis almost bought all of the new software in the catalog.

3. During the meeting, we nearly finished all of the doughnuts and coffee cake.

4. Congratulations, Jerry, you nearly have ten years on the job!

5. We will only need to purchase one computer for the research team.

Note: See page 412 for the key to the above exercise.

Double Negatives

To negate a statement, use only one negative. If you use a **double negative**—more than one negative in a sentence—your statement actually becomes positive.

The word *not* is commonly used word for negating; less common words used to negate are *nothing, never, hardly, barely,* and *scarcely.*

Incorrect:	I *can't hardly* get my work finished.
Corrected:	I *can hardly* get my work finished.
Corrected:	I *can't* get my work finished.
Incorrect:	The crew *wasn't barely* finished before the rain started.
Corrected:	The crew *was barely* finished before the rain started.
Corrected:	The crew *had just* finished when it started to rain.

The negative form of the word *regard* is *regardless*. However, some speakers add the prefix *ir* to the already negative form *regardless*, resulting in a word that has a built-in double negative: *ir-regard-less*. In short, the correct form is *regardless*.

PRACTICE 14.6

Double Negatives

Instructions: Correct the following sentences for incorrect forms of the negative.

Incorrect:	Jim couldn't hardly believe what the contractor said.
Corrected:	Jim *could hardly* believe what the contractor said.
Corrected:	Jim *couldn't* believe what the contractor said.

1. The receptionist wouldn't give us no information over the phone.

2. Martha didn't have no intention of helping us with the proposal.

3. Sylvestri couldn't barely wait to tell us his answer.

4. The contractors will not start construction irregardless of what we offer them.

5. The accountants won't give us nothing for the charity deduction.

Note: See page 412 for the key to the above exercise.

Hedges and Emphatics

A hedge qualifies a statement; an emphatic *supposedly* places emphasis on the word it describes. However, a message is clearer without hedges and emphatics. As Robert Browning said, *less is more*.

Weak: The meeting is *very* important, so you *certainly* must attend.

Revised: The meeting is important, so you must attend.

Here are some common hedges *to avoid*:

> kind of, sort of, rarely, hardly, at times, tend, sometimes, maybe, may be, perhaps, rather, in my opinion, more or less, possibly, probably, seemingly, for all intents and purposes, to a certain extent, supposedly, usually, often, almost always, and so on.

Example:

> *For all intents and purposes*, listening is an important part of communicating. Listening *may* help you connect with your audience by understanding *some of* their needs. By becoming a better listener, *to a certain extent* you become a better communicator, *at least in my opinion*.

Use the following emphatics sparingly, or they will detract from the meaning:

> very, most, many, often, literally, virtually, usually, certainly, inevitably, as you can plainly see, as everyone is aware, as you know, always, each and every time, totally, it is quite clear that, as you may already know, undoubtedly, first and foremost, and so on.

Example:

> *As everyone knows*, listening is a *really* important part of communicating. Listening *certainly* helps you connect with your audience by understanding *most, if not all, of* their needs. By becoming a better listener, you *literally* become a better communicator, *as you may already know*.

Without hedges and emphatics, here is the short paragraph:

> Listening is an important part of communicating. Listening helps you connect with your audience by understanding their needs. By becoming a better listener, you become a better communicator.

The next time that you use an emphatic or a hedge, assess if your point is clearer without it.

Fillers and Tag-Ons

Fillers and tag-ons are empty and add no value to your message. Two words that are often inserted as fillers in speech and writing are *just* and *like*.

Incorrect:	She *like just* said that we could *like* go to the meeting.
Corrected:	She said that we could go to the meeting.
Incorrect:	I *just like* went to the meeting before *like* I knew it was cancelled.
Corrected:	I went to the meeting before I knew it was cancelled.

In addition to fillers, pay attention to *tag-ons*. In general, sentences should not end in prepositions; at times, speakers and writers place a preposition unnecessarily at the end of the sentence as a tag-on. Tag-ons are grammatically incorrect. The word *at* is a common tag-on.

Incorrect:	Where do you work *at*?
Corrected:	Where do you work?
Incorrect:	Where did you go to school *at*?
Corrected:	Where did you go to school?

Have you ever used words such as *like*, *just*, or *totally* at times when those words were not needed?

Quantifiers

Quantifiers modify nouns; they tell us *how many* or *how much*. Some quantifiers are used with count nouns (for example, *trees*) and others with non-count nouns (for example, *dancing*).

- Use the following quantifiers with count nouns:

many	a few	a couple of
several	few	none of the

- Use the following quantifiers work with non-count nouns:

not much	a little	a good deal of
a bit of	a little	a great deal of

- Use these quantifiers with count and non-count nouns:

all of the	some	most of the
enough	a lot of	plenty of
a lack of		

In formal academic writing, use *many* and *much* rather than phrases such as *a lot of*, *lots of*, and *plenty of*.

Weak: *A lot* of the problems remain unresolved.

Revised: *Many* of the problems remain unresolved.

Complete the exercises at the end of this chapter before moving on Part 5: *Editing for Clarity*.

Recap

Use modifiers correctly and, for the most part, sparingly.

➤ Adjectives modify nouns and pronouns.

➤ Adverbs often end in –ly, and they modify verbs, adjectives, and other adverbs.

➤ When comparing *two* items, form the comparative by adding the suffix *–er* or by adding *more* or *less*.

➤ When comparing *three or more* items, form the superlative by adding the suffix *–est* or by adding *most* or *least*.

➤ Place modifiers close to the word or words that they modify.

➤ Do not use double negatives and avoid using *ir-regard-less*.

➤ Avoid using hedges, emphatics, fillers, and tag-ons.

ADVERBS AND ADJECTIVES

Adverbs modify verbs, adjectives, and other adverbs as well as infinitives, gerunds, and participles. Adverbs answer questions such as:

Why?   How?   When?   Where?   To what degree?

Adjectives modify nouns (including gerunds) and pronouns. Adjectives answer these questions:

Whose?   Which?   How much?   How many?   What kind of?

Use adjectives after linking verbs such as *be* (am, is, are, was, were) and *feel* when the verb expresses the condition or state of being of the subject.

> **Examples:**   The report is *good*.
> Sue feels *bad* about the changes.

USE ADJECTIVES AND ADVERBS TO COMPARE

Adjectives and adverbs indicate degrees of comparison through three forms:

- The *positive form* makes no comparison; the positive form is the simple form of the modifier: *red*, *slow*, *seriously*.
- The *comparative form* compares two things, indicating an increase or decrease over the positive form: *redder*, *slower*, *more seriously*.
- The *superlative form* indicates the greatest or least degree among three or more objects: the *reddest*, the *slowest*, the *most serious*.

IRREGULAR MODIFIERS

Positive	Comparative	Superlative
bad	worse	worst
good, well	better	best
far	farther, further	farthest, furthest
little	less, lesser, littler	least, littlest
many, some, much	more	most

Writing Workshop

Activity A. Writing Practice

Instructions: To gain more practice using modifiers, complete Part 1 and Part 2 below. For Part 1, work with a partner or in a small group. For Part 2, exchange your paragraph with a partner, and compare your use of modifiers.

Part 1.

In a small group, think of as many descriptive words as you can to describe the room that you are in now. When you have a substantial list, work together to write a paragraph describing the room. When you are finished, take turns with other groups to read each description out loud.

Part 2.

Step 1. Describe your favorite room or place. List the tangible elements first: tangible things are those that you can see, touch, and even smell. Next, explore the intangible aspects of the room: what kinds of activities and feelings are attached to the room and why? How does the room make you feel?

Step 2. Reread your paragraph describing your favorite room or place. How much sensory detail did you include? Make a quick list of the descriptive words and phrases that you used. Would someone else be able to visualize this place if you took away those descriptive phrases?

Experiment revising parts of your description by replacing abstract terms such as *cute dog* with concrete, specific words that help the reader get a visual picture, such as the *100-pound black Labrador wearing a red scarf and wagging his tail wildly* . . .

Activity B. Journal

Instructions: How do you use local language on a daily basis? Identify some of your local language patterns and their Edited English equivalents.

Are you more aware of how you use local language and Edited English than you were a month or two ago? Give examples of changes that you have made in your speech or writing. Is speaking Editing English proficiently important for a job search?

PART 5: EDITING FOR CLARITY

In earlier parts of this book, you learned principles about correct writing, which are elements of proofreading. Now you work with principles of editing. Editing improves the quality and style of writing, making it more readable and engaging.

Your writing style results from the decisions that you make about how to present your ideas. When you present your ideas in a clear, concise way, your writing style aids readers in understanding your message.

Though you had an introduction to active voice in Chapter 12, "Verbs," you work with active voice again in Chapter 15. Passive voice creeps into people's writing as they progress through the academic system. In other words, you will not find many eighth graders writing in the passive voice, but you will find a lot of college students writing passively. By graduate school, many writers use the passive voice without question.

Once writers start using the passive voice, they struggle to keep it. Because the passive voice becomes more prominent with more education, some writers think that passive voice makes them sound smarter: only smart people can produce complicated writing, right? Well, not everyone agrees:

Everything should be made as simple as possible, but not simpler.

—Albert Einstein

In today's fast-paced world, clear and concise writing is superior to complicated writing.

In this part, you also cover parallel structure and conciseness. Parallel structure is about keeping similar grammatical elements in the same form, giving writing rhythm and flow. Being concise involves cutting the clutter, such as background thinking and empty ideas as well as redundant words and phrases.

As you go through Part 5, Editing for Clarity, always keep in mind to apply the principles that you are learning as you edit, not as you compose. As you compose, you are clarifying your thinking (and probably putting a lot of clutter in your draft). Now you are learning how to cut the clutter.

The new tools that you learn in Part 5 will improve your ability to edit: a valuable skill that you will use to enhance the quality of your writing throughout your career.

As you edit, keep in mind that *less is more*.

15

Active Voice

If you find yourself struggling to understand what you are reading, your first thought may be that your reading skills need a tune-up. In fact, the more likely answer is that the writing is full of the passive voice and other complex constructions.

Passive voice complicates meaning because the passive verb does not create action, which is its prescribed job in a sentence. Active voice assists in making writing clear and concise precisely because the various sentence parts play their designated roles: the verb performs action, and a real subject drives that action.

- With **active voice**, the verb *performs* action.

- With **passive voice**, the verb *describes* action.

In fact, APA style recommends using active voice over passive voice, when possible. As you review active voice, realize that you are also developing an effective writing style in line with APA's recommendations.

Though active voice is generally the voice of choice, passive voice has a legitimate and necessary place in all types of writing when used purposely. In fact, in scientific writing, the passive voice is used to place focus on a method or procedure rather than the person who is carrying it out.

Since real subjects play a deciding role in the active voice, here is a review of the difference between grammatical subjects and real subjects.

Grammatical Subjects Versus Real Subjects

Real subjects drive the action of verbs; however, as you have already learned, the *grammatical subject* of a sentence is not always its *real subject*.

- The grammatical subject precedes the verb.

- The real subject drives the action of the verb.

When the real subject (RS) precedes the verb, the real subject and grammatical subject (GS) are the same, for example:

Jane's <u>manager</u> gave her a laptop.
       GS/RS

However, in the following sentence, the real subject (manager) is not the grammatical subject (Jane).

<u>Jane</u> was given a laptop by her <u>manager</u>.
 GS   RS

Since the real subject appears in the sentence, the above example is considered a **full passive**. In comparison, the following sentence has a grammatical subject, but not a real subject.

A <u>laptop</u> was given to Jane.   *What is the real subject?*
  GS

Who gave Jane the laptop? Based on the above sentence, we do not know. When a passive sentence does not contain a real subject, it is called a **truncated passive.**

Even though you covered active voice in Chapter 12, "Verbs," here is a review of active voice from the beginning. Active voice is that important.

Active Voice

The active voice is the most clear, direct, and concise way to phrase a sentence because each part of the sentences fills its prescribed role. Let us start with a passive sentence and then revise it to active voice:

Passive: The papers were sent to Sue by Bob.

To change the above passive sentence to active voice, first identify the main verb, which is *sent*. Next, identify the real subject by asking who performed the action: *Who sent the papers? Bob did.* Finally, change the order in the sentence so that the real subject (Bob) is also the grammatical subject.

Active: Bob sent the papers to Sue.

Here are the steps to change a sentence from passive voice to active voice:

1. Identify the main verb.
2. Identify the real subject by asking, *who performed the action of the verb?*
3. Place the real subject (along with modifying words) at the beginning of the sentence, which is the position of the grammatical subject
4. Follow the real subject with the verb, *adjusting for agreement.*
5. Complete the sentence.

In a shorter form, here is the process:

Step 1:	Main verb?
Step 2:	Real subject?
Steps 3 and 4:	Real subject + verb (*agreement and tense?*)
Step 5:	S – V – O.

Here is another sentence to revise from passive voice to active voice:

Passive: The merger was rejected by their new CEO.

Step 1:	Main verb?	Rejected
Step 2:	Real subject?	Their new CEO
Steps 3 and 4:	Real subject + verb	Their new CEO rejected
Step 5:	Complete sentence:	Their new CEO rejected the merger.

Here is the structure for the **active voice:**

Who *did/does/will do* what.

Here is the structure for the **passive voice:**

What *was done/is done/will be done* by whom.

This step-by-step analysis makes revising sentences from passive voice to active voice sound simple. In fact, the process is simple, even with complex sentences.

The challenges arise when you start revising your own writing because you also need to revise your thinking.

At first, it may be difficult to identify sentences that you have written in the passive voice. That's partly because writing in a complicated way is familiar to you and feels comfortable. Reading your own writing also feels comfortable because you are already familiar with the ideas. A place to start is to notice your reaction *as a reader* to various types of writing that others produce so that you can analyze your own writing with an open mind.

Work on the following exercise to practice the active voice.

PRACTICE 15.1

Active Voice

Instructions: Edit the following sentences by changing passive voice to active voice.

Passive: An urgent message was left by Miguel for my manager.

Active: Miguel left an urgent message for my manager.

1. Sean was asked by his manager to lead the diversity team.

2. Phelps was given another chance by his coach to swim in the relay.

3. The holiday event was hosted by our department last year.

4. A new policy on reimbursement for travel expenses was implemented by our president.

5. The program was cancelled by the mayor due to lack of interest.

Note: See page 412 for the key to the above exercise.

Passive Voice, the Tactful Voice

Since the real subject does not need to be present in a passive sentence, here are some times when passive voice is preferred over active voice.

• Whenever you do not want to focus on a specific person because it would be more tactful not sound accusatory, use passive voice, for example:

Passive: A mistake was made on the August invoices.

Who made the mistake? An active sentence needs an actor or agent performing the action of its verb; however, a passive sentence does not need an actor or agent because its verb does not create action.

- Whenever you do not know *who* performed an action, use passive voice, for example:

    Passive: The bank was robbed at gunpoint.

You will find that you use the truncated passive naturally in these situations. For these situations, the passive voice is natural and necessary. While truncated passives play a vital role in writing, full passives that are unnecessary interfere with the quality and the flow of writing.

Another element that complicates writing is nominals, which are often used in conjunction with the passive voice. After working on the Practice below, you will work on getting rid of unnecessary nominals.

PRACTICE 15.2

Passive Voice, the Tactful Voice

Instructions: Edit the following sentences by changing passive voice to active voice. Then determine which sentences would sound more tactful written in the passive voice.

Passive: Your check should have been mailed last week to avoid a penalty.

Active: You should have mailed your check last week to avoid a penalty.

Active or passive?   Passive is more tactful.

1. An error in invoicing was made on your account (by Meyers).

2. If you wanted to avoid an overdraft, your check should have been deposited before 4 p.m.

3. Your receipt should have been enclosed with your return item.

4. Your order was sent to the wrong address and apologies are being made.

5. Your invoice needed to be paid before the first of the month to avoid penalties.

Note: See page 413 for the key to the above exercise.

Nominalization

Verbs that change forms to function as nouns are call **nominals**. The actual term for transforming a verb into a noun is *nominalization*.

You have already worked with two forms of nominals: gerunds and infinitives.

- To form a gerund, add *ing* to the base form of a verb: *go* in its gerund form is *going*.

- To form an infinitive, add *to* to the base form of a verb, as in *to go*.

As they are nominalized, some verbs change forms completely, following no specific pattern. For example, the verb *analyze* turns into the noun *analysis* . . . the verb *fail* turns into the noun *failure* . . . and the verb *maintain* turns into the noun *maintenance*.

Many verbs, however, commonly turn into nominals by adding the suffix *–ment* or *–tion*; for example, *define* turns into *definition*, *commit* turns into *commitment*.

Verb	Nominal
accomplish	accomplishment
connect	connection
decide	decision
dedicate	dedication
develop	development
encourage	encouragement
evaluate	evaluation
facilitate	facilitation
institute	institutionalization
separate	separation
verify	verification

Obviously, nouns have no action and, for the most part, words originating as nouns cannot be used as verbs. When people use nouns as verbs, the construction often sounds awkward, as in "Let's *lunch* together" or "Do you *lotto*?" One word, however, has taken a unique place in English, and that word is *Google*. Google is a proper noun that also functions as a verb. Can you think of other proper nouns that can also function as verbs?

Nominalization changes a verb's *DNA*, so to speak, by stripping it of its action: nouns have no action. When writers use nominalizations unnecessarily, their writing becomes more complicated. However, just as passive voice at times adds value, nominalization can also add value when used effectively.

Here is an example of the verb *appreciate* used in its nominalized form *appreciation*.

Nominalized: I want to express my **appreciation** for your help.

Active: I **appreciate** your help.

In the nominalized version above, the weak verb *want* replaces the strong verb *appreciate*. As well as stripping *appreciate* of its action, the nominalized version is more wordy. However, at times nominalizations work well, as in the following:

I value your *appreciation*.

Without the nominalization, the same sentiment would be expressed awkwardly, as follows:

When you appreciate my work, I value it.

Here is an example using the verb *commit* and its nominalized form *commitment*:

Nominalized: A **commitment** of resources for the disaster in Haiti was made by our CEO.

Active: Our CEO **committed** resources for the disaster in Haiti.

Once again, the more complicated writing is, the less effective it is. When using nominals, use them purposefully, just as you must use passive voice with purpose.

When writers refuse to give up the passive voice, they may mistakenly believe that they sound sophisticated. Unfortunately, some writers fall into the same trap with nominalizations. Unnecessarily long four-syllable words do not improve the flow of writing. Follow Leonard DaVinci's advice when he said:

Simplicity is the ultimate sophistication.

As an effective writer, make complex messages as *simple* as you can: use nominalizations *only* when they improve the efficiency of your writing, and use passive voice *only* when it improves the tone of your writing.

Here is another example showing how the passive voice and nominalizations are used together:

Nominalized:	**Encouragement** was given to me by my coach and teammates.
Passive:	I **was encouraged** by my coach and teammates.
Active:	My coach and teammates **encouraged** me.

In the first sentence above, the nominalization *encouragement* is used in a passive sentence. In the second, the nominal is removed, but the sentence is still passive. In the third, *encourage* is used as an active verb in its past tense form.

Understanding these principles is much easier than actually applying them to your own writing. To achieve active writing, you need to be committed; the more committed you are, the more changes you will make in your writing.

To get practice, complete the following exercise.

PRACTICE 15.3

Nominals

Instructions: Rewrite the following sentences by changing nominalizations into active verbs.

Passive:	The distribution of the product was made by Mary Lou.
Active:	Mary Lou distributed the product.

1. The implementation of the dress policy was made official by management in August.

2. A suggestion was made by Jane that all new hires start on the first day of the month.

3. Information about that stock was given to us by our broker.

4. A discussion of the new account occurred at our last team meeting.

5. An announcement about the merger was made by our president before the deal was final.

Note: See pages 413 for the key to the above exercise.

APA Style, Active Voice, and Tone

Academic writing has a reputation of being passive, over-nominalized, and abstract—in other words, much academic writing is not reader friendly because it is more complicated than it needs to be.

In contrast, APA (2010) guidelines recommend active, clear, concise, readable writing as the preferred style of writing for academic papers (p. 26). However, many academic writers still cling to passive, complicated writing.

One of the biggest arguments against letting go of the passive voice is that changing a sentence from passive voice to active voice changes its meaning. However, shifting from one voice to another does not necessarily change the meaning, but it does change the tone.

When all actors are present in a sentence, changing from passive voice to active voice is an exercise in *translation*. Active voice is direct and clear. Passive voice is indirect and abstract to the point that the person performing the action is not necessarily in the sentence, for example:

Passive: The problem will be solved.

                      However, who *is solving the problem?*

Passive: A solution will be developed.

                      However, who *is developing a solution?*

For the above sentences to be active, each would need a *real subject* performing the action. Also, in sentences that do not include a real subject, no one is taking responsibility for any actions that the sentence may contain.

When sentences are long and complicated, the tone of the writing is much different from sentences that are clear and to the point. With passive voice, writers do not connect with their own words in the way that they must with active voice, for example:

Passive: A discussion of the issue ensued at length before an
                      acceptable compromise could be established.

Once again, *who discussed the issue*? By adding *actors* or *agents* (people) to drive the action of the verb, the sentence becomes more reader friendly, for example:

Active: We discussed the issue at length before we reached a
                      compromise.

Though passive voice sounds more formal, today's academic culture now recognizes that clear, concise, active writing can get the job done just as well. However, changing your style of writing is difficult: breaking out of a passive, nominalized writing style takes courage and commitment.

Always keep in mind that when you write in the active voice, your readers appreciate your clear, direct writing style because it saves them time and energy.

Style and Process

Even though you now have good editing tools in your writing toolkit, you still may be trying to get your words down in final form as you compose.

Remember, the *first and final draft approach* does not work: when you try to correct your words as you compose, you are sabotaging your writing. As you write, you need freedom to put ideas on the page in whatever way they take shape in your mind. If you interfere with that process, writing is much more challenging for you than it needs to be.

The next chapter covers parallel structure, another topic that ranks high along with the active voice in making your writing effective.

Recap

Using active voice improves the quality and readability of writing.

- ➢ Active voice is clear, concise, and direct.
- ➢ Passive voice is complicated and abstract but perfect for those situations that call for tact.
- ➢ Nominalization removes the action from verbs and complicates writing.
- ➢ Turn nominals back into active verbs.

If you have been able to identify passive sentences in your own writing and to revise them, savor your sense of accomplishment. Stay committed in your quest to write actively: active voice makes writing powerful because active voice brings writing to life.

Writing Workshop

Lessons Learned

Activity A. Writing Practice

Instructions: Take out a paper that you wrote a while back. Can you find any passive sentences that you could revise to the active voice?

Find a newspaper or a magazine article that interests you, and assess whether the writer uses the active voice or the passive voice.

Are you beginning to see the difference voice makes?

Activity B. Journal

Instructions: What is an important lesson that you have learned? Find a photo of yourself when you were ten or more years younger than you are now.

What advice would you give to that younger and more naïve person that you once were?

Skills Workshop

The active voice may be one of the most critical qualities of effective writing. For additional practice on the active voice, go to **www.thewriterstoolkit.com.**

Reference

APA. (2010). *Publication manual of the American Psychological Association* (6th ed.). Washington, DC: Author.

16

Parallel Structure

When writing sounds choppy and disjointed, check to see if it is lacking parallel structure. Parallel structure involves expressing similar sentence elements in the same grammatical form; that is, noun for noun, verb for verb, phrase for phrase, and clause for clause.

Parallel structure gives writing balance, rhythm, and flow; parallel structure also enhances understanding, which readers appreciate. In sentences, shifts in structure often occur with the following:

- Gerunds and infinitives

- Active and Passive Voice

- Verb Tense

Also check for parallel structure when using bullet points or creating lists. This chapter covers each of these topics and more.

Throughout the centuries, speakers and writers have used parallelism in a variety of ways to draw attention to their point. On a broad level, consider the parallel features of Dr. Martin Luther King's speech, *I Have a Dream*. Dr. King's repetition not only built up listeners' expectations but also added an indelible rhythm to his speech. When you listen to an especially effective speech, consider if the speaker uses parallel repetition to draw you in.

On a macro level, parallel structure involves using repetitive phrases or sentences to draw in readers and build their expectations. On a micro level, parallel structure involves putting similar sentence elements in the same grammatical form. On all levels, parallel structure creates rhythm and flow.

The smaller elements of parallel structure affect your writing on a daily basis, so those are the elements reviewed first.

Nouns

Writers have various ways of shifting structure when using nouns, thereby losing parallel structure.

Inconsistent: You need *rest*, *relaxation*, and *weather that is warm*.

Parallel: You need *rest*, *relaxation*, and *warm weather*.

Inconsistent: During summers, I worked as *a secretary*, *assistant cashier*, and *did tutoring*.

Parallel: During summers, I worked as *a secretary*, *an assistant cashier*, and *a tutor*.

Another common way to lose parallel structure is to shift from infinitives to gerunds. Infinitives and gerunds are nominals, so they function as nouns, not as verbs.

- An infinitive is the base form of the verb plus *to*, as in *to see*, *to go*, and *to keep*.

- A gerund is the base form of the verb plus *ing*, as in *seeing*, *going*, and *keeping*.

For parallel structure, the key to using gerunds and infinitives is using one or the other, but not both.

Inconsistent: My favorite activities are *to jog*, *swimming*, and *to go to the park and golfing*.

Parallel: My favorite activities are *jogging*, *swimming*, and *golfing*.

Next, you will work with parallel structure using adjectives.

Adjectives

With lists of adjectives, writers sometimes drift from an adjective to a phrase or a clause.

Inconsistent: Marguerite is *nice*, *pretty*, and *has a lot of talent*.

Parallel: Marguerite is *nice*, *pretty*, and *talented*.

Inconsistent:	The program is *short, intense,* and *many people like it.*
Parallel:	The program is *short, intense,* and *popular.*

When you see yourself shifting from an adjective to a phrase, revise your sentence so that it is parallel.

Phrases

Parallel agreement with phrases can be tricky, especially with prepositional phrases. For example, a preposition may not fit all of the phrases that follow it, necessitating the addition of a preposition that would fit:

Inconsistent:	I am disappointed *about the situation* and *the people* who caused it.
Parallel:	I am disappointed *about the situation* and *with the people* who caused it.

You may find a prepositional phrase followed by another type of structure:

Inconsistent:	Our company applauds them *for their dedication* and *because they are passionate about their cause.*
Parallel:	Our company applauds them *for their dedication to* and *for their passion about* their cause.

Once again, edit these kinds of inconsistencies out of your writing.

Clauses

When a sentence shifts from active voice to passive voice, or vice versa, the sentence lacks parallel structure, for example:

Inconsistent:	Bob received his brother's old car because a new car was bought by his brother. (active-passive)
Parallel:	Bob received his brother's old car because his brother bought a new car. (active-active)

Inconsistent:	We ran out of money in our budget, so that project was dropped. (active-passive)
Parallel:	We ran out of money in our budget, so we dropped that project. (active-active)

The following sentences will give you practice applying parallel structure.

PRACTICE 16.1

Clauses

Instructions: Edit the following sentences for parallel structure.

Inconsistent:	I am going to Florida and will be joined by my family.
Parallel:	I am going to Florida, and my family will join me.

1. My manager asked me to attend the annual meeting, and arriving early on Friday was his suggestion.

2. My family will join me in Florida, and reservations will be made for them by my assistant.

3. Though I gave input, my schedule was planned by my manager.

4. If my schedule can be adjusted, I will take time off for some fun with my family.

5. The extra time was approved by my boss, so now I must change my travel arrangements.

Note: See page 413 for the key to the above exercise.

Tenses

Do not shift verb tense unnecessarily. In other words, stay in present tense or past tense unless the meaning of the sentence requires that you change tense.

Inconsistent:	Tim *tells* me last week that the competition *was* over.
Parallel:	Tim *told* me last week that the competition *was* over.

Inconsistent:	Management *says* that our team won.
Parallel:	Management *said* that our team won.

For practice using verb tense consistently, complete the following exercise.

PRACTICE 16.2

Tenses

Instructions: The following sentences shift tense unnecessarily. Change the verbs so that tenses are consistent.

Inconsistent: The registrar says I needed to turn the form in yesterday.

Parallel: The registrar said that I needed to turn the form in yesterday.

1. The message is not clear and needed to be changed.

2. My boss says that their account was closed for some time now.

3. The new computers arrive today, so then I had to install them.

4. Yesterday my co-worker tells me that I was supposed to attend the budget meeting.

5. First Mary says that she wants the position then she says that she didn't.

Note: See page 413 for the key to the above exercise.

Lists

Pay special attention when listing items within a sentence or displaying items using bullet points or numbering.

When displaying lists, you can use various styles, but remain consistent. For example, you can display items using active voice, nouns, gerund phrases, or infinitive phrases.

When writing a list of instructions, by far the most effective style is to start each item with the base form of a verb; this style is equivalent to the *imperative mood or voice*: the imperative voice occurs only in the second person, and the subject is *you*. The imperative voice communicates to the reader what must be done in the most simple, direct way; for example, (you) *attend* the meeting and (you) *take* notes.

On the next page is an inconsistent list which is then displayed in the various styles: the base from of verbs, nouns, gerund phrases, and infinitive phrases.

Incorrect:

1. Paper on environmental risks

2. Selecting a location for meeting

3. Topics for meeting agenda

Corrected:

Verbs (base form or imperative voice):

1. Write paper on environmental risks

2. Select a location for meeting

3. Identify topics for meeting agenda

Nouns:

1. Paper on environmental risks

2. Location for meeting

3. Topics for meeting agenda

Gerund phrases:

1. Writing paper on environmental risks

2. Selecting a location for meeting

3. Identifying topics for meeting agenda

Infinitive phrases:

1. To write a paper on environmental risks

2. To select a location for meeting

3. To identify topics for meeting agenda

Here is a list of instructions that lacks parallel structure:

Instructions for Tallying the Call Volume

1. A tally should be taken of the call volume.

2. You need to complete the tally by 9 a.m. for the previous day's calls.

3. The call volume is recorded in the black binder labeled *Call Volume*.

4. Then you should report the number to the sales manager.

5. When you are finished, the binder must be returned.

Here is the same list using verbs (base form or imperative voice):

Call Volume Tally

1. Tally the previous day's sales calls by 9 a.m.

2. Record the number in the black binder labeled *Call Volume*.

3. Report the number to the sales manager.

4. Return the binder.

In the exercise below, put the items in parallel structure.

PRACTICE 16.3

Parallel lists

Instructions: Make the following list parallel by using the base form or the verb (or the imperative voice).

- Creation of High Performance Teams
- Development of Effective Communication Skills
- Effective Job Performance Coaching
- Conflict Resolution
- Recruitment and Retention of Managers
- Valuing Personality Differences in the Workplace
- Climate Assessment in Change Efforts

Note: See page 414 for the key to the above exercise.

Correlative Conjunctions

Here are common pairs of conjunctions—notice that the second word in the pair is a coordinating conjunction:

either . . . or

neither . . . nor

both . . . and

not . . . but

not only . . . but also

whether . . . or

When using correlative conjunctions, follow the second part of the correlative with the same structure as the first part.

Inconsistent: We will *not only* upgrade your account *but also* are providing monthly reports.

Parallel: We *not only* will upgrade your account *but also* will provide monthly reports.

Parallel: We will *not only* upgrade your account *but also* provide monthly reports.

Complete the following exercise for additional practice.

PRACTICE 16.4

Correlative Conjunctions

Instructions: Edit the following sentences for parallel structure.

Incorrect: Barbara will either go to the meeting or she will not go.

Corrected: Barbara will either go to the meeting or not (go to the meeting).

1. My boss not only asked me to complete the report but also presenting it at the meeting was required.

2. Milly applied both for the job and got it.

3. Our team neither focused on winning the game nor to show good team spirit.

4. The solution makes not only sense but also saves time.

5.   Neither my new car has a warranty nor does it run well.

Note: See page 414 for the key to the above exercise.

Recap

Parallel structure comes in all shapes and forms. Developing a keen eye for similar sentence elements takes time and commitment. As you focus attention on parallel structure, you will see connections that you did not previously see.

➢   Express similar sentence elements in the same grammatical form: noun for noun, verb for verb, phrase for phrase, and clause for clause.

➢   Start bulleted lists with gerunds, infinitives, or verbs.

➢   Use the imperative voice when writing instructions (which is equivalent to using the base form of the verb).

➢   Pay special attention to parallel structure when using correlative conjunctions.

Writing Workshop

Activity A: Writing Practice

Use your newly refreshed understanding of parallel structure to give instructions on how to accomplish a task. Start by selecting a task that takes several steps to complete, such as cooking a recipe, completing a chore, or following directions to a specific location. Then break the task down into steps, and list each step in the active voice.

In other words, write your list of instructions so that anyone could pick up your list and accomplish your chosen task. (See an example on page 197.)

Activity B: Journal

Instructions: Short of telepathy, one person cannot transfer feelings and thoughts to another person in pure form. In other words, something is always lost in translation when words leave one person's lips and enter another's ears.

1.   Describe an experience in which you misinterpreted someone's words or actions.

2.   What did you learn from the experience?

COACHING TIP

Create a Positive Tone

Everyone appreciates positive words; even subtle comments add energy. To stay positive, focus on *what will go right if procedures are followed* rather than on what will go wrong if they are not.

In fact, even valuable services can sound threatening if stated in the negative, for example:

Negative: If I don't hear from you within a week, I'll assume you are not interested.

Positive: If you are interested, please contact me within the next week.

Another way to improve tone is to avoid the word *not*:

Negative: You cannot schedule any time off until you complete the project.

Positive: Once you complete the project, you can take time off.

Whenever you edit a sentence so that you state the same message without the word *not*, the tone sounds more positive.

Negative: You are not qualified for the position.

Positive: You are better qualified for other positions and would benefit from exploring other options.

When a situation is inviting, people are more inclined to put positive energy toward accomplishing the task.

17

Conciseness

When you write, do you ever have magical moments? You know the ones—when you can simply sit down and write what you mean without effort. Most of the time, writing does not work that way. Even seasoned writers struggle with their words until their thoughts become clear. The real magical moments are the insights, the clarity, the next step revealed.

Adapt your expectations so they are in line with the reality of the writing process, and writing will not disappoint you. Writing develops your thinking: compose freely until you understand your point. Once you understand your purpose, you can edit your writing so that you say what you mean in the most simple and most concise way. That's because your purpose clarifies the difference between information that is important from information that is unimportant or even irritating for the reader.

To get rid of the clutter in your writing, you may need to change some ways of thinking, giving up security blankets and old habits. This chapter shows you the kinds of information to edit out of your writing, and here is the principle to follow:

Less is more.

If you find yourself in a mire of words, remember the following:

1. Simple words and short messages convey information more effectively than complex words and long messages.

2. Using big, four-syllable words is *not* a sign of intelligence.

In other words, along with empty information, let go of artificial and abstract language.

The more you explain it, the more I don't understand it.

—Mark Twain

Let us get started by examining how purpose relates to being concise.

Put Purpose First

When you are composing, you eventually reach an insight that clarifies your key point. Those are the moments of insight when you say to yourself, "Wow, that's what I was trying to say—now I can stop writing and start editing."

Those light-bulb experiences are the best moments of writing, making the struggle worthwhile. Once you know your key point, follow these steps:

1. Paste your key point to the beginning of your message.

2. Identify and cut information that the reader does not need to know.

You may find yourself cutting quite a bit of irrelevant or empty information. You see, you reader does not need to know the background information that led you to your key point.

As you read the following e-mail, take special note of where in the message the writer's purpose finally becomes clear:

Dear Ms. Holloway:

My name is Donald Draper, and I recently attended a local job fair where I met an associate of yours. His name is Roger Sterling, and he was representing your company at the job fair.

Mr. Sterling suggested that I write you because you are the person in charge of the intern program at your company. To give you a little background about myself, I am currently completing my degree at Best College, and I am scheduled to receive my degree in marketing next spring. My purpose in writing you is to find out if you have any openings in your intern program this coming winter. I would be pleased to send you my resume. I look forward to hearing from you.

Best regards,

Donald Draper

To revise the above message, follow these steps:
1. Identify the key point.
2. Bring the key point to the beginning of the message.
3. Cut irrelevant information.
Revise the above message before reviewing the revision on the next page.

Here is a revision with the key point up front:

Dear Ms. Holloway:

Do you have any openings in your intern program this winter?

At a recent job fair, your associate Roger Sterling suggested that I write you. I will receive my degree in marketing from Best College this spring, and my résumé is attached.

I will follow up with you in a week or so; in the meantime, I look forward to hearing from you.

Best regards,

Donald Draper

Was the revised message more accessible? How did the tone change? What other changes improved the message?

Empty information comes in various categories—the smaller details relate to redundancies and outdated language, which are reviewed next.

Eliminate Redundant Pairings

Some redundant pairings have been passed on for centuries, such as *various and sundry* and *first and foremost*. Do you even know what *sundry* means? If you list something *first*, isn't it also *foremost*?

Though redundant pairings seem to fit together like bookends, you need only one of the words: when you use both, you are automatically and unconsciously . . . oops, is that a redundant pairing?

For the pairings on the following page, which word would you cut? To turn this into a learning activity, cover the revised list as you go through the words on the original list.

Original	Revised
and so on and so forth	and so on
any and all	any *or* all
basic and fundamental	basic
each and every	each *or* every
fair and equitable	fair
first and foremost	first
full and complete	complete
if and when	if *or* when
hopes and desires	hopes
hope and trust	trust
issues and concerns	issues
more and more	more
null and void	void
questions and problems	questions
true and accurate	accurate

Also cut unnecessary verb add ons:

Verb Add Ons	Revised
add up	add
add together	add
advance forward	advance
continue on	continue
combine together	combine
refer back	refer
repeat again	repeat
rise up	rise

Cut Redundant Modifiers

Some words simply do not need to be modified. For example, have you ever wondered about *free gifts*? If gifts are not free, are they still gifts? What about *terrible tragedies* and *advance reservations*? Aren't all tragedies terrible and all reservations made in advance?

Redundant modifiers come in all shapes and sizes. Once again, cover the revised words as you work through the redundant modifiers.

Original	Revised
absolutely essential	essential
cold temperature	cold
combine together	combine
completely eliminate	eliminate
completely finish	finish
difficult dilemma	dilemma
end result	result
exactly the same	the same
final outcome	outcome
five different groups	five groups
foreign imports	imports
future plans	plans
general public	public
honest truth	truth
new breakthrough	breakthrough
one hundred percent true	true
past memories	memories
personal beliefs	beliefs
total of 12 attendees	12 attendees
true facts	facts
unexpected surprise	surprise
very unique	unique
12 noon/12 midnight	noon *or* midnight

Work on the following exercise to gain practice cutting unnecessary words.

PRACTICE 17.1

Cut Redundant Modifiers

Instructions: Edit the following sentences to remove empty information, redundancy, and outdated expressions.

Wordy: Before you finish this step to go on to the next step in the process, please review and examine all the items in your shopping cart.

Revised: Before you go on to the next step, review the items in your shopping cart.

1. We hope and trust that you find our services helpful and worthwhile.

2. Our new breakthrough in design makes our laptop even more perfect than it was before.

3. The final outcome of this project depends on each individual participant doing his or her best.

4. We want you to be absolutely certain that you have not ordered multiple items that are exactly alike.

Note: See page 414 for the key to the above exercise.

Cut Vague Nouns

If you use vague nouns as a lead in to your point, cut them. For example, nouns such as *area*, *factor*, *manner*, *situation*, *topic*, and even *purpose* are often fillers during the composing phase. Say what you mean and be specific.

Wordy: My field of study is the area of sociology.

Revised: I am studying sociology.

Wordy: I have found myself in a situation in which I am forced to make a decision.

Revised: I am forced to make a decision.

Wordy:	The topic that I have chosen to write about is gender differences.
Revised:	Gender differences answer common questions about miscommunication . . .
Wordy:	The purpose of my paper is to explore self-esteem in adolescents.
Revised:	The self-esteem of an adolescent is a critical factor in determining. . .

Can you think of any vague nouns that you use?

Eliminate the Obvious

Isn't *round* a shape and *red* a color? In the list below, cut the obvious.

audible to the ear	of an uncertain condition
brief in duration	period of time
bright in color	rate of speed
consensus of opinion	red in color
dull in appearance	re-elected for another term
extreme in degree	round in shape
filled to capacity	small in size
heavy in weight	soft to the touch
honest in character	visible to the eye

In fact, when you find yourself using the following phrases, simply delete them and get right to your point:

all things considered	in a manner of speaking
as a matter of fact	in my opinion
as far as I am concerned	my purpose for writing is
for the most part	the point I am trying to make
for the purpose of	what I am trying to say is that
I wish to take this opportunity	what I want to make clear is

Besides stating the obvious, writers often used canned and outdated phrases.

Update Outdated Phrases

Be confident about your writing and stop using outdated phrases, even if someone you respect still uses them. For example, writing experts have considered "thank you in advance" outdated for at least 30 years now.

Once again, to turn this into a learning activity, cover the right column that shows current use as you work through the outdated column.

Outdated	Current
attached please find	attached is
as per our discussion	as we discussed
as per your request	as you requested
at all times	always
at the present time	now, today
at your earliest convenience	give a specific date
attached please find	attached is
due to the fact that	because
during the time that	while
gave a report to the effect	reported
gave assistance to	helped
in the event that	if
in a situation in which	when
in almost every instance	usually
in the near future	soon
in receipt of	*Thank you for* . . .
in reference to	about
is of the opinion that	believes
I wish to thank you	do not wish *and* thank
may I suggest	do not ask permission
prior to	before
subsequent to	after

sufficient number of	enough
thank you in advance	thank you
thank you again	one thank you is sufficient
the manner in which	how
this day and age	today
with regard to	about or concerning

PRACTICE 17.2

Remove Redundancy and Outdated Expressions

Instructions: Edit the following sentences.

Wordy: In the event that you hear from George, give him the news.

Revised: If you hear from George, give him the news.

1. Attached please find the papers that you requested.

2. You have our complete and absolute confidence, and we appreciate and value our client relationship.

3. As per our discussion, the new policy should be received and reviewed this week.

4. You can completely eliminate any questions or problems by sending your agenda early in advance of the meeting.

5. I would like to thank you in advance for your cooperation, support, and assistance.

Note: See page 414 for the key to the above exercise.

Avoid Legalese

Today even attorneys avoid using the following terms:

Legalese	Revised
as stated heretofore	as stated
aforementioned	as mentioned

concerning the matter of	concerning
enclosed herewith please find	enclosed is
enclosed herein	enclosed is
notwithstanding	without
pursuant to	regarding
the writer/the undersigned	use *I* or *me*
until such time as	until

People who write passively and use outdated verbiage do so out of habit and are not yet conscious of the fact that canned language is "dead" language:

If you wouldn't say it that way, don't write it that way.

Use Simple Language

Some people think that using complicated words rather than simple ones make them sound smart. However, savvy writers choose simple words. As Leonardo da Vinci pointed out, "Simplicity is the ultimate sophistication."

Outdated	**Revised**
apprise	inform
ascertain	find out
cognizant of	aware of
contingent upon	dependent on
deem	think
endeavor	try
facilitate	help
implement	start, begin
initiate	begin
is desirous of	wants
methodology	method
prior to	before
render assistance	assist

referred to as	called
termination	end
transpire	happen
transmit	send
utilization	use

For example, instead of saying: **Say this:**

We *utilize* that vendor.

We *use* that vendor.

I am *cognizant of* the change.

I am *aware* of the change.

We *endeavor* to be the best.

We *try* to be the best.

Prior to working at Macy's . . .

Before working at Macy's . . .

Complete the exercise below to practice this principle.

PRACTICE 17.3

Use Simple Language

Instructions: Simplify the following sentences.

Weak: What transpired subsequent to their involvement?

Revised: What happened after they became involved?

1. We are utilizing that product, and the field supervisor is cognizant of our choice.

2. Subsequent to the change in policy, we have endeavored to compromise as much as possible.

3. As per your request, an omission of that information is being made.

4. If the merger is contingent upon our utilization of their facilities, we should endeavor to change locations.

5. If you are cognizant of their objections, endeavor to make respective changes.

Note: See page 414 for the key to the above exercise.

Modify Sparingly

In Chapter 14, "Modifiers," you reviewed two specific kinds of unnecessary modifiers that creep into writing, **hedges** and **emphatics**.

Example using hedges and emphatics:

> *As you may already know*, trust is best established from the beginning and, *in my opinion*, difficult to regain once breached. Assume that *each and every* communication *may* have the potential to build *some kind of* trust and also has the potential to *totally* destroy trust.

Without the hedges and emphatics, here is the short paragraph:

> Trust is best established from the beginning and difficult to regain once breached. Always assume that every communication has the potential to build trust as well as destroy trust.

PRACTICE 17.4

Modify Sparingly

Instructions: Remove unnecessary modifiers from the sentences below.

Wordy: First and foremost, editing is the kind of skill that is important to develop.

Revised: Editing is an important skill.

1. In my opinion, you should feel really certain what the true facts are before you sign the contract.

2. Can you confirm that it is totally true that they might possibly back out of their agreement?

3. I would kind of like for you to speak to the person who really knows a lot about this topic, literally.

Note: See page 415 for the key to the above exercise.

Edit Out Background Thinking

Background thinking is different from explaining an issue or giving evidence to support a point. Learn to identify the difference between your own background thinking and key information that makes a point.

As you compose your message, you may go down many different lines of thought to get to your main point. All or most of the details leading up to your main point could be background thinking. As you read the following, identify information to cut.

> After we spoke, I continued to think about the situation in which we find ourselves. Not that long ago, the economy was strong and we had an abundance of contributions coming in. The tax laws were also in our favor, encouraging wealthy constituents to make hearty contributions that were tax deductible. Now, with the sudden change in the economy and the changes in tax laws, we are faced with uncertainty—many of our contributors will be tightening their belts, and our clients will suffer from a lack of services and resources. Here's my point: we can sit back and hope that things get better or we can look for new, innovative ways to raise funds. Let's seek input from our staff and major donors to see what suggestions they come up with. What do you think?

Write your revision in the space provided below:

_____

_____

_____

_____

Note: See Endnote 1, page 298, for the key to the above example.

Leave Out Opinions and Beliefs

Though you may find that writing about your opinions helps you get to your key points, opinions are usually not relevant once you find your key point. If you find yourself rambling off the point, that is an indication to start cutting.

Be cautious when using phrases such as *I believe*, *I think*, and *I feel*. These types of phrases make you sound less sure of yourself; so unless you use these phrases as you give advice to a colleague, they are simply *I statements* that merit deletion.

Also, do not tell your reader *how* to interpret your message; these added comments may give the reader the impression that you are unsure of your message or that you lack confidence. Thus, remove phrases or sentences that tell your readers *how you think* they will react.

As you read the following example, identify the opinions and beliefs that you could cut.

> I'm not sure if you are going to like this idea, but I've been thinking about this for a few weeks now, tossing over the pros and cons. In fact, one of our guys in the field mentioned it to me, and I was surprised that he was thinking about it too. But if this is just another message suggesting something you are already thinking about or have decided won't work, sorry that I wasted your time.
>
> I am suggesting that we cut our annual conference by one day this year. Generally our productivity goes down by the last day, and we could save about 20 percent of our costs and probably accomplish just as much in the shorter time frame. Let me know what you think.

Write your revision in the space provided below:

_____

_____

_____

_____

Note: See Endnote 2, page 298, for the key to the above example.

Recap

Whenever you can, simplify your writing: *less is more*.

> ➤ Put purpose first, and you will have a clear idea of what to cut.

> ➤ Get rid of your background thinking and your opinions.

> ➤ Modify sparingly, paying special attention to hedges and emphatics.

> ➤ Be direct and say what you mean.

> ➤ Remember, compose freely—cut when you edit and revise.

Writing Workshop

Activity A. Writing Practice

Instructions: Select two or three pieces of your writing. Identify information that you could cut. Analyze the information by seeing if it fits in any of the following categories:

- Redundant pairings (including redundant subjects and redundant verbs)
- Vague nouns
- Hedges and emphatics
- Background thinking and opinions
- *I think, I believe, I feel* statements

Remember, *less is more*.

Activity B. Journal

Instructions: Write a short self-assessment identifying your strengths.

What do you do well? What have you accomplished that makes you feel good about yourself? What situations have you turned around, making something good come from something challenging? What are your personal qualities that assist you in getting a job done effectively?

Identify how you feel when you focus on your strengths, and then identify how you feel when you focus on your weaknesses. Do words make a difference? Can you affect your self-confidence with self-talk?

Skills Workshop

Using Simple Language

By using simple language, you connect with your reader effectively. For additional practice, go to **www.thewriterstoolkit.com**.

Endnotes

1. **Background Thinking Revised:**

    Since the economy and tax laws have changed, we need fresh ideas to raise funds. What do you think about seeking input from our staff and major donors?

2. **Reader's Perception's Revised**:

    How about cutting our annual conference by one day this year? Generally our productivity goes down by the last day, and we could save about 20 percent of our costs.

18

Formatting

Right now, you may be spending extraordinary efforts to craft your message while overlooking the obvious: how you format your document for your audience.

In academic and professional writing, formatting is an essential element that determines whether your document will be considered credible—and the reader can make the judgment *at a glance*.

Regardless of what you are writing, give your readers easy access to your ideas. When you use formatting effectively, formatting becomes a form of *visual persuasion* as well as an element of your writing style.

- Formatting speaks to your reader at first glance, and correct formatting gives your document credibility.

For example, if you are formatting a document in APA style, the reader can see instantly whether you have taken the time to learn formatting basics. Documents that do not have a correct *running head* or are not double-spaced throughout give the impression that the writer either did not know how to format or simply did not care. When documents are correctly formatted, credibility increases with a glance. However, well-formatted documents do more than present a professional image:

- Formatting gives visual cues to aid the reader in understanding the content.

Formatting tools include the use of headings, bullets and numbering, font, color, bold, underline, and italics. However, the most important element may be none of these, but rather the unused portions of the page, or **white space**. To present an effective finished product, all elements must work together harmoniously.

Special Features and White Space

To achieve rapport between your reader and your document, break your message into manageable chunks. Position your text so that it is well-balanced on the page, and display key ideas prominently. Such visual cues allow your reader to scan the document and understand its meaning before actually reading it.

Here is an overview of elements that affect formatting:

- Displaying key ideas with bullet points or numbering.
- Organizing a topic by using headings and subheadings.
- Incorporating special features such as bold, underline, and italics.
- Setting off explanations or descriptive information with parentheses.
- Selecting fonts for ease of reading.
- Following official guidelines for white space.

In addition to following official formatting guidelines, another way of adding white space is to break information into readable chunks. Just as a sentence is more readable under 25 words, a paragraph is easier to read when it does not appear too lengthy.

The following is an informal guideline: for papers, keep your paragraphs to about 8 lines in length or less; for letters, consider limiting paragraph length to 6 lines; for e-mail, keep your paragraphs to 4 lines or fewer. In fact, with e-mail, getting right to the point is critical, so messages are often short. As a result, even individual sentences can effectively be set off as paragraphs.

As you learn official guidelines for using formatting features and white space, you will see documents differently. In other words, you will build an expertise for knowing how to format a document so that it looks balanced and professional.

Bullet Points and Numbering

Have you ever written an e-mail message that included three or four questions; but when you received your response, only two questions were answered? Next time, consider numbering your questions, leaving a line of white space between each one.

Bullet points and numbering are strong visual cues. They not only make key points instantly visible for your reader but also organize and prioritize your key points. By the way, APA (2010) also suggests using bullet points and numbering in this manner.

- For items of equal importance, use bullet points.
- For items with different degrees of value, use numbers and list the most important items first.

For bullets or numbered items, you have a variety of different styles from which to choose. Stay consistent with the bullet or numbering style throughout your document, and shift from one style to another only if you have a special purpose for changing styles. For example, use a larger bullet for major points and a smaller bullet for minor points.

By numbering questions in an e-mail, you make it easier for your reader to respond to all of your questions. By making your key ideas instantly visible, you aid the reader in responding to your requests, which helps you get your job done.

Display bullet points in parallel structure: noun for noun, verb for verb, phrase for phrase. For example, if you start with an active verb, start every item in the list with an active verb in the same tense. Though you worked extensively with parallel structure in Chapter 16, "Parallel Structure," use the following examples as a brief review.

The following list is displayed as *nouns*:

Here are items to discuss at our next meeting:

- Employee Dress Policy
- Holiday Schedule
- Summer Hours

You can represent the same list using *verbs* (the *imperative voice*):

At our next meeting, we need to do the following:

- Revise employee dress policy
- Review holiday schedule
- Implement summer hours

Adding *–ing* to the verbs turns them into *gerunds* (a noun form):

The following are topics for our next meeting:

- Revising employee dress policy
- Reviewing holiday schedule
- Implementing summer hours

You can also use complete sentences:

Here is what we expect to accomplish at our next meeting:

- We will revise the employee dress policy.
- We will clarify our holiday schedule.
- We will establish summer hours and a date to implement them.

If you present your information in complete sentences or short phrases, you can end your bulleted or numbered points with a period. Experiment using bullets and numbering until you feel comfortable using them.

Formatting Features and Marks

Formatting features include **bold**, <u>underline</u>, and *italics*; special marks include parentheses and quotation marks.

You probably understand not to use all capitals (all caps) to stress words or phrases, as all capitals connote shouting. Instead, use bold, underline, or italics to stress words, as explained below:

- *Bold:* For professional writing, put words or key ideas in boldface type to make them stand out.

- *Brackets:* For APA style, enclose material in brackets that is inserted in a quotation by a person other than the original writer; also use brackets to enclose parenthetical material that is already within parentheses.

- *Italics:*
    - For APA style, use italics to stress words; also italicize the title of a periodical, book, brochure, or report.

    - For general use, also use italics to stress words as well as to give definitions; display book titles or foreign terms in italics.

- *Quotation Marks:* Enclose direct quotes and technical terms presented for the first time in quotation marks.

- *Parentheses:* Put parentheses around information that gives a brief explanation or that does not directly relate to your topic. Also put parentheses around a paraphrase or an abbreviation.

- *All capital letters (all caps):* Follow traditional capitalization guidelines; do not use all capital letters to make words stand out.

- *Underline:* Stress key words by underling them when you are using a typewriter or writing by hand. (When you are using a computer, stress words by using italics.)

Within a document, be consistent in the way that you display these features and marks. Since the bold and underline features provide a similar purpose, use one or the other, not both at once.

Sometimes, especially in e-messages, writers think they are making an idea stand out by using all capitals. Instead, readers may infer that the writer is shouting at them. To stress a word or phrase in any document, including e-mail, use bold *or* italics (but not all capital letters).

Many writers also think that putting a word between quotation marks makes the idea stand out (such as, *It's a really "good" idea*). Instead, when quotation marks are used for no valid reason, readers think that the writer is implying the *opposite* of what the word actually means. Be careful: Do not use quotation marks unless you are certain about how you are using them.

Use quotation marks to*:*

1. Enclose a direct quote of fewer than 40 words within the body of a document.
2. Identify technical terms, business jargon, or coined expressions which may be unfamiliar.
3. Use words humorously or ironically (if you think your reader will miss the humor).
4. Show a slang expression, poor grammar, or an intentionally misspelled word.

Use italics to:

1. Refer to a word as a word; for example, the word *listen* has many shades of meaning.
2. Emphasize a word, phrase, or entire sentence.
3. Display foreign terms (such as *Merci, Grazie, Dobra, Domo Arigato*) and Latin abbreviations (such as *i.e.* and *e.g.*).
4. Display book titles. In the past, book titles were underlined. However, now that we have access to the variable spacing and special features of computers, using italics is the preferred method.

Use parentheses to:

1. Include a brief explanation within a sentence.
2. Insert a sentence that does not directly relate to the topic of your paragraph.
3. Supply abbreviations.

Using parentheses tells the reader that the information relates to the broader topic without going into detail of how or why. Thus, you can sometimes avoid writing a lengthy explanation by enclosing a few words in parentheses.

Font Size and Color

For most professional documents, select conservative fonts and keep them to traditional sizes. Common fonts are Times New Roman for print material and Arial for electronic communication.

Most business and academic documents are written in a 12-point font, which means there are 12 characters per inch. The traditional color for print and e-mail messages is black. However, for e-mail, some professionals use blue. Colors other than blue or black may be considered unprofessional; in fact, some business executives are annoyed when untraditional colors or special features appear in an e-mail. These individuals may or may not be justified for feeling this way; however, entrants into the workforce should be aware of possible critics before being too creative. To avoid criticism, use accents of color conservatively. Also consider the following:

- Limit font types to two per document so that your work does not appear cluttered.

- For APA citation style, use only one style font throughout your entire paper (Times New Roman or Courier, size 12), including your title page.

- For documents formatted in styles other than APA, use a larger-sized font for the title of your document (size 14) and major text headings (title, chapter, and section headings).

If you know that your reader has visual difficulty, increase font size; you may also use the bold feature to make the message especially clear.

White Space and Balance

The term **white space** refers the unused areas of your document, such as top and side margins and spacing between lines. Official guidelines dictate a range of minimum to maximum spacing to leave between parts. After you learn official guidelines for spacing, which are reviewed in the following pages, you develop a trained eye for document placement—*only then should you vary from guidelines.*

White space gives your readers' eyes a place to rest and delineates the various parts of your document. White space also gives readers a place to make notes and comments. White space controls the way your document looks at a glance. Therefore, before you consider a document complete, ask the following questions:

- Does this document look balanced, appealing, and professional?
- Does the document look as if it has a *picture frame* of white space?

Manual Spacing Versus Automatic Spacing

Most documents in this chapter show *manual spacing guidelines*. However, for manual guidelines to work, **paragraph spacing** must be set at **0**. Otherwise, you will leave extra white space automatically each time that you hit *Enter*, and your document will look unprofessional and thus unappealing.

Until you have a trained eye for vertical spacing, use manual spacing guidelines for business letters (see page 309). In fact, for APA formatting, double spacing is *not* double spacing at paragraph breaks unless paragraph controls are set at **0**. Set controls correctly for each document, starting with basic settings:

- Set margins for 1-inch default margins top, bottom, and sides.
    - Go to the **Page Layout** tab: click on **Margins** and select **Normal.**
- Set paragraph spacing at **0 pt** for **Before** and **After** (see page 306).
- For business letters and APA formatting, use a serif font such as Times New Roman, size 12.
- For most documents, including APA, select *Align Text Left*, leaving right margins ragged; in other words, do not select *Justify*.

Paragraph

Spacing Chart

For documents that are single-spaced, manually space down 2 times (or ↓ 2) between most parts of your document.

When you space down 2 times, you *double space*, which leaves 1 blank line; however, when you space down 3 times, you leave 2 blank lines:

Single spacing	Double spacing ↓ 2	Triple spacing ↓ 3
Single spacing	x	x
Single spacing	Double spacing	x
Single spacing		Triple spacing
Single spacing	Double spacing	
Single spacing		
Single spacing	Double spacing	Triple spacing

- Start counting at the end of a line—each time that you hit *Enter* counts.
- Also make sure that your *paragraph controls are set 0 and single spacing*. (See page 306 for step-by-step instructions.)

To see if need to make any vertical adjustments on your document *before* you print it, click on *Print*; on the right side of the screen, you will see a preview of your document.

Until you have expert skills, follow these guidelines closely.

Paragraph Settings

For spacing guidelines to be effective, *paragraph controls must be set correctly*. For Microsoft Word 2010, adjust paragraph controls for each document you create:

1. Go to the **Home** tab.

2. Open the **Paragraph** tab by clicking on the arrow.

3. At the **Indents and Spacing** tab, find **Spacing**.

4. Set **Before** and **After** at **0 pt**.

5. For *business letters*, set **Line spacing** at **Single**; *or*

   for *APA formatting*, set **Line spacing** at **Double**.

6. To set tab stops for the *body* of an APA paper, under **Special**, select **First line**; then set **By** at **0.5"** (0.5 inches).

   Note: For the *reference page* tab stop, under **Special** select **Hanging, 0.5"**.

7. To make settings default, click **Set as Default**, located left of **OK**.

8. Click **OK**, so that you are back at the **Home** tab; then set font at Times New Roman, 12 points, and margins at 1" on all sides.

In short:

1. Home → Paragraph → Spacing → Before and After → 0 pt

2. Home → Paragraph → Line Spacing → Single (*or Double for APA*) → Default → OK

3. Home → Times New Roman, Size 12

4. Page Layout → Margins → Normal (1" on all sides)

Creating a Header for Letterhead or APA Running Head

At times, you will use a header, such as when you create a personal letterhead for your job-search documents or a running head for papers formatted in APA style.

To create a personalized letterhead, insert your personal information in a style of your own design into the header. For APA formatting, creating a header is more complicated because it involves multiple pages that are numbered, and the page 1 header is different from second page headers. Set up the header when you start your paper; here is one way to do it in Word 2010:

1. On the Word toolbar, click on **Insert** (located next to **Home** tab).
2. Click on **Page Number**.
3. Select the option **Top of Page** and then select the **plain number** option at the upper right of the page.
4. Check the box, **Different First Page**—*this is key to setting up headers correctly.*
5. Set **Header from Top** at **0.5"**.

When you check the box, **Different First Page**, if the page number disappears, repeat steps 2 and 3 above. Next put in your running head, which needs to be at the left margin; here is one way to get your running head at the left margin:

1. Move your cursor to the left of the page number "1."
2. Type your page 1 running head (Running head: FIRST 50 CHARACTERS OF TITLE).
3. Then hit the tab key (or space bar) until your running head is at the left margin. (If you add too many spaces, you will need to delete the extra or it will not align properly.)
4. Next, go to the page 2 header: insert the title of your paper in all caps to the left of the page number, and then once again hit "Tab" until the title aligns at the left margin.

Make sure that the font for your running head and page number are both set at Times New Roman, size 12.

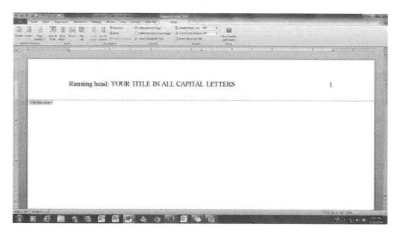

Parts of a Business Letter

1. *Letterhead.* For a company, a letterhead contains the name, address, phone number, fax number, web address, and company logo; for personal business correspondence, design your own letterhead with your contact information.

2. *Dateline.* The date appears at least 3 lines below the letterhead and no more than 2.5 inches from the top of the page.

3. *Inside Address.* The inside address contains the name of the recipient, his or her title, the company name and address. Use two-letter state abbreviations, but avoid using other types of abbreviations in addresses.

4. *Salutation.* Use the recipient's last name or first name in the greeting:
   o   For example, *Dear Mr. Jones:* (formal) or *Dear George:* (familiar).
   o   Follow the salutation with a colon, *not* a comma (and never a semicolon).

5. *Body.* Single space; block paragraphs at the left (do not indent); leave 1 blank line between paragraphs; break paragraphs into *intro*, *body*, and *conclusion*.

6. *Closing.* Use the standard closing *sincerely*; use less formal closings for e-mail.

7. *Writer's Signature Block.* Type your name along with your title, when used.

8. *Reference Initials.* Indicate a typist's initials, *if different from the writer*.

9. *File Name Notation.* To indicate where a document is stored, you may use a code. When used, file names often have three components: a name, a dot used as a separator, and an extension consisting of 1 to 3 characters.

10. *Enclosure Notation.* Use this notation to alert the recipient (and remind the writer) that something is enclosed with the letter.

11. *Delivery Notation.* Use this notation to indicate that a letter was sent in a special way, such as UPS, FedEx, Express, and so on.

12. *Copy Notation.* Include a *cc* notation (courtesy copy) to indicate to whom copies of the letter are being sent.

13. *Postscript.* A postscript is an afterthought, represent it with or without periods and with or without a colon; however, use capital letters (PS, P.S., or PS:).

For most letters, use 1-inch default margins. For short or long letters, add or delete vertical space before the dateline, between the date and address, and between the closing and the signature line.

FIGURE 18.1. Blocked Letter Format

Before starting, set your paragraph controls on single spacing and 0 for "before" and "after." All lines are blocked at the left, producing a clean, uncluttered style. (Leave right margin ragged.)

Communication Network [1]

2300 North Lake Shore Drive
Chicago, IL 60610
312-555-5555 / cnwebsite.com ↓3+

August 3, 2011 [2]   ↓ 4 or 5 after date, depending on the length of letter

Mr. Reggie Piper [3]
All Pro Temps
333 West Wacker Drive
Chicago, IL 60610   ↓ 2

Dear Mr. Piper: [4]   ↓ 2

Thank you for your request for information on creating professional business letters. In the first paragraph, *connect* with your reader; and for most letters, state your main purpose.

The bulk of your information should be in the body. [5] Include details, examples, and rationale in the body. Use a conservative font, such as Times New Roman set at 12 points. If your letter is very short or very long, adjust the spacing and margins to allow more or less room, giving your letter balance. Use closed punctuation style: place a colon after the salutation and a comma after the complimentary closing.

In the last paragraph define *action needed* or next steps. Also invite the reader to contact you by including your phone number and Web address.   ↓2 before the closing

Sincerely, [6]   ↓ 3 to 5 after closing, depending on length of letter

Bob Allison [7]
Instructional Designer   ↓ 2 before notations

djy [8]
allison.711 [9]
Enclosure [10]
By UPS [11]
cc Michael Jones [12]

PS Before you print your letter, use the *print preview function* to make sure that margins are balanced, creating a "picture frame" effect. [13]

E-Mail Messages

For an e-mail, space down 2 times (DS) after the greeting, between paragraphs, and before your closing. By spacing down 2 times, you leave 1 blank line of white space. Here are some points to consider.

- When you expect recipients to take action based on information in your message, list their names in the *To* section, not the *Cc* section.

Reserve Cc use for when you copy a message to someone but do not expect the recipient to take action. With messages that you are forwarding, add a note at the top of the message stating expected action from recipients.

- Use an accurate **subject line** and update it as needed.

As your conversation evolves, update the subject line to reflect new information. Also, include due dates in the subject line to alert the reader to needed action.

- Use a **greeting,** even if it is as simple as the recipient's name.

Greetings personalize messages and engage the reader. When you write to several people, use a greeting such as *Hello team*, *Hi everyone*, or *Good day*. When you write to one person, use the person's name followed by a comma; if you wish, also use *Hi* or *Hello*. If the e-mail is formal, use *Dear*.

- Keep the message to about one screen in length.

If your message is long and detailed, consider phoning. Though e-mail may be a convenient way to communicate, consider other channels when communication becomes complicated or relationships become strained.

- Use a simple **closing**.

An e-mail is not as formal as a business letter, so you can use an informal closing such as *Best regards*, *All the best*, *Enjoy your day*, or *Take care*, among others. (Reserve the formal closing *Sincerely* for business letters.)

For professional messages, include a sign-off that lists your company name, address, phone number, and other relevant contact information.

FIGURE 18.2. E-Mail Format

Notice the use of white space in the e-mail message below. White space is an element of visual persuasion because it aids the reader in understanding your message.

Start messages with a greeting (or salutation) and an informal closing: "sincerely" is too formal for most messages.

Policy Manual Update - Message (HTML)

File | Message | Insert | Options | Format Text | Review | Adobe PDF

Arial | 10

Follow Up
High Importance
Low Importance

From ▾ dona.young@youngcommunication.com
To... Reginald Piper
Cc...
Subject: Policy Manual Update

Hi Reggie, ↓2 (DS) after the salutation

Thank you for asking our advice as you prepare your new company policy manual. ↓2

Because some employees use text messaging so often, please make sure that you stress the following: ↓2

1. Start with a salutation, addressing the recipient by name.
2. Leave adequate white space between each part of your message.
3. Use correct grammar and punctuation in all e-mail or the message loses credibility.
4. Follow standard rules for capitalization and abbreviation; for example, never use "i" in place of the personal pronoun "I" or "u" in place of "you." ↓2

Also, please include a section advising employees *not* to send messages if they have any doubts. Even e-mail messages that have been deleted can be retrieved and used in litigation, becoming part of the public domain. When employees feel unsure about a message, they should either save the message as a draft or make a phone call.

We look forward to seeing the first draft of your policy manual. ↓2

Best regards, ↓2 after the closing

Dona ↓2

Dona Young
Communication Network, Inc.
333 East Wacker Drive
Chicago, IL 60610
Phone: 312-555-1212
Fax: 312-555-1234

Create your automatic sign-off

Note: The example above shows how to add vertical space *manually*; however, some e-mail programs add a blank line of white space each time that you hit "Enter." When using those types of programs, *do not manually add extra line space between parts*.

Business Memorandum or Memo

To communicate within your organization, write a memorandum. Memos contain a heading and a list of guide words to route the message, and this information can be displayed in many ways. The traditional format is displayed below.

Many companies supply a template for their employees to use in writing e-memos. An e-memo differs from an e-mail. For example, use e-memos to make announcements or send out meeting agendas. Recipients do not reply to e-memos as they do with e-mail messages. In other words, e-memos are used as a one-way communication tool; in contrast, e-mail messages are exchanged back and forth.

When you create your own memo format, put the title, *Memorandum* or *Memo*, at the top. Use a slightly larger-sized font for the title, such as size 14 (or even larger), so that it stands out. Then space down 3 lines before typing the guide words, or heading.

FIGURE 18.3. Business Memo

Notice that the names following the guide words in the memo below are all aligned at least two spaces following the longest guide word, Subject. *Also notice that a memo does not contain a salutation (greeting) or closing.*

Memo

To: The name or names of the recipients
From: Your name
Date: The current date
Subject: A few words that reflect the purpose of the memo

Start the body of the memo 3 lines below the heading, and double space (DS) between paragraphs by hitting *Enter* two times.

Use a blocked style, which means paragraphs are not indented.

1. Align the information following the guidewords at the first tab stop after the longest guide word (subject).
2. Do not sign your memo; however, you can place your reference initials next to your name at the top or bottom of the memo.

Some companies design templates for interoffice memos that their employees send electronically.

Fax Cover Sheet

A fax is an efficient way to send a copy of an original document, especially one which contains an original signature. An alternative to faxing would be to scan a document and then send it via e-mail as an attachment.

Figure 18.4. Fax Cover Sheet

When faxing, create a cover sheet to ensure that those who receive your document know who sent the fax, who should it, and how many pages in total to expect.

FAX COVER SHEET

TO: Angelina Lopez   **FAX:**   800-555-9215

FROM: Jennifer Pitt   **PHONE:** 888-555-9242
                                 FAX: 888-555-9243

* 3 Pages Follow *

Angie, attached is the real estate contract for the property in Long Grove. The closing is next Friday at 10 a.m. Please call me if you have questions. I look forward to seeing you there.

                         Jenny

Business Letters: Connect – Tell – Act

The business letter is an excellent vehicle to build business relationships. Your letters may be the only image your client has of your and your company.

All letters should contain an *intro*, *body*, and *conclusion*; you can organize most letters successfully by applying the following structure:

- In the *introduction*, **connect** with the reader as one person to another, also connecting your purpose to the reader's needs and interests; be friendly.

- In the *body*, **tell** your reader details, explanations, and facts. Summarize and highlight information supporting your purpose.

- In the *closing*, state the **action needed** or next steps. Express good will; invite the reader to contact you for more information.

When you write a letter, determine whether you will communicate information using a **direct approach** or an **indirect approach**.

The Direct Message

Most letters take a direct approach by putting the purpose and main point in the first paragraph. Once readers understand the purpose, supporting information in the body confirms and expands their understanding of your message.

The bulk of the letter is in the body, which can consist of one paragraph (or as many paragraphs as it takes to convey your message). Give as many details as necessary, but do not stray from the principle *less is more*.

The closing in a direct message is usually short; the closing states the action or the next steps that you intend to take or that you request your reader to take. The closing also expresses good will and opens the door for additional communication.

The Indirect Message

Some letters purposely take an indirect approach. When conveying unexpected or bad news, first explain the rationale before stating your main point or decision. This approach equips the reader to accept the bad news by understanding the logic behind it. The indirect approach is tactful and shows respect to the reader.

In the introduction, state the purpose in a general way. Then give enough explanation so that the rationale leading to the news makes sense to the reader (or as much sense as possible). State your main point or bad news toward the end of the body or possibly in the conclusion.

Direct Message	Indirect or Bad News Message
Connect with the reader	Connect with the reader
State purpose/get to the point	State general purpose
Give supporting details	Give supporting details
Close with desired actions or next steps	State outcome or conclusion
	Close with cordial words (and next steps if they apply)

As in the direct message, the closing paragraph of an indirect message lets your reader know that he or she may contact you for additional information.

Recap

Here are some of the points stressed in this chapter:

➤ Ensure that you leave an appropriate amount of white space between each part of every document.

➤ Follow the salutation of a business letter with a colon (:), not a comma and especially not a semicolon (;).

➤ Structure business letters so that you include an *intro*, a *body*, and a *conclusion,* even when you write short letters.

➤ Adjust your computer settings so that spacing guidelines work.

➤ Create a header for documents that you format in APA style; also create a header when you design your letterhead for personal business documents.

➤ Use the **Print Preview** option to make sure your business letters look balanced on the page and have a picture-framed effect.

As you experiment using these tools to enhance the visual appeal of your documents, you will become more confident and use them with ease.

Writing Workshop

Activity A: Writing Activity

What Is Your Legacy? What do you want to be remembered for? Reflect on your strengths and values. Are you doing what you want to do? Are you in tune with your purpose and pursuing your life's mission?

Also reflect on your dreams. Are you following your passions? If not, what changes do you need to make to bring your dreams and passions into your life? When you were a child, what did you dream of becoming?

Activity B: Journal

Start a *joy journal.* Take a few minutes every day to list the things that you appreciate and that bring you joy. If you are writing daily in a personal journal or a work journal, finish each day's entry with this activity.

After a week or two, ask yourself it ending your journal entry this way makes a difference in your way of thinking or feeling.

APA Checklist

Below is a checklist for basic formatting elements for APA style.

Have you checked your paper for the following?

1. SETTINGS

____ Set margins for 1-inch at top, bottom, and sides

____ Use double spacing throughout document, including title and reference pages

____ Set paragraph controls at 0 pt (zero) for spacing **Before** and **After**

____ Set paragraph indentation at 0.5 inches (see page 306)

____ Use Times New Roman font, 12 points (or another serif font, such as Courier)

2. RUNNING HEAD

____ Page 1 running head: "Running head: TITLE IN 50 CHARACTERS OR LESS"

Note: "Running head" is followed by a colon and "head" is *not* capitalized.

____ Running head on second pages: Title only in all capital letters at left margin

____ On all pages, *including title page*, include page number in upper right corner

Note: See page 307 for details about creating a header for the running head so that page 1 is different from second pages.

3. TITLE PAGE

____ Center title and by line on the upper half of title page; 12 or fewer words for title

____ Use Times New Roman font, size 12, *not* in boldface

____ Include other information your professor may require

4. ABSTRACT

____ Develop a synopsis of your paper in one paragraph between 150-220 words

____ Block first line (and all lines) at left margin; *no paragraph indentation*

____ Include a keyword summary after the abstract, indenting and italicizing "Keywords" (*Keywords*: keywords follow . . .)

5. BODY

____ Present section titles differently from headings: do *not* put them in boldface type; section titles include title, abstract, reference(s)

____ Introduction of paper on page 3; title of paper as section head

_____ Present heading levels 1, 2, 3, and 4 in **boldface** font

_____ Space two times after a period

_____ Block margins at the left; margins are _left_ justified (not _full_ justified)

_____ Indent paragraphs 0.5 inches

_____ Integrate short visuals (tables, graphs, or charts) with the text of your paper

_____ Place large visuals on separate pages at the end of your paper or in an appendix

6. IN-TEXT CITATIONS

_____ Use the author's last name (surname) and year of publication:

- o   Jones (2010) found that at-risk youth were more likely to . . .
- o   At-risk youth were likely to have issues with self-esteem (Jones, 2010).
- o   In 2010, Jones' study of at risk youth showed that . . .

_____ In subsequent references within the same paragraph, the date is not necessary

_____ When a work has _two_ authors, cite both names each time they are referenced:

- o   Jones and Smithe (2011) found that among children who . . .

_____ When a work has _three_, _four_, or _five_ authors, cite all the first time; in subsequent references, use only the surname of the first author followed by _et al._:

- o   Jones et al. (2011) demonstrated that more than one study . . .

_____ For quotations longer than 40 words, double space and indent left margin 0.5 inches; do not use quotation marks; put period before the citation

_____ For short quotations, place the reference inside of the period:

- o   "Additional studies are needed to fill the gap" (Jones, 2010, p. 33).

7. REFERENCE PAGE

_____ List references in alphabetical order, leaving individual references in the order noted in the article or book

_____ Use last name and first initial (no first names)

_____ For books: author's last name and initials, publication date, title of work, and publication data: Jones, S., & Barker, D. (2012). _Title_. City, ST: Publisher.

_____ Block the first line of each reference at the left margin

_____ Indent second lines of references 0.5 inches (hanging indentation)

_____ Capitalize only the first word of book titles, the first word after a colon (subtitle), and proper nouns or proper adjectives

_____ Type the title of a book in _sentence case_, the title of an article in _sentence case_, and the title of a journal in _title case_

_____ Italicize the title of a book and the title of a journal and its volume number

Reference

APA. (2010). *Publication manual of the American Psychological Association* (6th ed.). Washington, DC: Author.

PART 6: MORE MECHANICS

Though you have already covered the critical elements of mechanics, many little details still linger. Since you are well on your way to becoming an incurable editor, now is the time to work on the final details to becoming an expert editor.

This part starts with similar words, such as *affect/effect* and *loan/lend*. Then you work with colons, ellipses, and dashes: these punctuation marks give you variety in the way you express yourself and give your writing flair.

Capitalization and number usage may give you headaches, but learning only a few simple rules will help clear up the confusion. Then there are quotation marks, apostrophes, and hyphens. Memorizing how to use these marks is unrealistic, so instead go over them with the goal of becoming familiar with them. You will know where to find the rules when you need to use them.

Grammar and mechanics are trivial compared to the critical thinking side of writing: Your ability to use writing to solve problems is one key to creating a successful career. However, knowing the grammar and mechanics of writing will give you more confidence and credibility. Now go have some fun with the mechanics of writing!

19

Word Usage

The English language has many common words that confuse writers. These are the words that sound alike but are spelled differently and have different meanings, such as *its* and *it's* or *affect* and *effect*. These kinds of words are called *similar words* or *homophones* and are presented in Section 1 of this chapter.

Section 2 of this chapter includes some *social work terms*. Take the time to become familiar with them: as you master the new language of your chosen field, you also improve your reading speed and comprehension.

Like any skill, the only way to build your vocabulary is through practice and repetition. Use new words in context, and you are more likely to remember them. Therefore, practice new words until you reach a comfort zone using them, building your vocabulary 10 words at a time. Start by using the spelling lists at the end of this chapter. Also, keep a running list of words that you are likely to misuse or misspell—especially those related to social work, your field of study.

The format of this chapter is different from the previous chapters in that you start with a short pretest. Take the pretest on the following page to identify *similar words* that give you problems.

Are you ready for some surprises? In all likelihood, this chapter will reveal several words that you regularly use without any clue that you are using the words incorrectly. For example, did you know that *alright* is not a Standard English spelling? Or when was the last time you *loaned* someone something or drove *thru* the car wash?

Pretest

Instructions: In the sentences below, cross out any words that are used incorrectly, and write in the correct word above it or to the right of the sentence.

1. Will that decision effect you in a positive way?

2. The principle on my loan is due on the 1st of the month.

3. My advise is for you to get a job before you buy that new car.

4. Please ensure my manager that I will return in one-half hour.

5. Its been a challenging day, but things are getting better.

6. Their are a few issues that we need to discuss.

7. The agency gave are report a new title.

8. Pat lives further from work than I do.

9. You can have a meeting everyday, if you prefer.

10. Whose going to the ballgame?

11. I enjoy movies more then I enjoy plays.

12. Megan assured that the project would be successful

13. It's alright for you to contact the manager directly.

14. I didn't mean to infer that you were late on purpose.

15. Try and be on time for the next meeting.

Note: See page 415 for the key to the above exercise.

Section 1: Similar Words and Tricky Combos

This part contains some of the most common similar word combos. Write two or three sentences for each word that you are serious about mastering. With each new word that you learn, the next new word becomes a bit easier to learn. *Practice makes progress*—and enough practice makes *permanent*!

adverse/averse: *Adverse* is an adjective meaning *unfavorable or bad*; *averse* is an adjective meaning *reluctant or unenthusiastic*.

> I have an *adverse* reaction to dog racing.

> Jaclyn is *averse* to working on that project.

advice/advise: *Advice* is a noun and means *recommendation*; *advise* is a verb and means *to give advice or to make a recommendation*.

> Please give me some *advice* about my paper.

> I *advise* you to trust the writing process.

affect/effect: Though each of these words can be a noun and a verb, they are primarily used as follows:

> *Affect* is a verb meaning *to influence*.

> *Effect* is a noun meaning *result*.

When you cannot figure out which word fits, substitute its definition:

> How will this *affect* (influence) you?

> The *effect* (result) is good.

As a noun, *affect* refers to emotions and is used primarily within the field of psychology; as a verb, *effect* means *to cause to happen* or *to bring about*, for example:

> My sister was diagnosed with an *affective* (emotional) disorder.

> The new policy will *effect* (bring about) change within our organization.

When in doubt, use *affect* as a verb and *effect* as a noun.

alright/all right: *Alright* is not considered a Standard English spelling. Use *all right*. Here is a memory trick: something is either *all right* or *all wrong*, for example:

Are you feeling *all right* about the changes?

among/between: *among* is a preposition meaning *together with* or *along with*; *between* is a preposition that means basically the same thing as *among*. Use *among* when three or more people or objects are discussed, but use *between* when only two people or objects are discussed.

Among the three of us, we have all the talent we need.

Between the two of us, you have more time than I do.

appraise/apprise: *Appraise* is a verb meaning *to assess or evaluate*; *apprise* is a verb meaning *to inform*.

After the realtor *appraises* the house, she'll *apprise* you of your options.

are/hour/our: *Are* is a present tense form of the verb *to be*; *hour* is a noun that refers to 60 minutes of time; and *our* is the possessive pronoun for *we*.

What *are our* options? We have an *hour* to decide.

assure/ensure/insure: These three verbs are somewhat similar in sound and meaning, but they have distinct uses, for example:

assure: to give *someone* confidence

ensure: to make certain that some *thing* will happen

insure: to protect against loss

Here is the rule of thumb to follow: when you use *assure*, make sure that the object is a *person*, for example:

I *assure* **you** that we will meet the deadline.

When you use *ensure*, make sure that the object is a *thing*:

I *ensure* the **product** will arrive on time.

When you use *insure*, make sure that it refers to insurance.

You can *insure* against losses with our company.

breath/breathe: breath is a noun meaning *a lungful of air*; breathe is a verb meaning *to take in breaths*.

>   I need a *breath* of fresh air.

>   When I *breathe* fresh air, I feel much better.

don't/doesn't: *Don't* and *doesn't* are both contractions of *do not*. *Doesn't* is the contraction of *does not*, which is the third person –s form of Edited English. However, speakers often mistakenly use *don't* for third person singular subjects in place of *doesn't*.

>   She *doesn't* have a care in the world.

>> *Not:* She *don't* have a care in the world.

>   Bob *doesn't* go to school here anymore

>> *Not:* Bob *don't* go to school here no more.

everyday/every day: Use *everyday* as a modifier meaning *ordinary* or *daily*; if you can insert the word *single* between *every* and *day*, you know that it is two words.

>   That is an *everyday* routine.

>   We do that procedure *every (single) day*.

farther/further: Though similar in meaning, *farther* refers to actual distance that can be measured; *further* indicates progress that is intangible and not measurable, such as "to a greater or lesser degree or extent."

>   Sue lives *farther* from work than you do.

>   Let's discuss this proposal *further*.

has/have: *Has* and *have* are both present tense forms of *to have*. Use *has* for third person singular (he *has*, she *has*, and it *has*) and *have* for all other persons: I *have*, you *have*, we *have* and they *have*. However, writers sometimes use *have* for third person singular in place of *has*.

>   A block of rooms *has* been reserved.
>> *Not:* A block (of rooms) *have* been reserved.

>   The car *has* a few dents on its fender.
>> *Not:* The car *have* a few dents on its fender.

infer/imply: These two verbs are opposite in meaning: *infer* means *to deduce, conclude, or assume*; *imply* means *to express or state indirectly*.

From your statement, I *inferred* that Len was at the meeting; is that what you meant to *imply*?

its/it's: The word *its* is a possessive pronoun, whereas *it's* is a contraction of *it is* or *it has*, for example:

You can't judge a book by *its* cover.

It's been a great day.

Writing Tip

One way to improve your use of *its/it's* is to stop using the contraction *it's*; every time you use *it's*, see if you can substitute *it is* or *it has*.

---

loan/lend: Most people confuse these words without realizing it, even people in high level banking positions! Here is what you need to know:

Loan is a noun, not an action.

Lend is a verb; its past tense form is *lent*.

For example: The bank will give you a *loan*, but it will *lend* you money.

In other words, you cannot really *loan* someone your book, but you can *lend* it. Practice these words until the meaning becomes clear.

may be/maybe: *May be* is a verb form that suggests possibility; *maybe* is an adverb that means *perhaps*.

This week *may be* the right time to submit our request.

Maybe you can get the information from Fred.

Not: I *maybe* able to help you.

principal/principle: At one point, you may have learned that the *principal* of your school was your *pal*. That is true; however, *principal* has a broader meaning, which is *chief* or *main*.

Are you surprised to learn that your loan consists of *principal* and interest? *Principle* means *theory* or *rule of conduct*.

What is the *principal* on your loan?

We all try to live by our *principles*.

In fact, I would rather pay my *principal* than my interest!

saw/seen: *Saw* is the past tense of the verb *to see*; *seen* is the past participle. The past tense form of a verb does not take a helper verb; however, the past participle form must have a helper. Contrary to Edited English usage, in local language speakers sometimes use a helper with *saw* but leave out the helper with *seen*.

We all *saw* Tasha enter the conference room.

Not: We all *seen* Tasha enter the conference room.

We had *seen* that movie twice already.

Not: We had *saw* that movie twice already.

sight/site/cite: *Sight* is a noun referring to vision or mental perception; *site* is also a noun that refers to a location, as in website; *cite* is a verb meaning to *quote* or *to name*.

The pilot's *sight* was impaired due to the accident.

My website is under construction.

I was *cited* for driving without my license.

supposed to/used to: In speech the −ed ending of *supposed* and *used* is not always distinguished from the −t of *to*. Therefore, the −ed is often left off of these words erroneously. These words are regular verbs and as such require the −ed ending for their past tense and past participle forms.

You *are supposed* to attend that class. I *used* to go to that school.

Not: You are *suppose* to assist in the lab.

than/then: the word *than* is a conjunction used in comparisons; *then* is an adverb referring to time, as in *after that*. To help remember, use *then* when it has to do with *when*.

> I would rather get up early *than* sleep late.

> After you complete the project, *then* you will have more time.

their/there/they're: *Their* is the possessive form of *they* and will always be followed by a noun; *there* is an adverb meaning *in or at that place* or a pronoun which functions as an anticipating subject; *they're* is the contracted form of *they are*.

> *Their* apartment is next to mine.

> *There* are a lot of people in the lobby. Go *there* if you choose.

> *They're* standing next to the reception desk.

themselves/theirselves: *Themselves* is the reflexive form of *they*; *theirselves* is not a Standard English spelling.

> The team members can help *themselves* to refreshments.

through/threw/thorough/thru: *Through* is a preposition meaning *by means of; from beginning to end, or because of*; *threw* is a verb and the past participle of *throw*; *thorough* is an adjective meaning *carried through to completion*; and take special note: *thru* is an incorrect spelling of *through* (use *thru* as a hyphenated form of *drive-thru*).

> Walk *through* the room quietly.

> Jenkins *threw* the paper at the judge.

> We all did a *thorough* job on the report.

to/too: The preposition *to* is often used when the adverb *too* should be used. Remember, when you are describing something that relates to quantity, use the adverb *too*. *Too* also means *also*.

> It's *too* late to go to the meeting.

> The proposal has *too* much fluff and *too* little substance besides being *too* late to make a difference.

> I will go to the conference *too* (also).

try to/try and: The verb *try* is not followed by the word *and*. Instead, *try* is followed by an infinitive, such *to be, to see, to go,* and so on. Many people inadvertently say "*Try and* be on time" when they really mean to say "*Try to be* on time."

Try to get your work done early.

Try to be there before anyone else.

were/we're/where/wear: *Were* is one of the past-tense forms of the verb *to be* (as in *you were, we were, they were*). *We're* is a contraction for *we are*. The adverb *where* (pronounced the same as *wear*) is often confused with the past tense verb *were*. The verb *wear* means *to dress in*.

Where were you when the decision was made?

We're about to enter a new phase.

Wear that suit to the meeting.

who's/whose: The contraction *who's* stands for *who is* or *who has*. *Whose* is the possessive pronoun of *who*.

Who's chairing the meeting?

Whose book is that?

you/yous/y'all: *You* is a subjective pronoun, and *you* is singular or plural. In some areas, such as Chicago, the word *yous* is used as a local language plural form of *you*, as in *yous guys*. While this is considered colloquial in the United States, *yous* is an acceptable pronoun in Ireland.

You all should go to the game this Friday.

In southern and southwestern portions of the U.S., the equivalent to *yous* is *y'all*, with *all y'all* being used with larger groups. An additional form is *you'uns* or *you'ins*.

These variations add life and color to the language when speaking; however, edit them to standard usage in your writing so that people from all parts of the globe can understand the meaning of your message.

you're/your: *You're* is a contraction for *you are. Your* is a possessive pronoun for *you.*

> *You're* the one I want on my team.

> *Your* personality makes the difference.

The similar words listed in this part are only a handful of similar words that you will come across. If you have a question about a word that is not listed here, go to the Internet and do a search. Several professional sites are likely to offer a complete explanation of the word in question.

Section 2: Social Work Terms

This part contains some basic terms used in social work. Write two or three sentences for each term or a paragraph using several of the terms. With each new term that you learn, the next one becomes a bit easier to learn, even if it does not feel that way at the moment. In addition, as your vocabulary becomes stronger, so do your reading skills.

adaptation: in social systems theory, one of the four functional variables in which the system attempts to adapt to its external environment to facilitate goal attainment.

boundary: a hypothetical construct that defines the border that separates the system from its suprasystem; for example, personal boundaries and generational boundaries.

case management: a method of professional practice conducted by an individual or team that involves an ongoing responsibility to help functionally impaired clients.

> Professional social workers help their clients by: (1) developing goals and making informed choices; (2) helping them access and effectively use services; (3) developing services needed but not otherwise available; and (4) advocating in a manner that promotes the clients' own efforts to achieve goals that will increase their sense of well-being.

casework: a method of direct practice generally conducted on a face-to-face basis with a client and focused on improving the client's level of social functioning.

client system: an individual, group, family, organization, or community that is the beneficiary of a helping effort.

community organization: a method of social work practice that helps individuals, groups, organizations, and other collectives from a community (the same geographic area) to deal with shared interests, opportunities, or problems to enhance their state of well-being.

direct practice: social work practice that involves direct client contact, usually face-to-face, such as casework.

focal system: a system that is the subject of attention. (If a family is a focal system, the siblings are a subsystem and the community is a suprasystem.)

generalist practice: a professional social work practice that can be conducted in a variety of settings with client systems of varying size, addressing the several levels of prevention and applying a transferable body of knowledge, values, and skills.

group work: a method of social work practice that consists of a small group of people with common interests who meet regularly working toward their common goals.

indirect practice: social work practice that involves indirect contact with clients., such as social work administration that is conducted on behalf of clients but does not usually involve direct contact with them.

input: all of the resources that are required by a social system to accomplish its purposes, including people and money.

logic modeling: a tool for applying critical thinking skills to identify an underlying system of reasoning as the means of explanation.

macro: a large social system such as a formal organization or community.

micro: a small social system such as a social group or family.

output: the status of signal/task and maintenance inputs following a conversion cycle of a social system.

practice: the process of providing professional assistance to clients so that they make planned changes to move to a state of well-being.

social services: a program of activities directed toward helping people to meet their needs and/or to enhance their level of social functioning.

social system: a social entity possessing functionally interdependent relationships with each other, for example a family, agency, or community.

social systems model: a particular representation of a social system.

social systems perspective: a set of assumptions on which social systems theory is based.

social systems theory: a set of assumptions and concepts that seeks to explain behaviors exhibited in the functioning of social systems and how such systems achieve well-being.

strengths perspective: an approach that focuses on the strengths and capacities of people and their organizations to achieve a sense of well-being.

subsystem: a component element of focal system that displays all the attributes of a system, but can be located within a larger designate system; for example, a married couple functions as a system and is a subsystem of the total family unit.

suprasystem: a part of the social environment to which a subject system is functionally linked; for example, birth families are relevant parts of a family's suprasystem.

theory: a logically derived set of assumptions and concepts used to explain something; for example, social systems theory.

value: a belief pertaining to what is right and good, comprising the normative structure of a social system; for example, values form the foundation on which social systems develop.

Section 3: Spelling Tips

One of the reasons spelling is difficult is that only about 40 percent of English words are spelled according to phonetics, which is how they sound. In other words, about 60 percent of English words are written with silent letters or other non-phonetic qualities, thereby requiring them to be memorized.

Use these suggestions to improve your spelling and vocabulary usage:

- *Make a running list of words that you find challenging.*

  The way that you use language is unique. Your reading, writing, and spelling skills have different strengths and weaknesses from everyone else. The way to become stronger is to learn the specific words that challenge you. As you read, circle the words that you do not understand, and look them up.

- *Subscribe to online vocabulary-building newsletters.*

  For example, Merriam-Webster (www.merriam-webster.com) has a *word of the day* as does Wordsmith (www.wordsmith.org).

- *Use new words in context: write two or three sentences with each new word.*

  To learn a new word, practice it in context. By writing two or three sentences, you are applying the new word in a way that will make it easier to remember and use correctly.

- *As you learn a new word, check the correct pronunciation.*

  Break up the new word into syllables and use the dictionary guidelines for pronunciation. Ask a friend to pronounce the word for you; say the word out loud several times until you feel comfortable.

- *Use spelling rules that are easy to remember.*

  Use spelling rules that you find helpful. For example, the rule "use *i* before *e* except after *c* or when the sound is like *a* as in *neighbor*" is easy to remember and helpful. However, learning complex spelling rules that have a lot of exceptions may not be as helpful. Go to the Internet and Google *spelling rules*. Glean what you need, and then move on.

- *Learn some of the Latin and Greek roots of words as well as prefixes and suffixes.*

  Learning roots, prefixes, and suffixes will help you figure out new words and gain a deeper understanding of the words you already know. A few are listed below.

Section 4: A Sampling of Roots, Prefixes, and Suffixes

Root	Meaning	Origin
anthrop	man	Greek
biblio	book	Greek
cent	one hundred	Latin
equ	equal, fair	Latin
geo	earth	Greek
hydro	water	Greek
ortho	straight	Greek
psych	mind, soul, spirit	Greek
sci	to know	Latin
techn	art, skill	Greek
viv, vit	life	Latin

Prefix	Meaning	Example
a- or *an-*	not, without	amoral, apolitical
ab-	away from	abduction
ambi-	both	ambidextrous
anti-	against	antisocial
bene-	good	beneficial
bi-	two	biannual
contra-	against	contradict
de-	not	derail
dis-	not	disengage
ex-	out from	exhale
hyper-	over	hypertension, hyperactive
il-, im-, in-	not	illegal, impossible, indivisible
inter-	between	interstate

ir-	not	irreversible
macro-	large	macrocosm
micro-	small	microcosm
mis-	not	misconduct, misplace
mono-	one	monologue
post-	after	postpone
pre-	before	pretest
pseudo-	false	pseudonym
re-	again	repeat
semi-	half	semiannual
sub-	under	subversive
trans-	across	transport
un-	not	unable

Suffix	**Meaning**	**Example**
-able	able to	durable
-age	result of action	courage
-er	doer of	teacher
	more	greater
-ectomy	cutting	appendectomy
-ful	full of	peaceful
-ic, -tic, -ical	having to do with	dramatic, Biblical
-ism	the belief in	mysticism
-logy	the study of	psychology, biology
-ly or -y	like	friendly
-ment	state of	judgment
-ness	quality	kindness
-phobia	fear	claustrophobia
-ship	condition, status	ownership
-ous	full of	ridiculous

Recap

Improving your vocabulary improves your critical thinking skills as well as your writing skills. Practice new words in context: write two or three sentences with each new word so that you can use it with confidence.

Writing Workshop

Writing Practice

Instructions: In the Skills Workshop, you will find 5 lists of spelling words that were taken from the 100 most commonly misspelled words. Select one of those lists for this exercise.

Break into small groups of three or four. Allow ten minutes for each group to develop a paragraph using as many vocabulary words from the list as possible. Now determine which group used the most words in their paragraph. Make sure, however, that the paragraph makes sense!

Work through each list (one list per week). Write two sentences for each word to ensure that you can use it in context.

Posttest

Instructions: In the sentences below, cross out any words that are used incorrectly, and write in the correct word above it or to the right of the sentence.

1. The affect of that decision is not yet known.

2. When you know principle on your loan, let me know.

3. Her advise was that you take the other part-time job.

4. Can you assure the quality of your work?

5. The dog chased it's tail, amusing several children.

6. They are a few issues that we need to discuss.

7. Is that are new computer?

8. You are farther along on the project than I am.

9. We meet everyday at 3 p.m.

10. Who's book is that?

11. Sue was taller then Mary last year.

12. Melanie ensured me that we would be finished by Friday

13. Its alright for you to contact the manager directly.

14. I'm not trying to infer that you were late on purpose.

Note: See page 415 for the key to the above exercise.

Spelling Lists 1 - 5

Each of the following 5 lists contains 10 of the 100 most commonly misspelled words. Master these words by using them in sentences.

Spelling List 1

1.	acceptable	adj: satisfactory
2.	believe	v: consider, accept as true
3.	calendar	n: agenda, schedule
4.	definitely	adv: absolutely, without doubt
5.	existence	n: survival, subsistence, life
6.	leisure	n: free time, relaxation
7.	maintenance	n: preservation, looking after
8.	neighbor	n: fellow citizen
9.	privilege	n: honor, opportunity
10.	separate	v: divide, break away; adj: unconnected, distinct

Spelling List 2

1.	amateur	n: layperson, not professional
2.	embarrass	v: humiliate, make self-conscious
3.	conscience	n: sense of right and wrong
4.	conscious	adj: aware, mindful, awake, deliberate
5.	foreign	adj: overseas, unfamiliar, unrelated
6.	inoculate	v: immunize, vaccinate
7.	miniscule	adj: very small, tiny
8.	precede	v: to go before, to lead
9.	proceed	v: to go on, to carry on, to continue
10.	relevant	adj: pertinent, applicable, important

Spelling List 3

1.	accommodate	v: to house, to have capacity for
2.	conscientious	adj: reliable, diligent, thorough
3.	equipment	n: gear, tools, paraphernalia
4.	hierarchy	n: rank order of things or people
5.	jewelry	n: adornments
6.	mischievous	adj: ill-behaved, bad, harmful
7.	medieval	adj: pertaining to the Middle Ages
8.	noticeable	adj: visible, evident, in plain sight
9.	possession	n: ownership
10.	questionnaire	n: survey, opinion poll, feedback form

Spelling List 4

1.	acquire	v: to obtain, to attain
2.	experience	n: knowledge, skill, familiarity; v: feel, live through
3.	gauge	v: measure, estimate, judge
4.	immediate	adj: urgent, high priority, instant
5.	knowledge	n: information, expertise, skill, familiarity
6.	license	n: authorization, permit, certificate
7.	millennium	n: a thousand years
8.	misspell	v: to spell incorrectly
9.	occurrence	n: incident, happening, event
10.	reference	n: mention, citation, note; v: to mention, to cite

Spelling List 5

1.	argument	n: quarrel, disagreement
2.	discipline	n: self-control, strictness, branch of learning
3.	humorous	adj: funny, amusing, witty
4.	ignorance	n: lack of knowledge, unawareness
5.	intelligence	n: cleverness, aptitude, astuteness
6.	kernel	n: core, essential part, seed
7.	perseverance	n: insistence, resolve, determination
8.	referred	v: recommended
9.	schedule	n: agenda, timetable, plan
10.	weird	adj: unusual, peculiar

20

Colons, Dashes, and Ellipses

Since you have already mastered commas and semicolons, the minor marks of punctuation in this chapter should seem easy for you.

One reason that writing seems so difficult for many people is that they try to make a multitude of decisions all at once. The principles that you learn here allow you to make decisions about mechanics without effort, freeing your energies to create a writing style that is reader-friendly and clear.

Colons, dashes, and ellipses enhance writing because they add variety and energy. Incorporating these marks into your writing sparingly, but correctly, until you feel comfortable using them.

The Colon

In general, the colon alerts readers that information will be illustrated, making the colon a strong mark of punctuation that commands attention. Use the colon for the following purposes:

1. After salutations of business letters and formal e-mail messages.

2. At the end of one sentence when the following sentence illustrates it.

3. At the end of a sentence to alert the reader that a list follows.

4. After words such as *Note* or *Caution*.

Each of these categories is explained below.

1. *Colons after salutations.* The most common use of a colon is after the salutation in a business letter, which is the most formal type of written communication. Only when you write a letter to a personal friend should you relax that tradition, using a comma instead of a colon. Here are some examples of salutations using a colon:

Dear Mr. Jones:	Dear Dr. Wilson:	Dear Professor:
Dear Jorge:	Dear Mia:	Robert:

Notice that even when you use the recipient's first name, the colon is appropriate. You could also use the above salutations in an e-mail if the message were formal, such as an inquiry for a job. However, for the most part, business professionals use a comma after the greeting of an e-mail as in the following:

Dear Janet,	Jack,	Hi Carolyn,

The one mark of punctuation that you would *never* use for a salutation is the semicolon; however, some writers mistakenly use it, for example:

Incorrect:	Dear Charles;
Corrected:	Dear Charles:
Corrected:	Dear Charles,

Next, examine how to use the colon to add variety to your writing style.

2. *Colons after sentences.* You have probably noticed that a colon is used to introduce lists, but have you noticed a colon sometimes occurs at the end of one sentence when the following sentence illustrates it?

Using a colon to illustrate a complete sentence is probably the colon's least common use, but possibly its most powerful use. This type of colon use adds a nice dimension to writing style, conveying the message in a slightly more emphatic way.

Here are some examples of one sentence introducing another:

The colon is a strong mark of punctuation: it draws the reader's attention.

Johnson Ecology accepted our proposal: we start on Monday.

For general usage, the first word of the independent clause following a colon should be in lower case. However, capitalize the first word if you are placing special emphasis on the second clause or the second clause is a formal rule, as shown below:

> Here is the principle that applies: A colon can be used in place of a period when the sentence that follows illustrates the one that precedes it.

> Update your report by Friday: The accrediting commission's site visit is next week.

In contrast to general usage, APA guidelines recommend *always* capitalizing the first word after the colon when a full sentence follows it.

When you use a colon to illustrate a sentence, use it sparingly. While there is no hard and fast rule, limit yourself to using no more than one or two colons per page this way.

If you have never used a colon in this way, try it. Once you do, you may enjoy having this punctuation alternative. Experiment by writing a sentence or two on the line below to illustrate this principle.

---

3. *Colons to illustrate lists.* Using the colon to illustrate a list of words or phrases generally requires using words such as *these, here, the following,* or *as follows* within a complete sentence. Here are some examples:

> These are the materials to bring to the meeting: your annual report and current data.

> Bring the following identification: driver's license, social security card, and current utility bill.

> Here are writing samples that you can use: Myers, Jones, and Riley.

However, do not use a colon after an incomplete sentence, for example:

Incorrect: The items you need to bring are: a tent, a sleeping bag, and a light.

Corrected: The items you need to bring are a tent, a sleeping bag, and a light.

Incorrect: This package includes: a stapler and 3-hole paper punch.

Corrected: This package includes a stapler and 3-hole paper punch.

Also notice that the colon can be used after the adverbial conjunction *for example* to alert the reader that an example follows.

4. *Colons after* Note *or* Caution. Use a colon after a word of caution or instruction, for example:

Note: All meetings are cancelled on Friday.

Caution: Do not use the staircase.

If a complete sentence follows *Note* or *Caution*, capitalize the first word, as shown above. Space one or two times after the colon, but be consistent in the style you choose.

PRACTICE 20.1

The Colon

Instructions: Place colons where needed in the following sentences.

Incorrect: The materials we need are: blankets, water, and cell phones.

Corrected: The materials we need are blankets, water, and cell phones.

1. I have some exciting news for you, Jeremy proposed on Friday.

2. Note, the office is closed on Monday for the 4th of July holiday.

3. The supplies we need are as follows; markers, copy paper, and staplers.

4. Giorgio said that we need: cereal, coconut milk, and bananas.

5. Here is what you should do, complete the inventory list and then work on the schedule.

Note: See page 416 for the key to the above exercise.

The Dash

The dash is the most versatile mark of punctuation, at times replacing the comma, the semicolon, the period, and even the colon.

Here are some examples using the dash:

> Bob called on Friday—he said he'd arrive by noon today.
>
> Thanks—your package arrived right before our meeting.
>
> Feranda Wilson—our new executive VP—will host the event.

The dash adds energy, making information that follows one dash or that falls between two dashes stand out. Though you can use the dash in formal documents, you will find yourself using it most often in informal communications. However, when overused, the dash gives the impression that the writer is speaking in a choppy and haphazard fashion. Limit yourself to no more than one or two dashes per page or e-mail message.

Though the dash is different from the hyphen, the hyphen is used to create the dash. Here are two ways to create a dash using hyphens:

1. Use two hyphens without a space before, between, after them; some software will create an *em* **dash**, as illustrated in the sentences above.

2. Use two hyphens, but this time place a space before and after the hyphens to create an *en* **dash**, as follows:

    The London – Paris train arrives at 2 o'clock this afternoon.

    Chicago defeated Green Bay, 13 – 6.

The *em* dash is the traditional choice when using the dash for general writing; however, the *en* dash is often used to connect words in directions or with scores, as illustrated above.

If you work for a company, check your company policy manual to see if the manual states a preference—some companies state a preference so that corporate communications remain consistent.

Once again, overusing dashes is similar to overusing colons or exclamation points. Writers enjoy using them, but readers tire of them easily. Thus, hold yourself back and use them sparingly. However, if you have never used a dash in your writing, try it. Dashes definitely add energy and are fun to use.

PRACTICE 20.2

The Dash

Instructions: Place dashes where needed in the following sentences; make any other corrections, as needed.

Incorrect: Mark scheduled the meeting, how could I refuse to go?

Corrected: Mark scheduled the meeting—how could I refuse to go?

1. Margie called on Friday George is home!

2. Mike's parents are visiting he invited me to have dinner with them.

3. Helen Jones the new CEO asked me to join her team.

4. Call if u need anything Im always here to support you.

5. Give as much as you can to that charity it's a good cause.

Note: See page 416 for the key to the above exercise.

The Ellipses

Ellipses is the plural form for *ellipsis marks*. Ellipses indicate that information is missing, thereby removing an otherwise awkward gap.

In formal documents, ellipses allow writers to adapt quotations by leaving out less relevant information, making the main idea stand out. In informal documents, ellipses allow writers to jump from one idea to another without entirely completing their thoughts. Ellipses also allow the writer to convey a sense of uncertainty without coming right out and stating it.

- Ellipsis marks consist of three periods with a space before, between, and after each one, for example:

   This doesn't make sense to me . . . let me know what you think.

- Some software programs create ellipses when you space once, type three periods in a row, and then space once again, as follows:

   Vic was not pleased ... he will call back later.

Before using the unspaced ellipses described above, check to make sure that it is acceptable practice within the domain you are submitting your work, as the unspaced ellipses may not be acceptable.

Many writers are unsure of how to display ellipses vary the number of periods they use each time, not realizing that rules surround the use of ellipses. The only time a fourth period would be used is when the missing information is at the end of the sentence in a formal quotation, for example:

According to Goleman (1995), "[T]he topics taught include self-awareness, in the sense of recognizing feelings and building a vocabulary for them, and seeing the links between thoughts, feelings, and reactions . . . ." (p. 268)

Use ellipsis marks sparingly, but correctly, even for informal use.

PRACTICE 20.3

The Ellipses

Instructions: Use ellipsis marks to show how to adjust the following quotations while retaining the key meaning of each quote; **for example:**

Original Quote by John F. Kennedy:

The great enemy of the truth is very often not the lie—deliberate, contrived and dishonest, but the myth, persistent, persuasive, and unrealistic. Belief in myths allows the comfort of opinion without the discomfort of thought."

Abbreviated Quote:

"The great enemy of the truth is very often not the lie . . . Belief in myths allows the comfort of opinion without the discomfort of thought."

1. Original Quote by Albert Einstein:

"The important thing is not to stop questioning. Curiosity has its own reason for existing. One cannot help but be in awe when he contemplates the mysteries of eternity, of life, of the marvelous structure of reality. It is enough if one tries merely to comprehend a little of this mystery every day. Never lose a holy curiosity."

Abbreviated Quote:

_____

_____

2. Original Quote by Victor Frankl:

"Don't aim at success—the more you aim at it and make it a target, the more you are going to miss it. For success, like happiness, cannot be pursued; it must ensue, and it only does so as the unintended side-effect of one's dedication to a cause greater than oneself or as the byproduct of one's surrender to a person other than oneself. Happiness must happen, and the same holds true for success: you have to let it happen by not caring about it. I want you to listen to what your conscience commands you to do and go on to carry it out to the best of your knowledge. Then you will live to see that in the long run—in the long run, I say!—success will follow you precisely because you had *forgotten* to think of it."

Abbreviated Quote:

_____

_____

_____

Note: See page 416 for suggested revisions to the above exercise; answers may vary.

Recap

Below is a summary of the colon, dash, and ellipses: three marks that can give your writing variety and flair as long as they are not overused.

➤ The colon illustrates information that follows it; here are some basic guidelines:

- Use the colon at the end of one sentence when the following sentence illustrates it.

- Use the colon after a complete sentence that includes words such as *these* or *the following* to indicate that a list follows.

- Use the colon after the words *Note* and *Caution*; if a complete sentence follows the colon, capitalize the first word of that sentence.

➤ The dash emphasizes information that falls between two dashes or after one dash; create a dash as follows:

- Use two hyphens without spaces before, between, or after them to create an *em* dash.

- Use two hyphens with a space before (but not between) and after them to create an *en* dash.

➢ The ellipses fill gaps and allow the reader to express uncertainty; create ellipses as follows:

- Use three periods and include a space before, between, and after each period.

- Use a fourth period at the end of sentence.

Writing Workshop

Activity A. Writing Practice

Instructions: Identify an historical figure whom you respect, and then log on to the Internet to find a long quotation by that person.

- Search the following: "quotations by (insert the name)." Several quotation sites should become available. Select a quotation, and then use ellipsis marks to shorten your quote, making a key point of the original quotation stand out.

- After you have worked with the quote, write about what the quote means to you.

Activity B. Journal

Instructions: Experiment using dashes, colons, and ellipses as you write your journals this week.

Go back to some of your earlier journal entries and notice how you used punctuation. Choose one entry from the first or second week that you started your journal; correct and revise the punctuation of that journal entry.

Write one journal this week that discusses how your thinking about punctuation has changed . . . or not changed.

References

Albert Einstein Site Online. (2014). Retrieved from http://www.alberteinsteinsite.com/

quotes/einsteinquotes.html

Frankl, V. (2006). *Man's search for meaning*. Boston, MA: Beacon Press.

Goleman, D. (1995). *Emotional intelligence*. New York, NY: Bantam Books.

JFK Experience. (2014). Retrieved from http://www.jfkexperience.com/jfk-resources/

favorite-jfk-quotes/

21

Capitalization and Number Usage

Capitalization decisions can be confusing. Some words and titles sound official, so they simply *must* be capitalized, right? However, you may be surprised to learn that most of the time those official-sounding words and titles are not capitalized: they are not proper nouns. Instead of wasting time and energy guessing, this chapter gives you the information that you need to make most capitalization decisions.

Then there is number usage. When you stop to decide whether to spell out a number in words or to use numerals, you waste time. Knowing a few basic number rules makes a big difference in how you use numbers in your writing.

Before you review number usage, work on capitalization, a more common issue in writing.

SECTION 1: CAPITALIZATION

Many writers are naïve about capitalization. Instead of respecting the basics and staying safe, they capitalize words almost randomly. However, this problem is an easy one to solve if you use the following as your motto:

> When in doubt, do not capitalize.

In other words, unless you know for sure that a word should be capitalized, leave the word in lower case. Here are the two major categories of words that should be capitalized:

- Proper nouns
- First words of sentences, poems, displayed lists, and so on

The challenge then becomes knowing which words are proper nouns and which are common nouns, which is the starting point before identifying some of the most common types of capitalization errors.

Proper Nouns and Common Nouns

To avoid capitalizing common nouns, you must first learn the difference between common nouns and proper nouns. The chart below helps illuminate some of the differences:

Proper Noun	Common Noun
John Wilson	name, person, friend, business associate
Wilson Corporation	company, corporation, business
Southlake Mall	shopping, stores, shops
New York	state, city
Italy	country

Words derived from proper nouns become proper adjectives and are capitalized:

Proper Noun	Derivative or Proper Adjective
England	English language
Spain	Spanish 101
Italy	Italian cookware
French	French class

Names are proper nouns, and that includes the names of people as well as the names of places and things, such as the following (Young, 208):

Titles of literary and artistic works	Chicago Tribune, the Bible
Periods of time and historical events	Great Depression
Imaginative names and nicknames	Big Apple
Brand and trade names	IBM, 3M, Xerox copier
Points of the compass	the North, the South, the Southwest *(referring to specific geographic regions)*
Place names	Coliseum, Eiffel Tower
Organization names	National Business Education Association
Words derived from proper nouns	English, South American
Days of the week, months, and holidays	Thanksgiving, Christmas, Chanukah

Articles, Conjunctions, and Prepositions in Titles

Not every word of a title is capitalized, and the types of words in question are articles, conjunctions, and prepositions. Here's what to look for:

Articles: the, a, an

Conjunctions: and, but, or, for, nor

Prepositions: to, at, in, from, among, over, and so on

Here are rules about capitalizing articles, conjunctions, and prepositions:

1. Capitalize any of these words when it is the first word of a title or subtitle.

2. Capitalize a preposition when it is the first or last word of a title or subtitle.

Sources vary about the capitalization of prepositions in other positions in a title. For example, though some sources require prepositions to remain in lower case even when they consist of five or more letters, *APA requires the following:*

- Prepositions of *three or fewer letters* must be in *lower case.*
- Prepositions of *four or more letters* must be *capitalized.* (In fact, any word that has four or more letters would be capitalized in APA style.)

Here are some examples:

The University of Chicago

Pride and Prejudice

Tuesdays With Morrie (APA style)

Tuesdays with Morrie (most styles other than APA)

First Words

As you have already seen, the *first word* is given special designation. Make sure that you capitalize the first word of each of the following:

Sentences

Poems

Direct quotations that are complete sentences

Independent questions within a sentence

Items displayed in a list or an outline

Salutations/greetings and complimentary closings

Note: Also capitalize the first word of a complete sentence that follows a word of instruction or caution, such as *Note* or *Caution* (as illustrated here).

Hyphenated Terms

At times, you will need to determine how to capitalize hyphenated words, such as e-mail, long-term, up-to-date, and so on. Here are some guidelines:

- Capitalize parts of the hyphenated word that are proper nouns:

  If I receive your information by mid-December, you will qualify for the training.

- Capitalize the first word of a hyphenated word when it is the first word of the sentence, for example:

  E-mail is the preferred mode of communication.

  Mid-January is when the quarterly reports are expected.

- Capitalize each word of a hyphenated term used in a title (except short prepositions and conjunctions, as previously noted), for example:

  Up-to-Date Reports   Mid-July Conference

  E-Mail Guidelines   Long-Term Outlook

APA Style: Title Case and Sentence Case

For presenting titles, APA style employs two different types of capitalization styles, *title case* and *sentence case*.

- For *title case*, type titles in upper and lower case letters, following the basic guidelines for capitalization presented in this chapter. For example, capitalize all words in the title except for articles, coordinating conjunctions, and prepositions of three letters or fewer. Use title case for the following:

  o The title of your paper
  o The title of a book, article, or chapter *within the text of your paper*

- For *sentence case*, capitalize the first word of the title and the first word following a colon (the subtitle) as well as proper nouns and proper adjectives; all other words are typed in lower case. Use sentence case as follows:

  o The titles of books, articles, or websites (but not the title of the publisher or a journal) *with references listed on the reference page*

For example:

In text: *Tuesdays With Morrie: An Old Man, a Young Man, and Life's Greatest Lesson*

Reference: *Tuesdays with Morrie: An old man, a young man, and life's greatest lesson*

Organizational Titles and Terms

Most people believe that their job title is a proper noun, but professional titles are *not* proper nouns. Here are some rules to follow:

- Capitalize a professional title when it precedes the name.

- Do not capitalize a professional title when it follows the name.

- Capitalize organizational terms in your own company (but not necessarily other companies), such as the names of departments and committees.

Here are some examples:

Incorrect: John Smith, Vice President, will be meeting with the Finance Department.

Corrected: John Smith, vice president, will be meeting with the Finance Department.

Corrected: Vice President John Smith will be meeting with the Finance Department.

You may capitalize organizational terms from other companies to show special importance. In addition, the titles of high government officials are capitalized, for example:

The President had a meeting in the West Wing of the White House.

Finally, the following two types of capitalization errors are so pervasive that they merit special attention.

Two Common Capitalization Errors

You will have made important progress with capitalization if you stop capitalizing words randomly and follow the rules discussed above. However, the following two common types of errors fit into a special class of their own.

Error No. 1: Leaving the personal pronoun *I* in lower case.

The personal pronoun *I* is a proper noun and should always be represented in upper case. Partly due to text messaging, the problem of leaving the personal pronoun *I* in lower case has escalated, for example:

Incorrect:	A friend asked me if i could help, so i said that i would.
Corrected:	A friend asked if I could help, so I said that I would.

Whenever you use the pronoun *I*, capitalize it; and that includes its use in e-mail messages.

Error No. 2: Using all UPPER CASE or all lower case.

Another type of error that occurs, especially with e-mail, is typing in either all lower case or all upper case. Neither version is correct; using all upper case has earned the reputation that the writer is shouting. The truth is, the writer is not necessarily shouting. Most of the time, when writers use all capital letters (all caps), it is because they are unsure about writing decisions; putting the message in all capital letters (inaccurately) seems to be an easy way out.

When writers use all lower case, it often reflects a tradition within certain professional niches. For example, some computer professionals communicate primarily with other technical professionals, and they write to each other almost exclusively in lower case.

When communicating to professionals outside of their inner circle, these technical professionals sometimes continue to leave their words in lower case. For these professionals, adjusting to their audience is the key: Distinguish who is within your circle and who is not and then adapt accordingly.

Global Communication and the Rules

Most professional communication is now global communication: global communication involves speaking English with and writing English to those for whom English is a second language.

Global communication makes following the rules, such as the ones discussed throughout this book, critical for clear communication. That is because people for whom English is a second language find deviations from the rules difficult to understand. Using a second language according to the standard rules is hard enough, and adapting to the idiosyncrasies that result from misuse of any language adds another layer of confusion.

Rules create standards so that everyone can understand the meaning of the message, reducing confusion and misunderstanding among all readers. Following the rules is an important element of adapting to your audience. In addition, by writing correctly, you enhance your ability to communicate across borders and continents.

PRACTICE 21.1

Capitalization

Instructions: In the following paragraph, correct errors in capitalization.

Next year the President of my Company will provide a Financial Incentive for all employees, and i plan to participate in it. Jack Edwards, Vice President of Finance, will administer the plan. Everyone in my Department is looking forward to having the opportunity to save more. A Pamphlet entitled, "Financial Incentives For Long-term Savings" will describe the plan and be distributed next Week. If the Pamphlet has not arrived by friday, i will check with the Vice President's office to find out the details.

Note: See page 416 for the key to the above exercise.

SECTION 2: NUMBER USAGE

Many writers are unaware of how to display numbers in their writing, so they guess. Even worse, they go back and forth from one style to another, hoping they will be correct at least part of the time.

In addition, the rules for displaying numbers can be confusing. Different sources vary in their guidelines as to whether numbers should be written as numerals or spelled out as words.

In this section, you learn some general guidelines about how to display numbers according to APA citation style. Displaying numbers correctly in APA style is complicated at times. For example, one point is often related to another point, and you must understand the context to make the correct decision.

Therefore, read and study the entire section that follows before making decisions about how to display numbers. In fact, the best time to learn about number usage is when you are not pressured to make a decision.

The number rules are not that difficult to learn, and your only other option is to guess, which creates more confusion for you than it creates for your readers. However, when you do guess, at least represent numbers consistently—do not go back and forth, representing a number as a word in one place and then as a numeral in the next. By starting with the basics, you can stop guessing and start applying principles.

When in doubt about number usage, check the source: *Publication Manual of the American Psychological Association, Sixth Edition.*

Number Usage in APA Style

Here are some points about basic number usage in APA style. Also consult the *Publication Manual of the American Psychological Association* (2010) for more details.

Point 1: Spelling out Numbers

Spell out numbers in words for the following:

- Numbers one through nine within written text

- The first word of a sentence

- Fractions:

    o   one-half majority, two thirds of the participants

Point 2: Using Figures for Numbers

Use numerals for the following:

- Numbers 10 and above within written text

- Precise units of measurement:

    o   2 mm, 2 inches

- Statistical or mathematical functions, proportions, and ratios:

    o   6 divided by 2

    o   5 times as many graduates

    o   3 of the 4 applicants (proportion)

    o   a ratio of 3:1

- A sample size or specific number of participants:

    o   7 participants

- Percentages

    o   Use the percent symbol after a numeral: 10%

    o   Use the word "percent" after any number expressed as a word, such as a number that begins a sentence, title or text heading: "Five percent of the returns . . . ."

- o Use the word "percentage," not "percent" when no number appears with it: "a high percentage of respondents . . . ."
- Ages
  - o The sample included 9 to 12 year olds.
- Exact sums of money
  - o $15.92
- Numbered series, parts of books, tables
  - o Pages 53-64
- All numbers in an abstract

Point 3: Large Numbers

Combine numerals and words for the following:

- Numbers in the millions or higher can be written as a combination of figures and words if the number can be expressed as a whole number or as a whole number plus a simple fraction or a decimal amount.
  - o Our company extended their $1.5 million loan until April.

Point 4: Dates and Time

- Spell out the names of days and months; use figures for dates
  - o September 12
- Use figures for time and use the abbreviations *a.m.* and *p.m.* or the word *o'clock*, but not both.
  - o 4 p.m.
  - o 4 o'clock in the afternoon
- For time on the hour, you may omit the :00 (unless you want to emphasize time on the hour).
- Use the ordinal ending for dates only when the day *precedes* the month.
  - o 21st of February

Note:

1. When you start a sentence with a number, for consistency spell out the rest of the numbers in that sentence.

    Example: Five of the sixteen applicants were hired.

2. Use the same form for related numbers within a sentence: When a number above 9 is in the same sentence as a number below 10, use figures for all of the numbers.

    Example: In all, 6 of the 12 options were accepted.

3. Use a combination of numerals and words to express back-to-back modifiers.

    Example: The Beck Depression scale has four 10-point subscales.

4. Write indefinite numbers, such as *thousands* or *hundreds*, in words.

    Example: We were pleased with the hundreds of positive responses.

Next is a review of how to represent addresses and phone numbers.

Addresses and Phone Numbers

As with dates, parts of addresses should not be abbreviated. So before reviewing the rules for addresses and phone numbers, here is a guideline:

> When in doubt, spell it out.

Abbreviate parts of addresses when space is tight or when you are following a specific system of addressing. However, do not abbreviate simply for convenience.

Here are some rules for displaying addresses:

- Spell out parts of addresses: Do not abbreviate points of the compass such as *North* or *South* or words such as *avenue*, *street*, or *apartment*.

- Spell out street names *One* through *Ten*.

- Use figures for all house numbers except the number *One*.

- Add ordinal endings only when points of the compass (North, South, East, and West) are not included, for example: 1400 59th Street.

- Use two-letter state abbreviations; leave one or two spaces between the two-letter state abbreviation and the zip code.

- Do not place a period after a two-letter state abbreviation.

Here are some examples:

Mr. Alistair Cromby
One West Washington Avenue
St. Clair, MN 56080

Dr. Michael Jules
1214 79th Place, Suite 290
Chesterton, IN 46383

Mrs. Lionel Hershey
141 Meadow Lane South
Seattle, WA 92026

Ms. Lorel Lindsey
Associate Director
The Fine Arts Studio
500 North State Street, Suite 311
Chicago, IL 60611-6043

In general, the broadest part of an address is on the last line (the name of the country or the name of the city and state), as shown above and below.

Mr. Lucas M. Matthews
72 O'Manda Road
Lake Olivia, VIC 3709
AUSTRALIA

Pierluigi e Sylvia D'Amici
Via Davide Bello No. 1
00151 ROMA
I T A L I A

Display phone numbers by using parentheses around the area code or by using a hyphen or period between parts.

For example: Please call (212) 555-1212 at your earliest convenience.

You can reach me at 312-555-1212.

I left the message at 502.555.1212.

When phone numbers are written without any sort of

PRACTICE 21.2

Numbers

Instructions: Make corrections to the way numbers are displayed in the following sentences.

Incorrect: Reggie sent ten copies of the report, but I received only 5.

Corrected: Reggie sent 10 copies of the report, but I received only 5.

1.   We r meeting on Jan. 5 at 10 AM at our offices on Lake St.

2.   Call me on Mon. at 4075551212.

3.   Alex lists his address as 407 S. Maple St., Hobart, Ind. 46368.

4.   We received 100s of calls about the job opening but only five résumés.

5.   Purchase 12 laptops but only seven new printers for our department.

Note: See page 416 for the key to the above exercise.

Two-Letter State Abbreviations

State	Abbr.	State	Abbr.
Alabama	AL	Montana	MT
Alaska	AK	Nebraska	NE
Arizona	AZ	Nevada	NV
Arkansas	AR	New Hampshire	NH
California	CA	New Jersey	NJ
Colorado	CO	New Mexico	NM
Connecticut	CT	New York	NY
Delaware	DE	North Carolina	NC
District of		North Dakota	ND
Columbia	DC	Ohio	OH
Florida	FL	Oklahoma	OK
Georgia	GA	Oregon	OR
Guam	GU	Pennsylvania	PA
Hawaii	HI	Puerto Rico	PR
Idaho	ID	Rhode Island	RI
Illinois	IL	South Carolina	SC
Indiana	IN	South Dakota	SD
Iowa	IA	Tennessee	TN
Kansas	KS	Texas	TX
Kentucky	KY	Utah	UT
Louisiana	LA	Vermont	VT
Maine	ME	Virgin Islands	VI
Maryland	MD	Virginia	VA
Massachusetts	MA	Washington	WA
Michigan	MI	West Virginia	WV
Minnesota	MN	Wisconsin	WI
Mississippi	MS	Wyoming	WY
Missouri	MO		

Note: Do *not* put a period after a two-letter state abbreviation.

Recap

Below is a summary of the rules and guidelines reviewed in this chapter.

Capitalize the following:

➢ The personal pronoun *I*.

➢ Proper nouns and their derivatives, such as *England* and *English*.

➢ The first words of sentences, poems, displayed lists, and so on.

➢ Titles that precede a name, such as *President Gerry Smith*.

➢ The names of departments within your own organization.

Guidelines for representing numbers are as follows:

➢ Spell out numbers 1 through 9; use figures for numbers 10 and above.

➢ If numbers above and below 9 are in a sentence, use figures.

➢ Use the percent sign (%) with numerals; write out the word *percent* with numbers expressed as words.

➢ Use the word *percentage* (rather than *percent*) when used without a number.

For dates, times, and addresses, do the following:

➢ Do not abbreviate: *When in doubt, spell it out.*

➢ Omit the :00 for time on the hour.

➢ Use a.m. and p.m. or o'clock, but do not use both.

➢ Use two-letter state abbreviations.

Writing Workshop

Activity A. Writing Practice

Instructions: Write a Personal Mission Statement

While most companies have mission statements that reflect their core values and purpose, many individuals also write their own personal mission statement.

Personal mission statements help individuals become more aware of what is important in their lives. By writing your own personal mission statement, you focus on your goals and prioritize your actions. In the process, you enhance the likelihood that you will achieve them.

Use the prompts below to begin your personal mission statement.

The achievement in my life that I am most proud of is . . .

Each day I will try to be . . .

The things I value most in life are . . .

The most important of these is . . .

Each day I will contribute to others by . . .

In the future, I hope my successes will include . . .

To achieve these goals, I plan to . . .

The most important thing in the world to me is . . .

Your mission statement will change over time; so if this exercise gives you insight, you may consider repeating it in the future.

Activity B. Personal Journal or Work Journal

Instructions:

What did you learn about yourself as a result of doing the above exercise?

1. Are you following the 2 x 4 approach: writing two pages, four times a week in a personal journal?
2. Have you been making entries in your work journal?
3. Have you identified experiences from your work journal that you expand upon using the DEAL Model?

References

APA. (2010). *Publication manual of the American Psychological Association* (6th

ed.). Washington, DC: Author.

Young, D. (2008). *Business English: Writing for the global workplace.*

Burr Ridge, IL: McGraw-Hill Higher Education.

22

Quotation Marks,
Apostrophes, and Hyphens

Quotation marks, apostrophes, and hyphens are minor marks of punctuation, but they occur frequently: using them correctly improves the quality of writing and enhances its credibility.

SECTION 1: QUOTATION MARKS

The primary reasons for using quotation marks are as follows:

1. Inserting a direct quote of three or fewer lines within the body of a document.

2. Identifying technical terms or coined expressions that may be unfamiliar.

3. Using words humorously or ironically.

4. Showing a slang expression or an intentionally misused word.

However, do not use quotation marks to make a word stand out, for example:

> That is a really "good" idea.

In the above example, your reader will assume that you really do not mean the idea is *good* because the reader may assume you were being sarcastic. To avoid overuse of quotation marks, follow this motto:

> When in doubt, leave quotations out.

Quotation Marks with Periods and Commas

One of the reasons that quotation marks confuse writers is that there are two basic ways to display them: the *closed style* and the *open style*. Here is the major difference between the two:

- **Closed style:**

  Place quotation marks on the outside of commas and periods.

- **Open style:**

  Place quotation marks on the inside of commas and periods.

Here are a few examples:

Closed: Bill's exact words were, "That dog can't hunt."

The president said, "I would like to have that data," but which data was he referring to?

Open: Reginald described the situation as "grim but not hopeless".

Terry instructed me to put the package in the "boot of the car", so I did.

If you live in the United States, use the closed style; if you live in Great Britain, use the open style. (This book and APA apply the *closed style*.)

Quotation Marks with Semicolons and Colons

For semicolons and colons, *always* place the quotation marks on the inside of the semicolon or colon, for example:

Senior management wants us to "go the extra mile"; however, everyone seems to be burnt out already.

Bryan said, "George's bid is overpriced": Is that correct?

According to policy, "Distribution of funds can be made only before the 15th of the month"; therefore, your funds will be sent in 10 days.

Quotation Marks with Questions and Exclamations

When using quotation marks with a question mark or an exclamation point, determine whether the question or exclamation is part of the quote or the entire sentence, for example:

Did Margarite say, "Rose is getting married next month"?

Fred asked, "How do you know?"

Margarite said, "Rose is getting married next month!"

I just won "the grand prize"!

Short Quotes and Long Quotes

Display short quotations less than 40 words with quotation marks, leaving the quote in the body of the paragraph. However, for quotations 40 words or more, do not use quotation marks; instead set off the quote from the body of your writing by indenting it 0.5 inches from the left margin.

Here is an example of a short quote:

According to *The China Study* by Campbell and Campbell II (2004), "[p]rotein, the most sacred of all nutrients, is a vital component of our bodies and there are hundreds of thousands of different kinds" (p. 29). Different kinds of proteins play different roles in health and nutrition, and some of these are discussed.

Quotation within a Quotation

When you need to display a quotation within a quotation, use the single quotation mark (') for the inner quotation and the double quotation mark (") for the outer quotation, for example:

Bob said, "I'm not going to 'insult' George by inviting him to the meeting."

Complete the following exercise using *closed quotation style*.

PRACTICE 22.1

Quotation Marks

Instructions: Place closed quotation marks where needed in the following sentences.

Incorrect: Beth's exact words were, "I'll be in Boston next week".

Corrected: Beth's exact words were, "I'll be in Boston next week."

1. My answer to your request is an enthusiastic "yes".

2. If you think that's a "good idea", then so do I!.

3. The code was "307A", not "370A".

4. All he wrote was, "Our dog can hunt".

5. If you call that "good timing", I don't know how to respond.

Note: See page 417 for the key to this exercise.

SECTION 2: APOSTROPHES

The apostrophe (') is used for contractions and possessives. Possessives are a bit more complicated than contractions, so possessives are reviewed first.

Possessives

When a noun shows possession, use the apostrophe to show ownership. Regular nouns are made possessive as follows:

- For a singular possessive noun, place the apostrophe before the s ('s).

- For a plural possessive noun, place the apostrophe after the s (s').

- If a noun ends in an s, add an apostrophe and s ('s) or simply an apostrophe (').

Singular Possessive	**Plural Possessive**
the cat's whiskers	the cats' toys
the dog's scarf	the dogs' bones
Mary's books	my friends' books

Here are a few examples of names and other nouns ending in *s* and showing possession:

> Francis' new job *or* Francis's new job
>
> Mr. Jones' office *or* Mr. Jones's office

When pronunciation would sound awkward with the extra syllable, do not add the *s* after the apostrophe, as follows.

> Los Angeles' weather
>
> the witnesses' replies

For irregular nouns, place the apostrophe before the s ('s) for both singular and plural possession:

Singular Possessive	**Plural Possessive**
the child's coat	the children's toys
the woman's comment	the women's association
a man's advice	the men's sporting event

The easiest way to work with plural possessives—whether regular or irregular—is to make the noun plural first and then show the possession.

To show joint possession, place the apostrophe after the second name, for example:

> Janet and Bob's car

To show individual possession, place the apostrophe after each name, for example:

> Janet's and Bob's cars

Next is a category of possessives that often goes unnoticed, *inanimate possessives.*

Inanimate Possessives

Possessives are easier to spot when a person possesses an object, such as *Bob's car*. However, an inanimate object, such as *wind* or *newspaper* can also show possession, for example:

the wind's force   the newspaper's headline

To know if a word shows possession, flip the phrase around. If you need to use the word *of*, in all likelihood the word shows possession, for example:

the headline of the newspaper	the newspaper's headline
the force of the wind	the wind's force
the ending of the play	the play's ending
the work of the day	the day's work
the cover of the book	the book's cover
the fender of the car	the car's fender

Another common use of apostrophes occurs in contractions, which create a major spelling error for many writers.

Contractions

Contractions are acceptable for use in e-mail; however, avoid using contractions for formal or academic writing. For example, *APA does not accept contractions.*

The most common contractions are verbs, which can be shortened by omitting a few letters and using the apostrophe in their place, for example:

Verb	Contraction
will not	won't
cannot	can't
did not	didn't
should not	shouldn't

One contraction that creates a lot of problems for writers is "it's." *It's* is the contraction for *it is* or *it has*. The possessive pronoun *its* has no apostrophe.

Caution: When writers misspell contractions by leaving out the apostrophe, they are making serious spelling errors that result in lost credibility.

PRACTICE 22.2

Apostrophes: Possessives and Contractions

Instructions: Make corrections where needed in the following sentences.

Incorrect: Its all in a days work.

Corrected: It's all in a day's work.

1.   My supervisors report wont be ready until next week.

2.   The weather report says its going to rain later, but I dont believe it.

3.   Though its Junes responsibility, its in Jacks best interest to complete the task.

4.   Dr. Jones office isnt located down the hall; its next to Dr. Raines.

5.   If you tell me its Tess project, i'll adjust my expectations.

Note: See page 417 for the key to the above exercise.

SECTION 3: HYPHENS

Here are some of the primary uses of hyphens:

1.   To divide words.
2.   To form group modifiers.
3.   To display fractions and numbers above twenty-one.
4.   To form certain prefixes and suffixes.

Each of these uses is reviewed below.

Word Division

Because computers have eliminated the need to divide words at the end of lines, here is the most important current principle about word division:

> When dividing words, divide only between syllables.

If you are unsure of a word's syllabication, look it up: *When in doubt, check it out.* However, avoid dividing words whenever possible.

Compound Modifiers

Using hyphens for compound modifiers merits attention. Compound modifiers are formed when two adjectives modify a noun jointly, for example:

long-term project	two-word modifiers
first-quarter report	short-term earnings
second-class service	first-class accommodations

When the modifier follows the noun, do not use a hyphen. In fact, that is one way to check usage, for example:

meetings that are high powered	high-powered meetings
information that is up to date	up-to-date information
a woman who is well dressed	a well-dressed woman

Another way to test if you need a hyphen is to check one word at a time to see if the combination makes sense; for example, the *long-term report* is neither a *long report* nor a *term report*. Both words together form *one unit of meaning*, which adding the hyphen accomplishes.

When two or more compound modifiers occur in sequence, use a suspension hyphen at the end of the first modifier and follow it with a space:

The short- and long-term prognoses are both excellent.

The 30- and 60-day rates are available.

Hyphens are also used in compound numbers, which are reviewed next.

Compound Numbers

Compound numbers from twenty-one to ninety-nine are hyphenated. Here are a few examples:

thirty-three	forty-nine	seventy-three

When you write a check, apply this rule to display compound numbers correctly!

When fractions are used as adjectives, they are hyphenated:

one-half complete   two-thirds gone   one-quarter Irish

However, fractions that are treated as nouns are not hyphenated:

George spent one half of the budget renovating his office.

Prefixes

Rules about prefixes can be complicated, but here are a few points about common uses of hyphens with prefixes:

- Use a hyphen after the prefix *self*, for example:

    self-confidence   self-esteem   self-employed

- Use a hyphen after the prefix *re* when the same spelling could be confused with another word of the same spelling but with a different meaning: [2]

    I re-sent the papers.   I resent your comment.

    He will re-sign the contract.   I will resign immediately.

    Sue will re-lease her car.   Sue will release her car.

- Use a hyphen after a prefix that is attached to a proper noun, as follows:

    ex-President Carter   trans-Atlantic flight

    pro-American policy   pre-Roman period

Work on the practice below, applying the principles you have just learned.

PRACTICE 22.3

Hyphens

Instructions: Make corrections as needed in the following sentences to show correct use of hyphens.

Incorrect: The short term progress is good.

Corrected: The short-term progress is good.

1. Your first class treatment has impressed all of us.

2. Our budget is one half spent.

3. The short and long term outlooks are quite different.

4. Twenty five people attended the conference.

5. Do you have funding for your 30 and 60 day payment schedules?

Note: See page 417 for the key to the above exercise.

Recap

Below is a summary how to use quotation marks, apostrophes, and hyphens.

➤ Use quotation marks with closed punctuation as follows:
  - Place periods and commas inside of quotation marks.
  - Place semicolons and colons outside of quotation marks.
  - Place question marks and exclamation marks based on the meaning of the sentence.

➤ Use the apostrophe to show possession:
  - With singular nouns, use an apostrophe plus *s*: *cat's meow*.
  - With plural nouns, use an apostrophe after the *s*: *dogs' bones*.
  - With inanimate objects, use an apostrophe, as in the *wind's force*.
  - For joint ownership, place the apostrophe after the second noun: *Reggie and Grey's vacation*.
  - To show individual ownership, place the apostrophe after each noun: *Janet Sue's and Dinkie's cars*.

➤ Use hyphens as follows:
  - In group modifiers, such as *first-quarter report*.
  - With compound numbers *twenty-one* through *ninety-nine*.
  - For certain prefixes, such as *self-confident*.
  - For words that would otherwise be confused, such as *re-sent*.

Writing Workshop

Activity A. Writing Practice

Instructions: What is listening?

Write a short paper on the topic of listening, defining what effective, active, and engaged listening is and what it is not. Before you begin to write, discuss the topic with a partner. Then mind map your response, and use major topics from your mind map to create a page map. Spend about a twenty minutes composing your response, and then another five minutes editing and revising your paper.

Activity B. Journal

Instructions: What do you value most in your life?

As a follow up to writing your personal mission statement, list the five things that you value most, such as education, secure finances, family, health, and so on. Before moving to the next step, force yourself to rank order your list.

Next, identify how much time and effort you are devoting to the things you value most. For example, if you value health, what are you doing (or not doing) to ensure good health. Finally, identify if there is an incongruence or inequality between what you value in life and how you spend your time and money. If you are not committing the time and money to the things and people that you value, what does this mean?

Reference

Campbell, T. C., & Campbell II, T. M. (2004). *The China study*. Dallas, TX:

Bendella Books.

Quick Guide to
Job-Search Tools

*It is not the strongest of the species that survive, nor the most intelligent,
but the ones most responsive to change.* –Charles Darwin

Though you may expect that this chapter is about learning how to use the Internet to find a job, it is not: this chapter is actually about helping you define your unique career profile so that you can develop your career portfolio. Then searching online at sites such as SocialWorkers.org and CareerBuilder.com will be more meaningful. As you complete your portfolio, you may also feel motivated to network in local or national social work organizations, on site or online.

Regardless of your achievements, looking for a job can make you question everything that you have ever achieved. That is because the job-search process is different from other activities and projects. You are not just using your talents to solve a problem: you have become the *central theme* of the project. Finding a job is a full-time job; whether you like it or not, *you* are the focal point, and the job itself is secondary.

You may feel more confident using your skills than talking about them. Verbalizing your job survival skills equates to marketing yourself; to do that, you first need to identify your unique qualities so that you can prepare your résumé and ready yourself for interviewing.

Career Portfolio

All job seekers need to be organized and ready to present their credentials so that employers recognize their skills at a glance.

In fact, the first screening of an applicant lasts only seconds. Today employers are looking to eliminate applicants at the beginning of the process. Something as small as using a comma (instead of a colon) after the salutation in your cover letter can be reason enough for some to toss out your letter and résumé.

However, stay optimistic: if you are good at what you do, there will always be a place for you. You may find, though, that you need to continue to reinvent yourself throughout your career. If you keep your mindset geared toward change, you will succeed.

Here are some suggestions about what to include in your portfolio:

- *Purpose Statement.* To gain clarity and make effective career choices, write a purpose statement that reflects your life's mission.

- *Résumé.* Prepare your traditional and electronic résumés, tailoring your résumé for each job. Keep your résumé to two pages at *most.* For international corporations, prepare a curriculum vitae (CV).

- *Work Samples.* Select a few exhibits of your best work from previous jobs or classes: a letter, a report, a paper, and so on.

- *Reference Letters.* Ask for letters now, before you need them, using the salutation, *To Whom It May Concern.*

- *Networking contacts.* Become an expert at networking on site and online. Networking is still the best way to find a job; and, like it or not, e-networking is here to stay.

- *Business Card.* Design your own job-search card with your name, e-mail address, phone number, and vital points about your skills.

Start with a three-ring binder; use tabs to organize the various parts. Keep an electronic file of everything that you collect so that you can transform your hard copy into an *e-portfolio.*

If you have a Facebook page, now is the time to edit it: prospective employers routinely screen applicants' social networking activity and photos. Also, make sure that you have a professional-sounding e-mail address!

The most important part of your job search is being able to verbalize your skills, qualities, and experience, so keep that in mind as you work through the remainder of this chapter.

Skills, Not Titles or Degrees

Has anyone ever asked you, *what do you want to be when you . . . ?*

Most of us fumble with this question until we can answer it with a job title: teacher, accountant, mechanic, doctor, nurse, lawyer, engineer, and so on. However, titles and majors are *labels*, and they do not accurately reflect who you are or what you are capable of doing.

Do not limit yourself in the job market by being too attached to a job title or your college major. Keep your objective flexible—new job titles are created every day as traditional titles are eliminated.

Though a title will not follow you throughout your career, your skills, talents, and achievements will. Identify how your skills transfer to *any* business environment, and you gain a broader understanding of what you can offer.

Transferable Skills

Defining marketable skills is a challenge, especially when you think that you do not have any. By defining what you have achieved, you are able to see the unique qualities that you bring to an employer. Every exercise that you do in this chapter helps ready you for your interview.

Some of your skills have come from interests or hobbies, and you may not even be aware of what you have learned. Start to develop your job search profile by exploring these basic areas:

- Working with People
- Identifying Knowledge You Can Apply
- Identifying Personal Qualities

Working with People   *How do you work with people?* Consider formal and informal experiences at school, at your place of worship, with volunteer groups, on part- and full-time jobs, in sports activities, and in associations.

Here are some terms to open up your thinking. As you go through the list, notice your impressions as well as specific experiences that come to mind.

Counseling	Giving Feedback	Receiving Feedback
Working on Teams	Supervising	Working Independently
Marketing	Expressing Humor	Listening Actively
Leading	Organizing Projects	Organizing Events
Delegating	Care Giving	Selling
Advising	Negotiating	Mediating
Entertaining	Serving	Phoning/Soliciting
Cleaning	Being Compassionate	Fixing
Training	Evaluating	Facilitating

Identify three of the terms listed above that seem to stand out among the others and that describe you. For each term, recall an experience in which you used your people skills successfully, for example:

> *Giving Feedback:* When working on a team project, I gave objective feedback that kept our team focused and on track. I deal well with conflict, so I was able to negotiate communication challenges among team members. As a result, we ended up with a successful project.

> *Serving:* I work part-time at a local nursing home and take pride in assisting our patients in whatever they need. Sometimes they need more help than I can provide alone, so I call on team members for support. I enjoy advocating for people who have special needs.

For each of the three terms you choose, give an example of how you used your people skills successfully, giving a specific example to demonstrate it.

Identifying Knowledge You Can Apply

What are your areas of expertise? In addition to formal learning, consider hobbies and interests. Read through the list below and circle three or more of the items that reflect your abilities:

Writing (composing, editing, revising) / Communication / Languages (speaking, writing, translating, interpreting) / Research / Social Policy / Group Practice / Global Communication / Communities and Societies / Business Management / Accounting / Psychology / Sociology / Social Work / Counseling / Physical Sciences / Math / Statistics / Budgeting / Biology / Medicine / Pharmaceuticals / Music / Instruments / Child Care / Early Child Development / Elementary or Secondary Education / Voice / Theater / Film Making /Art / Archeology / Anthropology / Law / Criminal / Civil / Police Science / Political Science / History / Social Sciences / Sports / Nutrition / Cosmetology / Physical Therapy / Organizational Development / Human Resource Development / Fundraising / Graphic Arts or Design / Interior Design

What other subjects or major areas can you identify? If need be, take out your college catalog and list specific classes and assignments that were particularly meaningful.

Can you come up with three or more areas in which you feel especially competent? For example:

I feel confident with my *writing* skills. I can compose, edit, and revise e-mail messages, letters, and reports.

I like working with *numbers*. I make a budget, follow it, and balance my checking account online; I also have good *computer skills*.

Nutrition and *sports* have always been major interests. I *coach* my friends when we're at the gym and they've seen good results.

In the spaces below, identify three subjects and for each one write a sentence describing your experience or competence.

1._____

2._____

3._____

Working on Tasks   *What kinds of tasks can you perform?* Consider all of the classes that you have taken as well as job experience, paid or volunteer. Also consider your hobbies and interests; these activities are important to employers.

Which tasks can you perform well? Which tasks do you enjoy? (Later in this chapter, you will list part- and full-time jobs.) Use the list of nouns and verbs below to generate a list of tasks that you do well:

Work with Children / Counsel / E-Mail / PowerPoint / Case Notes / Web Design / Manage / Solve Problems / Crisis Management / Analyze / Trouble Shoot / Survey / Care for Children and Elderly / Design / Paint / Draw / Sketch / Sculpt / Construct / Gather Information / Organize and File / Spreadsheets / Tables / Graphs / Letters / Behavior Management Plans / Agendas / Minutes / Reports / Proposals / Set Goals / Meet Quotas / Read / Write / Edit / Coach / Supervise / Anger Management / Greet and Receive / Clean Houses or Offices / Play Music / Compose / Style Hair / Drive / Word / Excel / WordPerfect / Harvard Graphics / Calendar Creator Plus

What other tasks relate to your experience?

Though some of these tasks may not seem relevant to your ultimate career goal, every task you do well contributes to your unique career profile. Give examples of successful experiences, for example:

> During my free time, I enjoy assisting my elderly neighbor. When I noticed that she was not able to take her dog on walks through the neighborhood anymore, I offered to walk her dog. Once I started walking her dog, another neighbor, who had recently broken his ankle, asked if I could walk his dog too. Soon walking dogs turned into a part-time job. The dogs are fun to work with, and their owners are grateful that I can help them out in a bind.

> My mother is a member of an organization that helps raise funds for the disease lupus. I helped the director by taking minutes at one of their meetings and then organized and filed papers in their office. My phone work is good. I enjoyed making follow-up calls to tell people about a meeting or to let them know what we did at a meeting that they missed. Every part of it was fun because I was helping people.

What tasks do you do well and enjoy? Give at least one detailed example below:

_____

_____

_____

In addition to the specific tasks that you performed, also describe what you learned about yourself and others from performing these tasks, for example:

> When I volunteered at the lupus organization, I acted friendly and confident, even though I didn't feel secure at first. I was also patient with clients on the phone. When I made a mistake, I took responsibility for it and corrected it quickly.

> When I helped my neighbors with their dogs, I showed initiative. By volunteering to help people in need, other people sought out my services, and I ended up creating a small business. I was very exciting to fill a need, and I learned a lot about dogs!

This exercise is difficult because most people are used to doing a task rather than analyzing what they learned from it. Select three of your tasks or work experiences and record what you learned about your skills and attitudes.

The unfamiliar is challenging for everyone—until it becomes *familiar*. Reviewing tasks you do well builds your confidence, reminds you of your competence, and puts your job search into perspective.

Identifying Personal Qualities

You are unique whether or not you realize it. *What are your personal qualities that shape you into who you are? Which of the following qualities describe you?*

reliable	dependable	motivated	self-starter
persistent	optimistic	self-reliant	strong
independent	capable	fast learner	supportive
eager	focused	purposeful	task-oriented
disciplined	friendly	persuasive	artistic
committed	easy-going	encouraging	flexible
balanced	open minded	accepting	prompt
courteous	patient	dedicated	supportive
loyal	adaptable	credible	ethical
competent	kind	helpful	determined
confident	decisive	creative	enthusiastic
honest	responsible	self-learner	passionate

Close your eyes and reflect for a moment. *What adjectives come to mind when you think of yourself?*

_____

Next, write three of your positive qualities below, and give examples of times when you displayed them to get a job done or help someone.

1. _____
   _____

2. _____
   _____

3. _____
   _____

Now that you have established several good qualities, list an area or two that you wish to improve; call them your *growing edges* if you wish.

Prospective employers do not expect you to be perfect, and they will ask about your weaknesses. By responding effectively, you have the perfect opportunity to show that your self-awareness leads to self-growth.

Because they interview hundreds of applicants, human resource (HR) professionals can see through insincere answers. By being honest yet optimistic about your weaknesses, you will actually score points. State your weakness in a constructive way. For example:

Do Not Say: I'm late getting my work done sometimes, and I need to get control of my schedule.

Do Say: Sometimes I get so involved in solving a problem that I lose track of time. I'm working on time management so that my schedule is more balanced. Overall, it feels as if I have more time and more control over my time.

Do Not Say: I feel frustrated working on a team, especially when others don't hold their weight. Sometimes I'm very critical.

Do Say: I prefer working independently than working on a team because I have more control over a project, but I am becoming more patient as well as learning how to give constructive feedback to move a project along.

Asking for Feedback   When you are on a job interview, one of the questions that you may be asked is, *How do others perceive you?*

To prepare, ask three people who know you well to describe your skills and attitudes. Choose people who are positive and supportive. Let them know that you are doing research for your job-search profile. If they are willing, ask if you could receive your feedback in writing via a short note or e-mail so that you are able to refer to it later.

Here are some questions that you can ask:

- What are three adjectives that you would use to describe me?
- What are some tasks that you have seen me do well?
- In your eyes, what achievements have I made?
- Do you consider me a team player? A leader? A self-starter?
- What do you think are my growing edges or areas in which I can improve?

Take a few moments to reflect on the input that you have received and record it, especially if it is all verbal.

You may be surprised at how positively others perceive you. If you feel uncomfortable when you hear good things about yourself, simply say *thank you* and move on. The same advice is true if you hear negative things. Keep an open mind, and use the feedback to develop objectives for self-growth.

Work Experience

Make a list of all paid or volunteer jobs you have had; for each, specify how long you had the job. Instead of giving start and end dates, you can just list the months and years and then quantify the time. For example:

Supportive Care, part-time caregiver	January to March, 2012	7 weeks
	July to August, 2012	6 weeks
	December, 2012	3 weeks
	Total	about 4 months

Though you are concerned with dates, you also want to have an idea of the amount of time on the job. Quantify your experiences in terms of years and months or even weeks.

After you tally the specifics, you can list your experience as follows:

Supportive Care, part-time caregiver

January to December, 2012 4 months

Now take a moment to record the jobs you have held and tally your job experience in months and years.

For each position, write a sentence or two that demonstrates the skills that you applied. Write active sentences using strong verbs, and avoid filler verbs and phrases, such as "I learned how to" or "I gained experience doing," as shown in the examples that follow.

Weak: While working as a caregiver at Supportive Care, *I learned how to communicate* with all types of clients.

Revised: While working as a caregiver at Supportive Care, *I communicated* effectively with all of our clients.

Weak:	While I volunteered at Benevolent Hospital, *I gained experience from assisting some of the* nurses distribute medication.
Revised:	While volunteering on the children's ward at Benevolent Hospital, *I assisted* nurses distribute medicine to children.
Weak:	As a coaching assistant at Boys and Girls YMCA, *I was able to learn how* to provide personal attention to each child.
Revised:	As a coaching assistant at Boys and Girls YMCA, *I assisted each child based on their individual needs, giving feedback and encouragement to keep them motivated.*

When you go on an interview, be prepared with an example to demonstrate one of your achievements.

For example, perhaps you are the first person in your family to graduate from college or maybe you recently won an award. These types of notable experiences give prospective employers insight into your personality and interests as well as how you apply your skills.

Of course, use discretion in choosing which achievements to cite. A prospective employer does not want to hear about personal milestones such as engagements or weddings; and no matter how cute your children are, save those stories for your friends and relatives.

COACHING TIP
Voicemail Messages

Have you ever received a rambling voicemail message? Have you ever left one? To get the best results, plan your message before you call.

Here are guidelines for leaving voice mail messages:

1. Mind map the message before you call.
2. Start your message by *slowly* stating your name and phone number.
3. State the purpose of your call: give the most important details first.
4. Include a time frame: when do you need the information you are requesting?
5. Make sure you include the best times you can be reached.
6. Repeat your phone number *slowly* at the end of the message.

Business Cards

Especially if you are new to the job market, create a business card. Select a few accomplishments and list them as bullet points on your card:

<table>
<tr><td>Jane Addams</td><td>312.555.1212</td></tr>
<tr><td></td><td>ja@email.com</td></tr>
</table>

BSW, Rockford University

- Three years of caregiving experience
- Compassionate, Creative, Focused, and Motivated
- Excellent GPA and References

Your new business card is a useful tool for networking, providing your contact information and reminding associates of your skills.

Networking

Networking is the best way to secure a job. You may find out, for example, that you have a better chance of getting an interview by contacting someone you know at an agency than by contacting human resources.

Networking has changed dramatically in recent years; the sooner you become networking savvy, the better. In her book *Graduate to LinkedIn: Jumpstart Your Career Network Now*, author Giovagnoli-Wilson (2010) adds science to the art of networking, coining the term *networlding*.

Professional networking groups give you a steady stream of new contacts. By doing an online search of professional groups in your field, you will discover many groups in which you can use your social skills to build your reputation and credibility.

- *Connect with people who have similar goals and values.* Stay active and involved on site and online.

- *Build your network before you need it.* Start now and network on an ongoing basis so that you make contacts, remain visible, and get the support you need.

- *View networking as a communication exchange, not a one-sided dialog.* Before you call on someone to network, articulate why the meeting would be *mutually* beneficial. Look for common interests, experiences, or shared acquaintances.

- *Reciprocate favors: when you ask people for help, also ask what you can do for them in return.* You may find that an opportunity that did not work out for you is perfect for someone else.

- *View organizations within your field as career opportunities.* Through professional organizations, you will meet new people and have experiences that enhance your leadership skills.

- *Continue to network within your organization.* By networking within your organization, you build relationships as you promote your visibility and flexibility.

Volunteer to serve on committees, participate in focus groups, and attend social work-related activities. Find new friends by attending fund-raising events for not-for-profit organizations. Treat everyone with respect, including support staff such as mailroom and cleaning personnel.

Job-Search Letters

Letters are important tools for initiating, developing, and following up with contacts and job prospects. Even though everyone seems to be using e-mail for everything, a hard-copy letter still makes a strong impression. Here are two types of letters that are part of the job search process:

1. Cover Letter
2. Thank-You Letter

Tailor every letter that you write to the specific position that you are going after and the organization to which you are sending it. In addition, some prospective employers prefer that all application letters and résumés be submitted online; others prefer to receive hard copies. Check each organization's preference as you engage in your job search.

Next, you will review how to customize your letter.

Cover Letters

Send a cover letter with your résumé; or a *cover message*, if you send your résumé online. State why you would be the best person for the job and highlight your accomplishments. While your letter—or message—may not get you the job, a poorly written one will keep you from getting in the door to apply. Here are some guidelines that relate to job-search letters.

- *Know the name and title of the person to whom you are writing.* Do *not* address a letter to *Dear Sir* or *Dear Madam*. Go to the company website or call to find out the addressee's name and its correct spelling.

- *Find out whether the preference for receiving résumés is online or through the mail.* If you submit an application letter and résumé online, e-mail it to yourself first and print out your file to make sure it looks professional.

- *Stress what you can offer the organization.* Rather than focus on what you are looking for in a position, instead stress how your skills can benefit the organization.

- *Develop a plan for follow-up.* Take charge: do not expect others to contact you after they receive your information.

- *Aim for perfection: your written communication creates a strong first impression.* A letter of application presents high stakes. Write in active voice, use *you viewpoint*, and be concise.

A strong cover letter has an opening to capture the reader's attention but also identifies the job for which you are applying.

Example: The opportunity listed with CareerBuilder for a home health care social worker is a great fit with my background and qualifications; my résumé is enclosed.

Example: Our mutual colleague Jennifer Lopez suggested that I have the talent and qualifications that you are looking for in a bi-lingual social worker. My enclosed résumé highlights some of that experience.

In the next paragraph, explain your special skills by listing some of your major accomplishments or qualifications that are relevant to the position you are seeking.

Example: As a recent college graduate, I have experience in youth and family services. My degree in social work includes a three-month internship. As an intern, I supported three case managers who trusted me with clients and managing their paperwork.

In the last part of your cover letter, request an interview. State that you will call within a specific time frame to find a mutually agreeable time to meet.

Example: I'd appreciate the opportunity to meet with you to discuss how my background can benefit your agency. I will contact you the week of June 12 to see if we can meet.

Thus, the first paragraph identifies the job, the second paragraph explains your special skills, and the third paragraph is the call to action.

Be sure to follow up with your commitment to call. If the person is not available, ask if there is another time that would be convenient for you to call back. Leave your name and number, but do not feel slighted if you do not get a callback: the responsibility for communication is on your shoulders.

Follow-Up Letters and Thank-You Notes

Two of the most powerful tools in your job search toolkit are a follow-up e-mail and a handwritten thank-you note.

Your note will make a new networking associate or potential employer feel good for meeting with you or for making a call or two on your behalf.

By writing a formal thank-you letter, you have another opportunity to sell yourself. Your letter allows you to restate your skills and accomplishments. Write a letter that is simple, friendly, and genuine. Do not use a boiler-plate, *one-size-fits-all* message. Customize each letter, e-mail message, and handwritten note by specifically referring to something you discussed.

Get a business card from each of your contacts so that sending a note or e-mail takes less effort. Surprisingly, no matter how good the results are when thank-you notes are received, few people actually send them.

Figure QG.1. Sample Thank-You Note

Elaine:

Thank you for sharing your valuable time and advice for my job search.

I have contacted Joe, as you suggested, and will keep you informed on my progress. If I can assist you in any way, do not hesitate to contact me. I would be pleased to put my strong computer skills to use on your behalf!

Good luck with assisting your clients at the new community center.

All the best,

Sophie

Figure QG.2. Sample Cover Letter

Keep your cover letter short, and a prospective employer is more likely to read it. Write your letter so the reader can pick up key information from a glance.

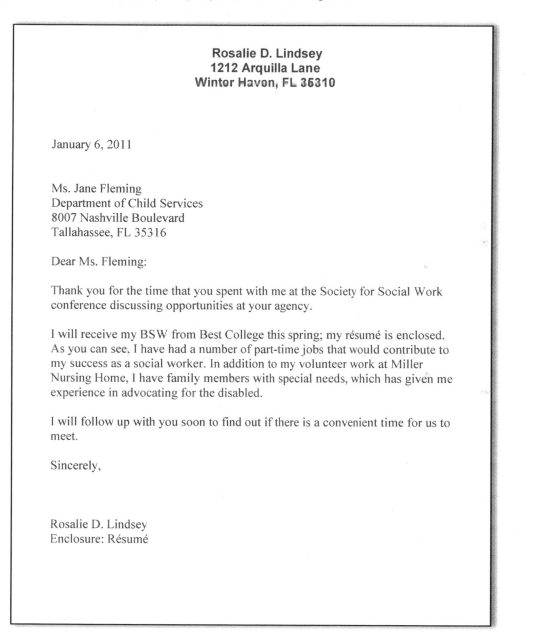

Rosalie D. Lindsey
1212 Arquilla Lane
Winter Haven, FL 36310

January 6, 2011

Ms. Jane Fleming
Department of Child Services
8007 Nashville Boulevard
Tallahassee, FL 35316

Dear Ms. Fleming:

Thank you for the time that you spent with me at the Society for Social Work conference discussing opportunities at your agency.

I will receive my BSW from Best College this spring; my résumé is enclosed. As you can see, I have had a number of part-time jobs that would contribute to my success as a social worker. In addition to my volunteer work at Miller Nursing Home, I have family members with special needs, which has given me experience in advocating for the disabled.

I will follow up with you soon to find out if there is a convenient time for us to meet.

Sincerely,

Rosalie D. Lindsey
Enclosure: Résumé

The Résumé

Human resource executives and hiring managers receive hundreds of résumés for every job opening. What will make your résumé stand out among others?

Brevity is critical: highlight your experience effectively on one page; at any rate, do not exceed two pages. Also, do not use flamboyant fonts or fancy paper: use conservative fonts such as Times New Roman and Arial; use one style of font for the body and another for your letterhead and headings. Also use crisp, white heavy-weight bond paper. Customize your résumé for each potential position.

Chronological Formatting

The *chronological format* lists your education, work experience, and accomplishments in order, starting with the most recent and working backward.

This format is the more traditional, so readers find it easy to see a history of steady promotions or increased responsibility. Here are some tips:

- Use *career focus* or *summary* rather than *objective*.

- Make sure that prospective employers can tell at a glance the job or job category for which you are applying; tailor your résumé for each job you seek.

- Be specific about accomplishments; quantify your achievements when possible.

- Apply parallel structure (represent words in a consistent form).

- Keep your résumé to one page if you can, two pages if you cannot.

Write your résumé to answer questions *before* they arise. On your cover letter, fill in gaps of unemployment that might appear on your résumé. Employers assume you are telling the truth until they find out otherwise. When employers check specific details, they usually do so only after they have already decided to hire you.

Figure QG.3. Sample Chronological Résumé

Rather than use a template, develop your own résumé design by incorporating the latest job-search language, such as "career focus" rather than "objective." Also, add contrast to the design by using a serif font for the body and a non-serif font for the headings.

ROSALINE D. LINDSEY

1212 Arquilla Lane
Winter Haven, FL 35319
(813) 555-1212 (H) • (813) 555-1212 (C)
pv@email.com

CAREER FOCUS

Dedicated ***advocate for children with special needs*** with extensive experience as a caregiver at home and in nursing homes. Committed to assisting others; effective leader who can train and motivate.

EXPERIENCE

Supportive Care, Tampa, Florida   **June 2010 to Present**
Senior Care Assistant

- Assisting with bathing, grooming, and incontinence issues.
- Providing stabilization and assistance with walking.
- Preparing meals and cleaning up meal-related items.
- Providing medication reminders and appointment reminders.

EDUCATION

BSW, Best University, 2014
A.A., Communications, Everglade State College

SKILLS

Word, Excel, PowerPoint, WordPerfect, Lotus Notes, Calendar Creator Plus, Outlook (e-mail), Internet (Orbitz and Expedia)

Electronic Formatting (E-Résumés)

Your job-search portfolio is not complete unless you have an electronic résumé (e-résumé). For example, some companies screen applicants as a first step by having them submit an e-résumé.

Here are tips for your e-résumé:

- Use a maximum of 65 characters per line.
- Omit italics and underlines.
- Include a key-word summary at the top of the page.
- Adhere to parallel structure and end verbs in their *ing* form, for example, *answering phone and e-mail messages*.

For an online application, send your electronic résumé attached to an e-mail or post it on the Internet within personal Web pages. On your electronic résumé, include a *key word summary*.

Place a *key word summary* that consists of 20 to 30 words at the top of the page after your name and contact information:

- Use words and phrases that highlight your education and experience.
- Customize your summary with words used in the description of the job for which you are applying.

On a traditional résumé, you describe your work experience in verb phrases that begin with strong action verbs (such as managed, supervised, processed). Instead, on an e-résumé, key word summaries consist of noun and adjective phrases, such as "fluent in Spanish," "team-oriented," or "strong communication skills." Emphasize your knowledge, experience, and skills that are likely to attract prospective employers.

Employers report receiving thousands of résumés for jobs listed online. Unless the job advertisement calls for "apply by e-mail only," the best approach is to respond with a traditional résumé and cover letter. At one time you would have gotten noticed in a good way by dropping off your résumé in person; however, that is not the case in the current job market.

Figure QG.4. Sample E-Résumé

Customize your key word summary for each position for which you apply.

PAT VINCENT
109 Hillcrest Avenue,
Downers Grove, IL 60615
E-mail: pv@email.com
630-555-1212

KEYWORDS

direct youth services, client-focused, collaborative, diverse computer skills, multi-disciplinary team member, youth and senior advocate for community services, high caseload ability, leadership, communication and writing skills, college graduate

OBJECTIVE

A position in which I can use my case management, communication, and leadership skills to grow within a social service organization that has a client focus.

EDUCATION

MSW, Best University

BSW, Ivy College

Related courses: social policy, research, group practice, communities and societies

Diploma, South Side High School, Downers Grove, Illinois
Graduated 2006

WORK EXPERIENCE

Case Manager, Department of Child Services, Chicago, Illinois, 2008 to present
Facilitating life skills group, maintaining a caseload of 20 families, creating behavior management plans, creating goals and objectives with clients, transporting clients to public aid appointments, recording daily and weekly case notes, providing crisis management to clients.

SKILLS

Word, Excel, PowerPoint, WordPerfect, Lotus Notes, Calendar Creator Plus, Outlook (e-mail), Internet (Orbitz and Expedia)

Though traditional résumés contain tabs and bolding for headers such as *Education* and *Experience*, e-résumés lack tabs and highlighting. E-mail programs usually have difficulty reading tabs and highlighting, so remove both to ensure your recipient receives your résumé intact.

Here's how to change your traditional résumé into an electronic one:

1. Remove all highlighting: bolding, underlining, and italics.
2. Eliminate bullets, and replace them with dashes, small o's, or asterisks.
3. Move all your text to the left.
4. Remove returns except for those separating major sections.
5. Use all capitals for headers.
6. Provide an additional line or two of spacing between sections.
7. Save the file in ASCII or Rich-Text Format.

To send your electronic résumé, start with a *subject line* that states the title of the job for which you are applying, such as "Graphic Arts Applicant." Then copy and paste your cover letter followed by your résumé within an e-mail.

Check first before sending your traditionally-formatted résumé as an attachment. Employers are reluctant to open attachments from applicants whom they do not know. In your cover letter, refer to the résumé that follows. Then copy and paste your letter into the e-mail first and follow it with your résumé.

Quick Introductory Pitch

By developing a quick introduction pitching your skills, you will be ready for any networking event or even the impromptu meeting of a potential employer.

Think of the quick introduction as an *elevator speech: a short monologue that provides vital information*, keeping the listeners' attention and garnering their interest. Create an actual script that you memorize—but be sure to sound natural when you use it.

Here is an example of a quick introductory pitch:

> Hi. My name is Rose Lindsey, and I have a bachelor's degree in social work. As well as having extensive experience working with the elderly and disabled, I am a good team player with strong leadership qualities. Would you be interested in receiving my résumé, or do you have any positions that I might apply for?

Your elevator speech should take no more than *ten seconds*. Give the listener enough honest information that highlights key reasons how you could contribute to his or her company.

Before you finish your conversation, get contact information and find out how you should send your information: electronic copy or hard copy.

Recap

Finding a job is itself a job. Commit to preparing your career portfolio as well as preparing your mindset toward success.

You have worked hard to build your skills. Though searching for a job might feel daunting, the best response is to take action and stay active until you achieve your dreams.

> *Inaction weakens the vigors of the mind . . . action strengthens*
> *the essence of creation.*   —Leonardo daVinci

Take action: *Do the work, and you will see the results.*

Job-Search Checklist:

_____ Write your career objective or personal mission statement.

_____ Create a personal business card.

_____ Collect samples of your written work.

_____ Compose a sample cover letter.

_____ Prepare your résumés: chronological and electronic format.

_____ Ask two to three contacts for a letter of reference.

_____ Prepare a list of networking opportunities.

_____ Buy heavy-weight bond paper and envelopes for résumés and letters.

Writing Workshop

Topic A: Writing a Self-Appraisal

Instructions: Write an honest self-appraisal; start with the following questions:

• What are my strengths and best qualities?

• What are some recent accomplishments?

• What are my growing edges?

As part of this activity, write two or three goals, identify specific steps to achieve them, and include a time frame for each step. By including a time frame, you are creating an *action plan.*

Finally, write yourself a letter of recommendation identifying your best qualities and highlighting your skills and abilities. Give yourself the same kinds of words of encouragement that you would give your best friend. Keep your letter and refer to it periodically.

Topic B: Researching Social Work Organizations

What are some social work organizations that you can join now while you are a student or in the future as a professional?

Research your community as well as do a search online for professional organizations that can offer you the benefit of gaining experience and networking. What are some other benefits of joining a professional social work organization?

Topic C: Researching Careers in Social Work

What are some different types of positions that are available in social work? Research opportunities by doing an Internet search: go to www.careerbuilder.com or careers.socialwork.org, along with other sites.

What positions are available? What qualities, skills, and types of experience are organizations seeking? What are some goals that you can set for yourself to become more marketable in finding your dream job?

Topic D: Writing a Thank-You Message

Thank-you messages are important job-search tools. Who would you like to recognize for assisting you? *A networking contact? An interviewer? A friend or family member?*

By taking the time to send a thank-you note, you are setting yourself apart from the crowd.

Résumé Worksheet

Career Focus

_____

_____

Summary

_____

_____

Education

School/College   **Degree to Be Conferred**

_____   _____

Major: _____   **Minor:** _____

School/College   **Degree Conferred**

_____   _____

Major: _____   **Minor:** _____

Skills and Training

_____

_____

Clubs and Extra-Curricular Activities

_____

_____

Job Experience Summary

For each position, list several job duties or tasks that you performed. Start each with a strong verb and maintain parallel structure.

Position	Job Duties or Tasks
1._____	_____
From _____to _____	_____
	_____
Total time: _____	_____
2._____	_____
From _____to _____	_____
	_____
Total time: _____	_____
3._____	_____
From _____to _____	_____
	_____
Total time: _____	_____

Reference

Giovagnoli-Wilson, M. (2010). *Graduate to LinkedIn: Jumpstart your career network now.* Chicago, IL: Networlding Publishing.

Keys to Activities

Chapter 8

Practice 8.1: Sentence Core

1. <u>Social workers</u> <u>contained</u> too many unnecessary products.
2. <u>I</u> <u>thanked</u> them for their support.
3. (I) <u>Thank</u> you for asking that question.
4. Our new <u>program</u> <u>will begin</u> in one month.
5. (You) <u>Examine</u> the client's request before approving the program.

Practice 8.2: Redundant Subjects

1. My <u>friends</u> (or <u>associates</u>) <u>tell</u> me that being positive is an asset.
2. The <u>details</u> (or <u>specifics</u>) about the project <u>were</u> fascinating.
3. <u>Visitors</u> (or <u>guests</u>) <u>should sign in</u> at the front desk. ("sign in" is a verb phrase)
4. My <u>goals</u> (or <u>objectives</u>) <u>reflect</u> my dreams.
5. The <u>results</u> (or <u>outcomes</u>) <u>reflect</u> our success.

Practice 8.3: Redundant Verbs

1. Milton's <u>decision</u> (<u>uncovers</u> or) <u>reveals</u> his true motives.
2. Mark's <u>actions</u> ~~surprised me and~~ <u>caught</u> me off guard.
3. <u>We</u> ~~started the project and~~ <u>worked</u> on (the project) for two hours.
4. <u>I</u> ~~understand and~~ <u>appreciate</u> your commitment to our mission.
5. <u>Melanie</u> ~~greeted us and~~ <u>welcomed</u> us to the new resource center.

Practice 8.4: Parallel Phrases
List 1:

1. Order supplies   or Ordering supplies
2. Schedule appointment   or Scheduling appointment
3. Renew certificate   or Renewing certificate

List 2:

1. Coordinate schedules   or Coordinating schedules
2. Distribute supplies   or Distributing supplies
3. Phone clients   or Phoning clients

List 3:

1. Train staff   or Training staff
2. Develop policy   or Developing policy
3. Reconcile profit and loss   or Reconciling profit and loss

Practice 8.5: Sentence Fragments – Answers will vary.

1. Making the right decision at the right time *felt good*.
2. *We could all go to lunch* because he finished the project earlier than anyone expected.
3. After I made the decision to reclaim my spot on the team, *I was happy*.
4. To show interest in a project that no longer had merit *does not make sense*.
5. *Our goal was* going slower than planned but staying under budget.

Practice 8.6: Real Subjects and Strong Verbs

1. <u>Customer service</u> <u>needs</u> to fill five orders.
2. An electrical <u>problem</u> on the fifth floor <u>caused</u> the outage.
3. <u>Randy</u> <u>will revise</u> the document today.
4. A new <u>report</u> <u>arrived</u> earlier today.
5. <u>You</u> <u>can decide</u> tomorrow.

Practice 8.7: Information Flow--Answers may vary.

1. *Consumers* are not buying too many unnecessary and costly items at this time.
2. *Many consumers* are choosing to spend their money on good used items at a reduced price.
3. *A change in consumer attitudes* is partly due to the rapidly increasing cost of gasoline.
4. *For your next paper, consider the topic* of outsourcing jobs to third-world countries.
5. *As you complete your report,* please consider the cost as well as the time required to make the revisions.

Chapter 9

Practice 9.1: Paragraphs and Information Flow—answers may vary.

Good writing is about composing and editing. As you compose, allow yourself to write freely and make mistakes. When you edit, identify the mistakes that you have made and correct them. Once you understand how to manage the writing process, good writing becomes much easier to produce.

Practice 9.2: Pronoun Point of View and Consistency

1. I usually work late on Thursdays because *I* can get a lot done at the end of the week. When *I* work late, I usually see other people working late also. Having *my* boss notice that *I am* putting in extra time always makes me feel good.

2. Good nutrition leads to good health. When *you* eat well, you are likely to feel better. *You may* not find it easy to eat in a healthful way, though. *You may* prefer to eat fast food at the end of the day when you are tired.

    Or: Good nutrition leads to good health. When *I* eat well, *I* feel better. *I* do not find it easy to eat in a healthful way, though. I usually prefer to eat fast food at the end of the day when *I am* tired.

Practice 9.3

The construction for the 9th floor conference room was extended two more weeks. *However, w*e were not informed until Friday. *As a result,* our meetings for the following week needed to be reassigned to different *rooms, but none* were available. *Fortunately,* Jane Simmons agreed to let us use her office, *and* several serious conflicts were avoided.

Chapter 10

Practice 10.1
Rule 2: Conjunction (CONJ)

1. <u>Mark Mallory</u> <u>is</u> the new case manager, and <u>he</u> <u>starts</u> on Monday. CONJ
2. <u>Mark</u> <u>will be</u> an inspiration to our staff and an excellent spokesperson for our agency. (no commas)
3. <u>You</u> <u>can leave</u> him a message, but <u>he</u> <u>will</u> not <u>be</u> able to reply until next week. CONJ
4. The <u>office</u> in St. Louis also <u>has</u> a new case manager, and her <u>name</u> <u>is</u> Gia Rivera. CONJ
5. <u>You</u> <u>can mail</u> your information now and <u>expect</u> a reply within the next two weeks. (no commas)

Practice 10.2
Rule 3: Series (SER)

1. <u>We</u> <u>were</u> <u>assigned</u> Conference Rooms A and B on the first floor. (no commas)
2. <u>(You)</u> <u>Make</u> sure that you bring your laptop, cell phone, and client list to the meeting. SER
3. <u>You</u> <u>should</u> <u>arrange</u> the meeting, call your supervisor, and submit your housing assessment. SER

4. <u>Mitchell</u>, <u>Helen</u>, and <u>Sally</u> <u>conducted</u> the workshop on anger management. SER
5. <u>They</u> <u>gave</u> a workshop for Elaine, Arlene, Donald, and Joanne on preparing housing packets for the elderly. SER

Practice 10.3
Rule 4: Introductory (INTRO)
1. Because the <u>letter</u> <u>arrived</u> late, <u>we</u> <u>were</u> not able to respond on time. INTRO
2. However, <u>we</u> <u>were</u> <u>given</u> an extension. INTRO
3. Although the extra <u>time</u> <u>helped</u> us, <u>we</u> still <u>felt</u> pressured for time. INTRO
4. To get another extension, <u>George</u> <u>called</u> their office. INTRO
5. Fortunately, the office <u>director</u> <u>was</u> agreeable to our request. INTRO

Practice 10.4
Rule 5: Nonrestrictive (NR)
1. Our <u>manager</u> *who specializes in project grants* <u>will</u> <u>assist</u> you with this issue. (restrictive: no commas)
2. <u>Tomas Phillips</u>, *who works only on weekends,* <u>will</u> <u>call</u> you soon. NR
3. The <u>therapist</u> *who researched this case* <u>is</u> not available. (restrictive: no commas)
4. <u>Nick Richards,</u> *who is in a meeting until 3 p.m.,* <u>can</u> <u>answer</u> your question. NR
5. Your new <u>contract,</u> *which we mailed yesterday,* <u>should</u> <u>arrive</u> by Friday. NR

Practice 10.5
Rule 6: Parenthetical (PAR)
1. <u>Clinical services</u>, I believe, <u>can</u> best <u>assist</u> you with this issue. PAR
2. <u>T. J.</u>, therefore, <u>will</u> <u>work</u> this weekend in my place. PAR
3. Our <u>invoice</u>, unfortunately, <u>was</u> <u>submitted</u> incorrectly. PAR
4. The new <u>contract</u>, in my opinion, <u>meets</u> specifications. PAR
5. <u>Brown Company</u>, of course, <u>recommended</u> us to a vendor. PAR

Practice 10.6
Rule 7: Direct Address (DA)
1. <u>(You)</u> <u>Give</u> your report to the auditor by Friday, Marcel. DA
2. Jason, <u>do</u> <u>you</u> <u>have</u> tickets for the game? DA
3. Doctor, <u>I</u> <u>would</u> <u>like</u> to know the results of my tests. DA
4. <u>Would</u> <u>you</u> <u>like</u> to attend the banquet, Alice? DA
5. (I) <u>Thank</u> you for inviting me, George. DA

Practice 10.7
Rule 8: Appositive (AP)
1. <u>Jacob Seinfeld</u>, our associate director, <u>decided</u> to hire Williams. AP
2. My lab <u>partner</u>, Carol Glasco, <u>applied</u> for a job here. AP
3. <u>Jim Martinez</u>, the registrar, <u>approved</u> your request. AP
4. The <u>department chair</u>, Dr. George Schmidt, <u>did</u> not <u>receive</u> your transcript. AP
5. The <u>director</u> <u>asked</u> Claire, my sister, to join us for dinner. AP

Practice 10.8
Rule 9: Addresses and Dates (AD)
1. <u>(You)</u> <u>Send</u> your application by Friday, December 15, to my assistant. AD
2. <u>San Antonio</u>, Texas, <u>has</u> a River Walk and Conference Center. AD
3. <u>Would</u> <u>you</u> <u>prefer</u> to meet in Myrtle, Minnesota, or Des Moines, Iowa? AD
4. <u>Springfield</u>, Massachusetts, <u>continues</u> to be my selection. AD
5. <u>We</u> <u>arrived</u> in Chicago, Illinois, on May 22, 2011, to prepare for the event. AD

Practice 10.9
Rule 10: Word Omitted (WO)
1. The <u>president</u> <u>shared</u> two intriguing, confidential reports. WO
2. The <u>crew</u> <u>scheduled</u> filming on Tuesday at 5 p.m., on Wednesday at 6 p.m. WO
3. The <u>problem</u> <u>is</u>, some of the results are not yet known. WO
4. <u>(You)</u> <u>Leave</u> the materials with Alicia at the Westin, with Marcia at the Hilton. WO
5. <u>Silvana</u> <u>presented</u> a short, exciting PowerPoint on Italy. WO

Practice 10.10
Rule 11: Direct Quotation (DQ)
1. Patrick shouted "Get back" before we had a chance to see the falling debris. DQ
2. According to Tyler, "All children can learn if they find an interest in what is taught." DQ
3. My father warned me, "When you choose an insurance company, find one with good customer service." DQ
4. Sharon encouraged me by yelling "Go for the gold!" as I was starting the race. DQ
5. Lenny said to me, "Good luck on your exam," before I left this morning. DQ (OR: no commas because it is a short quote)

Practice 10.11
Rule 12: Contrasting Expression or Afterthought (CEA)
1. <u>You</u> <u>will</u> <u>find</u> the manuscript in John's office, not in Bob's. CEA
2. <u>Marcus</u> <u>secured</u> the contract, but only after negotiating for hours. CEA
3. <u>(You)</u> <u>Chair</u> the budget committee, if you prefer. CEA
4. <u>Lester</u>, rather than Dan, <u>received</u> the award. CEA
5. <u>(You)</u> <u>Work</u> to achieve your dreams, not to run away from your fears. CEA

Chapter 11

Practice 11.1
Rule 1: Semicolon No Conjunction (NC)

1. <u>Keri</u> <u>will</u> not <u>approve</u> our final report; <u>she</u> <u>needs</u> more documentation.
2. (<u>You</u>) <u>Ask</u> Bryan for the report; <u>he</u> <u>said</u> that it was completed yesterday.
3. (<u>You</u>) <u>Arrive</u> on time to tomorrow's meeting; (<u>you</u>) <u>bring</u> both of your reports.
4. A <u>laptop</u> <u>was</u> <u>left</u> in the conference room; <u>Johnny</u> <u>claimed</u> it as his.
5. (<u>You</u>) <u>Recognize</u> your mistakes; (<u>you</u>) <u>offer</u> apologies as needed.

Practice 11.2
Rule 2: Semicolon Transition (TRANS)

1. <u>Carol</u> <u>suggested</u> the topic; fortunately, <u>Carlos</u> <u>agreed</u>.
2. The case management <u>team</u> <u>offered</u> assistance; however, their <u>time</u> <u>was</u> limited.
3. <u>Ken</u> <u>compiled</u> the data; therefore, <u>Mary</u> <u>crunched</u> it.
4. The <u>numbers</u> <u>turned out</u>* well; as a result, our new <u>budget</u> <u>was</u> <u>accepted</u>.
5. <u>Roger</u> <u>ran</u> in the marathon; unfortunately, <u>he</u> <u>was</u> unable to finish.

* "Turned out" is a verb phrase.

Practice 11.3
Rule 3: Semicolon Because of Commas (BC)

1. (<u>You</u>) Please <u>include</u> Rupert Adams, CEO; Madeline Story, COO; and Mark Coleman, executive president.
2. By next week <u>I</u> <u>will</u> <u>have</u> <u>traveled</u> to St. Louis, Missouri; Chicago, Illinois; and Burlington, Iowa.
3. <u>Mike</u> <u>applied</u> for jobs in Honolulu, Hawaii; Sacramento, California; and Santa Fe, New Mexico.
4. Your <u>application</u> <u>was</u> <u>received</u> yesterday; but when <u>I</u> <u>reviewed</u> it, <u>information</u> <u>was</u> missing.
5. <u>You</u> <u>can</u> <u>resubmit</u> your application today; and since my <u>office</u> <u>will</u> <u>review</u> it, <u>you</u> <u>can</u> <u>call</u> me tomorrow for the results.

Chapter 12

Practice 12.2: Regular Verbs in Past Time

1. The coach misplaced the roster before the game began.
2. My counselor suggested that I submit my résumé.
3. Bart received the award for most valuable player.
4. Last week no one on our team wanted the schedule to change.
5. When Jonika suggested that we meet after school, everyone was pleased.

Practice 12.3: Irregular Verbs in Past Time

1. We had already seen that movie last week. (Or: We already saw . . .)
2. The professor said that you wrote a good paper.
3. I brought my lunch today so I don't need to buy one.
4. Bob lent me $5 so that I could go to the game.
5. The assistant has taken all the papers to the office.

Practice 12.4: The –S Form

1. The coach says that we need to practice for one more hour.
2. Our team finishes in first place every year.
3. Taylor has chosen the players for both teams.
4. The coach has enough good players already.
5. If the group listens carefully, they will learn the information.

Practice 12.5: Verb Tense and Consistency

1. The note is not clear and needs to be changed.
2. My boss said that I arrived late to work every day this week
3. The new computers arrived today, so then I had to install them.
4. Yesterday my counselor told me I needed to take an extra elective.
5. Last week my teacher told me that I had to redo the paper.

Practice 12.6: Active Voice

1. My math instructor gave me the assignment.
2. My Uncle John purchased the car for me.
3. The entire team chose the new soccer jersey.
4. The Art Council will plan the annual art exhibit.
5. Please pay your invoice by the beginning of the month.

Practice 12.7: Parallel Structure

1. My professor asked me to submit a new paper and (to) hand it in on Friday.
2. My friends and I plan to visit a cathedral and (to) see the ancient ruins in Rome.
3. Everyone focused on showing good team spirit and winning the game.
4. Your attitude will go a long way toward achieving success and getting what you want in life.
5. I received the new soccer jerseys, and now I must pass them out.

Practice 12.8: Subjunctive Mood
1. The president insisted that Melba **attend** the reception.
2. Jacob wishes that he **were** on this year's team.
3. If Dan **were** your team captain, would you support him?
4. My mother said that it is imperative that my sister **complete** her college education.
5. If I **were** you, I would run for office.

Chapter 13

Practice 13.1: Subjects and Objects
1. If you can't reach anyone else, feel free to call **me**.
2. The director told Catie and **me** to role play again.
3. Fred and **she** collected for the local food drive.
4. His manager and **he** have two more reports to complete.
5. That decision was made by Jim and **me**.

Practice 13.2: Pronouns Following Between and Than
1. Between you and **me**, who has more time?
2. Beatrice sings better than **I do**.
3. The decision is between Bob and **you**.
4. The Blue Jays are more competitive than **we are**.
5. You can split the work between Margaret and **me** so that it gets done on time.

Practice 13.3: Pronoun and Antecedent Agreement
1. When **case managers** not relate well to their clients, they need more training.
2. **Servers** go beyond **their** job description when they prepare carry-out orders for customers.
3. A pilot has a challenging job because **he or she** works long hours under difficult conditions. **(Or: pilots have . . . they work)**
4. When **students do** not turn in their work, **they** should expect penalties.
5. **Writers need** to submit **their** work in a timely manner.

Practice 13.4: Point of View and Consistency
1. I enjoy jogging because exercise keeps **me** fit.
2. You should follow the guidelines until **you** finish the project. (Or change both pronouns to **we**.)
3. As long as **I** stay motivated, I won't mind finishing the project.
4. **You** should strive to get the best education possible so you can have a satisfying career.
5. Sue and Mary worked on the project together, and **Sue** will present it at the next conference. (Or **Mary**)

Practice 13.5: Relative Pronouns: Who, Whom, and That

1. **Who** wrote the monthly report?
2. **Whom** are you going to the meeting with?
3. Is Jim the person **who** spoke with you?
4. The doctor **who** saw you yesterday is not available.
5. Every person **who** arrives late will be turned away.

Practice 13.6: Indefinite Pronouns

1. Either one of the programs **works** perfectly.
2. Everyone who finished the project **is** free to go.
3. None of the employees **send** e-mail on Saturday.
4. Some of the assignments **need** to be distributed before noon today.
5. Everything **runs** much better when we are all on time.

Practice 13.7: Pronoun Consistency *Note:* Answers may vary.

I enjoy working on team projects because **I** learn so much from **my** teammates. **Team members need** to be helpful because they never know when they will need assistance from **their** colleagues. ~~When you are on a team, every~~ All members need to carry their weight. That is, teammates who do not do **their** share of the work can be a burden to the entire team and jeopardize their project.

Team members who stay motivated are more valuable to the team. I always strive to do my best because **I** never know when **I** will need to count on **my** team members.

Chapter 14

Practice 14.1: Modifiers and Verbs

1. Drive **slowly** so that you do not get in an accident.
2. George feels **bad** about the situation.
3. The trainer spoke too **loudly**, and our group was offended.
4. The music sounds **good** to all of us.
5. The entire group felt **bad** about the change in management.

Practice 14.2: Comparative and Superlative Modifiers

1. Use your editing skills to make this letter **better** than it was before.
2. Toni made the **silliest (or most silly)** comment at the board meeting on Tuesday.
3. I was the **hungriest (most hungry)** person in the room but the last to be served.
4. Of all the people at this college, I live the **farthest** from campus.
5. Our committee is **further** along on this project than I could have imagined.

Practice 14.3: Implied Words in Comparisons

1. Roger's office is nicer than our **manager's office**.
2. My office has more windows than **yours (your office)**.
3. Reggie learned to use the software sooner than **I did**.
4. The executives ordered their lunches before **we did**.
5. However, our desserts were much tastier than **theirs (their desserts)**.

Practice 14.4: Modifiers and Their Placement

1. The report *on policy change* is due in September.
2. Major issues *relating to dress policy* must be addressed at the fall meeting.
3. Filling out the forms, *the applicant* made a mistake.
4. The letter *giving details about the incident* was sent out yesterday.
5. *As I answered the phone,* my feet slipped right out from under me.

Practice 14.5: More on Correct Placement

1. I received *only* three copies of the report.
2. Louis bought *almost* all of the new software in the catalog.
3. During the meeting, we finished *nearly* all of the doughnuts and coffee cake.
4. Congratulations, Jerry, you have *nearly* ten years on the job!
5. We will need to purchase *only* one computer for the research team.

Practice 14.6: Double Negatives

1. The receptionist wouldn't give us **any** information over the phone.
2. Martha didn't have **any** intention of helping us with the proposal.
3. Sylvestri **could** barely wait to tell us his answer.
4. The contractors will not start construction **regardless** of what we offer them.
5. The accountants won't give us **anything** for the charity deduction.

Chapter 15

Practice 15.1: Active Voice

1. Sean's manager asked him to lead the diversity team.
2. Phelps' coach gave him another chance to swim in the relay.
3. Our department hosted the holiday event last year.
4. Our president implemented a new policy on reimbursement for travel expenses.
5. The mayor cancelled the program due to lack of interest.

Practice 15.2: Passive Voice, the Tactful Voice

1. Meyers made an error in invoicing on your account last week. (passive is more tactful)
2. If you wanted to avoid an overdraft, you should have deposited your check before 4 p.m. (passive is more tactful)
3. You should have enclosed your receipt with your return item. (passive is more tactful)
4. We sent your order to the wrong address and apologize for our mistake. (active)
5. You needed to pay your invoice by the first of the month to avoid penalties. (passive is more tactful)

Practice 15.3: Nominals

1. Management implemented the dress policy in August.
2. Jane suggested that all new hires start on the first day of the month.
3. Our broker gave us information about that stock.
4. We discussed the new account at our last team meeting.
5. Our president announced the merger before the deal was final.

Chapter 16

Practice 16.1: Clauses

1. My manager asked me to attend the annual meeting, and he suggested arriving early on Friday.
2. My family will join me in Florida, and my assistant will make reservations for them.
3. Though I gave input, my manager planned my schedule.
4. If I can adjust my schedule, I will take time off for some fun with my family.
5. My boss approved the extra time, so now I must change my travel arrangements.

Practice 16.2: Tenses

1. The message was not clear and needed to be changed.
2. My boss said that their account was closed for some time now.
3. The new computers arrived today, so then I had to install them.
4. Yesterday my co-worker told me that I was supposed to attend the budget meeting.
5. First Mary said that she wanted the position, then she said that she didn't.

Practice 16.3: Lists

- Create High Performance Teams
- Develop Effective Communication Skills
- Coach Effective Job Performance
- Resolve Conflict
- Recruit and Retain Managers
- Value Personality Differences in the Workplace
- Assess Climate Change Efforts

Practice 16.4: Correlative Conjunctions

1. My boss not only asked me to complete the report but also to present it at the meeting.
2. Milly both applied both for the job and got it.
3. Our team neither focused on winning the game nor showed good team spirit.
4. The solution not only makes sense but also saves time.
5. My new car neither has a warranty nor runs well.

Chapter 17

Practice 17.1: Cut Redundant Modifiers

1. We trust that you find our services worthwhile.
2. Our new design makes our laptop even better than it was before.
3. The outcome of this project depends on all participants doing their best.
4. We want you to be certain that you have not ordered multiple items that are alike.

Practice 17.2: Remove Redundancy / Outdated Expressions

1. The papers that you requested are attached.
2. You have our confidence, and we value our client relationship.
3. As we discussed, the new policy should be reviewed this week.
4. You can eliminate any questions by sending your agenda in advance of the meeting.
5. Thank you for your support and assistance. (or simply "support")

Practice 17.3: Use Simple Language

1. We use that product, and the field supervisor is aware of our choice.
2. After the policy change, we tried to compromise as much as possible.
3. As you requested, we are omitting that information.
4. If the merger depends on our use of their facilities, we should try to change locations.
5. If you are aware of their objections, try to make respective changes.

Practice 17.4: Modify Correctly

1. In my opinion, you should feel certain what the facts are before you sign the contract.
2. Can you confirm that they might back out of their agreement?
3. I would like for you to speak to the person who knows much about this topic.

Chapter 19

Key to Pretest

1. Will that decision ~~effect~~ **affect** you in a positive way?
2. The ~~principle~~ **principal** on my loan is due on the 1st of each month.
3. My ~~advise~~ **advice** is for you to get a job before you buy that new car.
4. Please ~~ensure~~ **assure** my manager that I will return in one-half hour.
5. ~~Its~~ **It's** been a challenging day, but things are getting better.
6. ~~Their~~ **There** are a few issues that we need to discuss.
7. The agency gave ~~are~~ **our** report a new title.
8. Pat lives ~~further~~ **farther** from work than I do.
9. You can have a meeting ~~everyday~~ **every day**, if you prefer.
10. ~~Whose~~ **Who's** going to the ballgame?
11. I enjoy movies more ~~then~~ **than** I enjoy plays.
12. Megan ~~assured~~ **ensured** that the project would be successful.
13. It's ~~alright~~ **all right** for you to contact the manager directly.
14. I didn't mean to ~~infer~~ **imply** that you were late on purpose.
15. Try ~~and~~ **to** be on time for the next meeting.

Posttest – Similar Words

1. The **effect** of that decision is not yet known.
2. When you know **principal** on your loan, let me know.
3. Her **advice** was that you take the other part-time job.
4. Can you **ensure** the quality of your work?
5. The dog chased **its** tail, amusing several children.
6. **There** are a few issues that we need to discuss.
7. Is that **our** new computer?
8. You are **further** along on the project than I am.
9. We meet **every day** at 3 p.m.
10. **Whose** book is that?
11. Sue was taller **than** Mary last year.
12. Melanie **assured** me that we would be finished by Friday
13. **It's all right** for you to contact the manager directly.
14. I'm not trying to **imply** that you were late on purpose.

Chapter 20

Practice 20.1: The Colon

1. I have some exciting news for you: Jeremy proposed on Friday.
2. *Note*: The office is closed on Monday to honor the Martin Luther King holiday.
3. The supplies we need are as follows: markers, copy paper, and staplers.
4. Giorgio said that we need cereal, coconut milk, and bananas.
5. Here is what you should do: complete the inventory list and then work on the schedule. (Or: Complete . . .)

Practice 20.2: The Dash

1. Margie called on Friday—George is home!
2. Mike's parents are in town—he invited me to have dinner with them.
3. Helen Jones—the new CEO—asked me to join her team.
4. Call if you need anything—I'm always here to support you.
5. Give as much as you can to that charity—it's a good cause.

Practice 20.3: The Ellipses—Answers may vary.

1. **Abbreviated Albert Einstein Quote:** "The important thing is not to stop questioning . . . Never lose a holy curiosity."
2. **Abbreviated Victor Frankl Quote:** "Don't aim at success—the more you aim at it and make it a target, the more you are going to miss it . . . success will follow you precisely because you had *forgotten* to think to it."

Chapter 21

Practice 21.1: Capitalization

Next year the president of my company will provide a financial incentive for all employees, and I plan to participate in it. Jack Edwards, vice president of finance, will administer the plan. Everyone in my department is looking forward to having the opportunity to save more. A pamphlet entitled, "Financial Incentives for Long-term Savings," will describe the plan and be distributed next week. If the pamphlet has not arrived by Friday, I will check with the vice president's office to find out the details.

Practice 21.2: Numbers

1. We are meeting on January 5 at 10 a.m. at our offices on Lake Street.
2. Call me on Monday at 407-555-1212.
3. Alex lists his address as 407 South Maple Street, Hobart, IN 46368.
4. We received hundreds of calls about the job opening but only five résumés.
5. Purchase 12 laptops but only 7 new printers for our department.

Chapter 22

Practice 22.1: Quotation Marks

1. My answer to your request is an enthusiastic "yes."
2. If you think that's a "good idea," so do I.
3. The code was "307A," not "370A."
4. All he wrote was, "Our dog can hunt."
5. If you call that "good timing," I don't know how to respond.

Practice 22.2: Apostrophes: Possessives and Contractions

1. My supervisor's report won't be ready until next week.
2. The weather report says it's going to rain later, but I don't believe it.
3. Though it's June's responsibility, it's in Jack's best interest to complete the task.
4. Dr. Jones's (or Dr. Jones') office isn't located down the hall; it's next to Dr. Raines' (office).
5. If you tell me it's Tess's (Tess') project, I'll adjust my expectations.

Practice 22.3: Hyphens

1. Your first-class treatment has impressed all of us.
2. Our budget is one-half spent.
3. The short- and long-term outlooks are quite different.
4. Twenty-five people attended the conference.
5. Do you have sufficient funding for your 30- and 60-day payment schedules?

GLOSSARY

A

abstract   A short, written statement that gives an overview of a report, study, or proposal; usually associated with scientific studies but equivalent to an executive summary or a synopsis.

academic writing   A formal style of writing in which a thesis statement is used to develop the introduction, body, and conclusion; it characterizes research papers, arguments, essays, and creative writing. Compare **business writing.**

acronym   An abbreviation pronounced as a word (for example, *AARP, SADD*).

action plan   A detailed plan for achieving a goal; includes action steps, deadlines for completing them, and a list of any obstacles and ways to overcome them.

action research   A research method for collecting information to use in an immediate environment: identify problem, gather information, analyze data, and take action to rectify problem.

action step   In an action plan, an identified task along with who will complete it when it is due.

action verb   A verb that transfers action from a subject to an object; in English, all verbs except 11 linking verbs. Also see **state-of-being verb**.

active listening   A listening skill that involves focusing on the meaning, intent, and feelings of the person who is speaking to gain a clear understanding of the message.

active voice   As applied to verbs, a term indicating that the subject performs the action of the verb (for example, "Bob *wrote the report*"). Compare **passive voice**.

adaptation   In social systems theory, one of the four functional variables in which the system attempts to adapt to its external environment to facilitate goal attainment.

adjective   A word that modifies a noun or pronoun.

adverbial conjunction   A word or phrase (for example, *however, therefore, thus*) that serves as a transition between sentences or paragraphs; shows the relationship between ideas, and plays a significant role in punctuation.

antecedent   The word or words to which a pronoun refers.

appositive   A restatement; a brief explanation that identifies the noun or pronoun preceding it. See also **essential appositive**.

auxiliary (verb)   A verb (such as any form of *be, have, do*) that is used with another verb to convey a different meaning or tense. Also called *helper* verb.

B

background thinking   A person's thoughts about how he or she arrived at a conclusion or how readers will interpret that conclusion; a type of meta-discourse that should be eliminated from writing.

bar chart   A graphics tool that displays information in vertical or horizontal bars; enables the reader to compare and contrast different items.

base form   The original state of a verb. See also **infinitive.**

base settings   Setting paragraph controls at single spacing with no added space before or after paragraphs.

bibliography   A comprehensive list of the sources cited in a document (and sometimes of sources consulted but not cited); follows a standard format, including author, title of work, and publication or other identifying data for each work.

bidialectual   Fluid in speaking two dialects of the same language; for example, the ability to speak Edited American English and a community dialect.

bilingual   Ability to speak two languages.

body language   The "language" of eye contact, gestures, and other body movements; conveys, often unintentionally, a message that contributes to the meaning of verbal and nonverbal communication.

boundary   A hypothetical construct that defines the border that separates the system from its suprasystem; for example, personal boundaries and generational boundaries.

business writing   A direct style of writing in which context is used to define the purpose of the message; it characterizes letters, memos, and e-mail that get to the point quickly. Key components are to connect with reader, relate main points, and clarify action to be taken. Compare **academic writing.** See also **professional writing.**

C

career portfolio   A collection of relevant job-search information and documents, including résumé, sample cover and contact letters, network contacts, among other items.

case   In grammar, the function a pronoun performs in a sentence, such as subjective (or nominative), objective, possessive, and reflexive.

case management   A method of professional practice conducted by an individual or team that involves an ongoing responsibility to help functionally impaired clients.

case notes   A professional record of the case worker's interaction with the client, documenting what was discussed, agreed upon, or unresolved with the client.

casework   A method of direct practice generally conducted on a face-to-face basis with a client and focused on improving the client's level of social functioning.

CAT (connect-act-tell) strategy   In e-mail messages, a structural approach that connects with the reader, states desired action, and then gives supportive information.

centered heading   In documents, a main heading that is centered between the margins to indicate a major break in content; typed in all-capital letters or bold cap and lowercase letters, followed by 1 blank line before the text below.

central idea   A thesis statement that expresses the main point of a paper.

chronological format   For résumés, a traditional structure that emphasizes job history; lists education, positions, and accomplishments in order, starting with the lists your education, positions, starting with the most recent and working backward in order of occurrence.

clarity   Clearness and simplicity.

cliché   A fixed or stereotyped expression which has lost its significance through frequent repetition.

client system   An individual, group, family, organization, or community that is the beneficiary of a helping effort.

closing   (1) The last paragraph of a letter, stating action the recipient needs to take; (2) a complimentary sign-off (for example, for letters, *Sincerely*; for e-mail, *Best regards* or *All the best*.

coherent   A term referring to a paragraph that presents a logical flow of ideas, developing a topic in a consistent, rational way. One idea leads to another.

cohesive   A term referring to a paragraph that presents one main topic along with details to support that topic, demonstrating connectedness among the ideas it contains. All ideas adhere together for a common purpose.

colloquial   Informal, conversational language patterns which include slang and nonstandard English. Also called *idiomatic*.

colloquialism   A saying that is not taken literally; expresses an idea unique to specific time and location; for example, "That dog can't hunt."

colon   A traditional mark of punctuation; alerts the reader that information will follow that explains or illuminates the information that preceded it.

comma splice   A grammatical error in which two independent clauses are joined with only a comma, causing a run-on sentence.

community dialect (CD)   Any language pattern which differs from Edited American English (Standard English); informally known as "home talk" or "talkin' country." Most people shift codes depending on context, speaking less formally when with family and friends.

community organization   A method of social work practice that helps individuals, groups, organizations, and other collectives from a community (the same geographic area) to deal with shared interests, opportunities, or problems to enhance their state of well-being.

comparative form   The form of an adjective that is used when two items are compared; for regular adjectives, formed by adding the suffix *er* or by using *more* or *less* before the adjective.

composing   Creating, inventing, discovering; planning or mapping your message; drafting your ideas on the page.

coordinating conjunction   A word that joins items of equal grammatical structure, such as independent clauses or items in a series. The seven coordinating conjunctions are *and, but, or, nor, for, yet, so*.

correlative conjunction   A pair of conjunctions (for example, *not only . . . but also*) that compares or contrasts ideas. The information presented after each conjunction must be presented in the same grammatical form (parallel construction).

courteous request   In written communications, a question that prompts the recipient to act rather than respond in words; ends with a period rather than a question mark.

cover e-mail   For online job searches, an e-mail message that indicates an electronic résumé is attached and that summarizes the sender's interest in a company and requests an interview. Also see *cover letter* and *cover message*.

cover letter   (1) Enclosed with a proposal, a letter summarizing key points in the proposal; (2) enclosed with a résumé, a letter that summarizes the senders interest in a company, highlights accomplishments, and requests an interview. Also called *application letter*. Also see *cover e-mail*.

cover message   For sending documents as attachments via e-mail, a message that fulfils the same function as a *cover letter*.

credibility   Believability; equates to trust, a critical element in all relationships.

critic's block   A barrier to writing that is caused by being too critical of one's ability to write well or improve writing skills.

cultural sensitivity   The dynamics of communication that relate to diversity, such as cultural, generational, gender, and personality differences.

D

dash   A substitute for the comma, semicolon, period, or colon, used to emphasize the information that follows it; appropriate in both formal and informal documents.

DEAL Model   A reflective practice tool: *describe* a specific experience, *examine* it closely, and *articulate learning*.

dependent clause   A group of words that has a subject and verb but does not express a complete thought; cannot stand alone as a sentence.

direct address   The use of a person's name or title in addressing the person directly.

direct approach   In written communications, a style that gets right to the point; conveys the purpose and main point in the first paragraph, followed by supporting information or details. Compare indirect approach.

direct practice   Social work practice that involves direct client contact, usually face-to-face, such as casework.

E

Edited American English (EAE)   The type of written and spoken language that, for the most part, follows the standard rules of English usage; used by formal media programs (such as newscasts) and academia. Another term for EAE is Standard American English or Standard English.

editing   Improving the flow of writing by changing the wording and cutting unnecessary words to make the writing more concise and readable.

editing strategy   An approach to editing that focuses on turning passive, wordy writing into simple, clear, and concise writing.

editor's block   Being overly concerned with product at the expense of process.

ellipsis marks   Three spaced periods used to indicate the omission of a word or words from a quotation. (Add a fourth period if the ellipsis [plural *ellipses*] occurs at the end of a sentence.)

e-mail   Electronic mail, the most widely used form of written communication; in business, used to communicate with colleagues in-house (on an *intranet*) or with associates outside of the company (on the *Internet*).

e-memo   An electronic memo sent on a company's intranet to its own employees; formatted like a traditional memo created by means of a template.

emphatic   An adjective or adverb used to place emphasis on the word it describes; can detract from the message rather than place emphasis on it, so should be used sparingly (for example, *very, really, incredible*).

empty information   Irrelevant or redundant information that adds nothing of value for your reader.

e-résumé   A résumé specifically formatted

for electronic transmittal; at the top, summarizes work skills and experience in keywords that are scanned by employers for matches with their needs.

essential appositive A word or phrase that identifies a particular person or thing in a sentence where the identity would not be clear without the appositive; should *not* be set off with commas.

essential element Any part of a sentence that cannot be removed without compromising meaning or structure; should *not* be set off with commas. Also called *restrictive element*.

evidence Proof of an assertion or research finding; typically consists of objective data, such as facts and figures, thereby eliminating bias.

exclamation point A mark of punctuation used to indicate surprise or excitement; can be used correctly after a word, phrase, or complete sentence. (Use exclamation points sparingly.)

executive summary A short, written synopsis that gives an overview of a report, study, or proposal; used in business, but equivalent to an abstract or a synopsis.

external due date A project completion date specified by the person or agency commissioning the project. Compare **internal due date**.

F

fax A copy of a document that is sent via phone lines to a fax machine or computer. (The term is derived from *facsimile*, meaning "a copy.")

feedback An objective appraisal based on specific details that offers a constructive description rather than a vague summary. Compare evaluation. See also constructive feedback, objective feedback.

filler An empty word that adds no value to a message (for example, *just*, *like*).

flowchart A graphic representation of information that depicts progression through a procedure or system.

focal system A system that is the subject of attention. (If a family is a focal system, the siblings are a subsystem and the community is a suprasystem.)

focused writing A writing technique that involves writing about a topic for 10 to 20 minutes simply to put ideas on the page, without expecting to produce usable material.

font The style of type face, such as Times or Arial. Fonts number in the hundreds, and each word processing program includes its own series of fonts. See also **serif** and **sans serif**.

forced writing A writing technique that involves writing about a topic for 10 to 15 minutes with the expectation of producing material that can be used.

format The overall appearance of a document, including placement of the entire text and of individual parts (for example, dateline and salutation) and the use of special features and white space.

fragment A phrase or dependent clause that is incorrectly punctuated as a complete sentence.

freewriting A writing technique that involves writing thoughts freely in a "stream of consciousness" to release feelings and stress and gain insight.

functional format For résumés, a nontraditional structure that highlights experience and accomplishments in each area of expertise; lists skills and education before work experience.

fused sentence   A grammatical error in which two independent clauses are connected without a comma or conjunction.

G

gender bias   In writing, the exclusion of one gender by using only masculine or feminine pronouns in contexts that apply to both genders. Plural pronouns and the phrase *he or she* are gender-neutral.

generalist practice   A professional social work practice that can be conducted in a variety of settings with client systems of varying size, addressing the several levels of prevention and applying a transferable body of knowledge, values, and skills.

gerund   The *ing* form of a verb (for example, such as *seeing*, *going*, *following*); functions as a noun.

gerund phrase   A gerund followed by a preposition, noun, and any modifiers (for example, *going to the meeting*, *being on time*); functions as a noun.

global communication   Communication across language and cultural borders.

goal   A broad statement of an intended achievement. Compare **objective**.

grammatical subject   A subject that generally precedes the verb but may or may not be the actor or agent that performs the action of the verb; in an active-voice sentence, the same as the real subject. Compare **real subject**.

group work   A method of social work practice that consists of a small group of people with common interests who meet regularly working toward their common goals.

groupthink   A phenomenon in which everyone "goes along to get along," agreeing with decisions regardless of quality; occurs when a need for approval (or a fear of disapproval) exists among members.

growing edge   An area in which a person needs more expertise or experience. Also called *weakness*.

H

hard copy   A paper copy of a document (as compared to an electronic copy). Compare **soft copy**.

hedge   A word or phrase that qualifies a statement by making it less than universal (for example, *sort of, kind of*); can weaken the message, so should be used sparingly.

helper (verb)   See **auxiliary**.

highly formal (writing)   A style of writing characterized by use of the passive voice, complicated language, abstract references, no contractions, and Latin abbreviations.

hypothesis   An explanation that can be tested.

I

idiolect   An individual's unique language pattern; differs from other's patterns on the basis of grammar, word use, and pronunciation.

idiom   An expression peculiar to a language, not readily analyzable from its grammatical construction or from the meaning of its component parts; for example, "to put up with" translates to "tolerate or endure." See **colloquial**.

independent clause   A clause that has a subject and verb and expresses a complete thought; can stand alone as a sentence.

indirect approach   In written communications, a style that presents details and explanations before getting to the main point; often used in messages that convey bad or unwelcome news. Compare **direct approach**.

indirect practice   Social work practice that involves indirect contact with clients., such as social work administration that is conducted on behalf of clients but does not usually involve direct contact with them.

infinitive   The base form of the verb preceded by *to* (for example, *to be, to see, to speak*); functions as a noun, adjective, or adverb.

infinitive phrase   An infinitive along with an object and any modifiers (for example, *to go to the store, to see the latest book reviews*); functions as a noun, adjective, or adverb.

informal speech   The language pattern used for speaking in everyday situations, as compared to doing a formal presentation; does not adhere strictly to standard rules of English usage.

information flow   In writing, the transition between ideas. Presenting old information that leads to new information creates smooth transitions and ensures that messages are cohesive and coherent.

initialism   An abbreviation pronounced letter by letter (for example, *IBM, NYPD*).

input   All of the resources that are required by a social system to accomplish its purposes, including people and money.

inside address   The part of a letter containing the name and address of the recipient. (The address on the envelope should mirror the inside address.)

internal due dates   A project completion date that group members set among themselves to ensure they will meet external requirements. Compare **external due date**.

intransitive verb   A verb that cannot transfer action to a direct object. Compare **transitive verb.**

introductory paragraph   In a letter, the opening paragraph; connects the reader with the writer's purpose.

irregular verb   A verb that forms its past and past participle in an irregular way (for example, *fly, flew, flown; sink, sank, sunk*).

J

jargon   using initials, abbreviations, technical, or occupational terminology as a sort of verbal shorthand.

job search profile   A compilation of information about a person's skills, qualities, interests, education, and employment history; serves as the basis for a résumé, job search, and jog interviews.

L

language pattern   A system of language, such as Edited American English or any form of community dialect. Most people speak several different dialects; social situations help determine which pattern to use at a given time.

linking verb   See **state-of-being verb**.

listener   In the communication process, the receiver of a message.

logic modeling   A tool for applying critical thinking skills to identify an underlying system of reasoning as the means of explanation.

M

macro   A large social system such as a formal organization or community.

main verb   The last verb in a string of verbs. In English, as many as five verbs can string together to form meaning.

memorandum (memo)   An internal communication tool used to inform or make announcements to peers, subordinates, and supervisors within an organization; in hard-copy form, sent via interoffice mail or posted on boards. See also **e-memo.**

meta discourse   As coined by Joseph Williams, author of *Style*, a term that refers to the language a writer uses to describe his or her own thinking process; usually consists of unnecessary information.

method   The "how, when, where, and who" of accomplishing a project.

micro   A small social system such as a social group or family.

mirroring   Paraphrasing what the speaker said to ensure the message was received clearly.

modified-block style   A letter style that follow the block style but starts the dateline and complimentary closing at the center (rather than the left margin).

modifier   A word or group of words that describes another word.

N

networking   Engaging in social and professional activities that facilitate interaction with people who can provide assistance with one's career or problem-solving endeavors

new information   Unfamiliar information; information that extends the reader's understanding.

nominal   A noun that originated as a verb; often formed by adding *tion* or *ment* to the base form of the verb (for example, *development* from the verb *develop*).

nominative case   Also called *subjective case*. The form of pronouns that function as subjects of verbs. Subject pronouns must be followed by a verb (either real or implied).

nonverbal behavior   Body language that communicates feelings and thus can affect the meaning of a verbal message.

nonverbal cues   Hand gestures, eye contact, and other types of body language that affect communication.

null hypothesis   A hypothesis that is negated so that statistical analysis can be used to disprove it, thus showing the likelihood that the original hypothesis is valid.

O

object   A word, phrase, or clause that follows a verb and receives the action of the verb.

objective   A narrow, precise statement of a specific and measurable intended action. Compare **goal.**

objective case   The form of pronouns that function as objects of verbs or prepositions (for example, *me, him, her, them*).

old information   Familiar information; information that is obvious or that the reader already knows; creates a context for new information.

open punctuation   In letters, a punctuation style in which no punctuation follows the salutation and the complimentary closing.

outcomes   The results a project will produce and how people affected by the project will change or grow.

output   The status of signal/task and maintenance inputs following a conversion cycle of a social system.

P

paraphrase   Putting someone else's ideas or words into one's own words; requires a citation to the original source. Incorrect paraphrasing (making a few changes in word order, leaving out a word or two, or substituting similar words) is a form of plagiarism.

passive voice   As applied to verbs, a term indicating that the subject does not perform the action of the verb (for example, " The report *was written* by Bob"—the subject, *report,* did not perform the action, *was written).* Compare **active voice.**

past   The simple past form of a verb, used without a helper verb (for example, *worked, did, was, followed).*

past participle   A verb form that consists of the past form preceded by a helper verb (for example, *have worked, had done, have been, had followed).*

PEER (purpose, evidence, explanation, recap) model   A guide to structuring information while composing or revising: define *purpose,* provide *evidence,* give an *explanation* or examples, *recap* main points.

period   A punctuation mark used to indicate the end of a statement; also used with some abbreviations and with Web addresses. Also called *dot.*

phrase   A group of words that form a unit but do not usually include a subject and a verb and cannot stand alone as a sentence; functions as a noun, adjective, or adverb. Types include prepositional, gerund, and infinitive phrases, among others.

pie charts   A graphics tool that displays information as "slices" of a circle; enables the reader to easily see both the relationship of one item to another and the relationships of all parts to the whole.

plagiarism   The use of another's ideas or words without crediting the source; constitutes a form of stealing. (The term is derived from the Latin *plagiarius,* "an abductor" or "thief.")

portfolio   For a job search, a collection of pertinent documents and information (for example, purpose statement, résumés, work samples, reference letters, networking contacts, business cards).

possessive case   The form of pronouns that show possession of nouns or other pronouns (for example, *my, mine, his, her, its, their).*

practice   The process of providing professional assistance to clients so that they make planned changes to move to a state of well-being.

prepositional phrase   A preposition along with an object and any modifiers (for example, *with* Bob*, to the* store); functions as a noun, adjective, or adverb.

prioritizing   Identifying the rank order of items on a list; identifying the level of importance.

professional writing   A direct style of writing characterized by use of the active voice, simple words, personal pronouns (for example, *I, you, we),* and at times contractions (for example, *can't* for *cannot);* used in most business communications. Compare **highly formal.**

profile card   A business card that includes a few simple bulleted points about the person's accomplishments; used in a job search.

progressive tenses   Verb tenses in which the main verb ends in *ing* and is preceded by a helper verb; used to indicate continuous action in the past, present, or future.

pronoun   A word (for example, *I, you, he, she, it, we, they)* that is used in place of a noun or another pronoun; must agree with its antecedent in number, person, and gender.

pronoun viewpoint The point of view that emanates from the number, person, and gender of a subjective case pronoun (for example, the "I" or "you" viewpoint); should be consistent within sentences, paragraphs, and at times documents.

proofread Correcting the grammar, punctuation, spelling, and word usage; part of the editing process but also stands on its own as the final, critical step in producing a document.

proofreader's marks A table of established marks that editors and printers use to show changes in a document.

protocols Formalities and rules of order and etiquette; play an important role in global business, governing interactions such as introductions, greetings and written communications.

Q

qualitative research Research that involves collecting narrative data to gain insight into phenomena of interest; often done by administering surveys and questionnaires.

quantify Express numerically; a way to describe an achievement or goal (for example, as a percentage, length of time, or amount of money) that shows its contribution to the bottom line.

quantitative research Research that involves collecting numerical data to explain, predict, and/or control phenomena of interest; often done by applying the scientific method, with experimental and control groups.

question mark A punctuation mark used to indicate a question the writer expects the reader to answer; sometimes can occur after individual words as well as

complete sentences structured as questions.

R

random sampling A research technique in which the researcher surveys a group of people who are chosen at random and thus believed to be representative of the broader population; reduces bias and enables calculation of a margin of error.

rate of speech The speed at which a person speaks. Listeners understand slow speech more effectively than fast speech.

real subject The actor or agent that performs the action of the verb but may or may not appear in the sentence; in an active sentence, the same as the grammatical subject. Compare **grammatical subject**.

reflexive case The form of pronouns that reflect back to subjective case pronouns (for example, *myself, yourself, ourselves*). Also called *intensive case*.

regular verb A verb that forms its past and past participle by adding *–ed* to the base (for example, *walk, walked, have walked*).

reliability In research, consistency of measure; for example, if the same study is repeated several times and the outcomes are the same, then it is *reliable*.

research The process of investigating, inquiring, and examining; involves seeking answers in a methodical, objective manner that includes an established line of thought and credible experience.

resistance A barrier consisting of beliefs, attitudes, and behaviors that keep people from moving forward with a decision, can stem from tangible sources (for example, lack of resources) or from intangible sources (for example, lack of trust) and from valid or invalid concerns.

results   See **outcomes**.

résumé   A concise document summarizing a person's education and work history. Also see **chronological format**, **e-résumé**, **functional format**, **scannable résumé**.

revise   Improve the way written ideas are presented by moving sentences or paragraphs and ensuring that major parts of the document achieve what is intended; intertwined with editing as the document progresses but on its own as a final check before proofreading.

run-on sentence   A sentence that consists of two independent clauses joined with only a comma.

S

"s" form   The third-person singular form of a verb in simple present tense (for example, *works, does, is follows*).

salutation   The opening greeting of a letter or e-mail message.

sans-serif   A font in which the top and bottom of the letters are uniform in thickness and look flat; literally, "without the line." Compare **serif**.

scannable résumés   A hard-copy résumé that summarizes work skills and experience in key keywords that are scanned by employers for matches with their needs. See also **e-résumé**.

scientific method   A rigorous process used to identify predictability of hypotheses in quantitative research, including a control group and an experimental group.

scholastic writing   See **academic writing**.

screening interview   A preliminary interview for the purpose of developing a pool of qualified candidates; may occur over the telephone, online, or in person.

semicolon   A punctuation mark used to separate two independent clauses and sometimes items in a series; stronger than a comma but weaker than a period, can be considered a "full stop that is not terminal."

sentence   A group of words that has a subject and a verb and expresses a complete thought; an independent clause.

serif   A font in which the edges of the letters end in short lines, creating a pointed or sharp look (for example, Times New Roman). Compare **sans-serif**.

set of commas   A pair of commas that set off nonessential information in a sentence.

side heading   In documents, a second-level heading that starts at the left margin; typed in bold, either all-capital letters or capital and lower-case, followed by 1 blank line before the text below. Also called *subheading*.

signal anxiety   A type of anxiety that has positive effects; alerts a person to a task that needs attention and provides the energy to achieve it.

simple, clear, and concise   The characteristics of a writing style that is effective for business writing.

simplified style   A streamlined letter style that follows the block style but emphasizes the subject of the letter and omits the salutation and complimentary closing; the style of choice when there is no specific recipient.

skill sets   Skills that a person perform in various areas of employment.

slang   Informal, nonconventional language (for example, jargon, colloquialisms) that reflect a dialect rather than standard English; not acceptable in multicultural communication exchanges.

social history   a client's formal record that details background, family relationships, special needs, mental illness, or medical conditions.

social services   A program of activities directed toward helping people to meet their needs and/or to enhance their level of social functioning.

social system   A social entity possessing functionally interdependent relationships with each other, for example a family, agency, or community.

social systems model   A particular representation of a social system.

social systems perspective   A set of assumptions on which social systems theory is based.

social systems theory   A set of assumptions and concepts that seeks to explain behaviors exhibited in the functioning of social systems and how such systems achieve well-being.

soft copy   An electronic version of a document. Compare **hard copy**.

speaker   In the communication process, the sender of a message.

Standard American English   The type of language that follows the standard rules of English usage; used in most books, in classrooms, and in public and professional forums. See also **Edited American English**.

standard punctuation   In letters, a punctuation style in which a colon follows the salutation and a comma follows the complimentary closing; the most common for business letters.

state-of-being verb   A verb that does not transfer action but instead links a subject to a subject complement (rather than direct object); any form of *to be* (*is, are, was, were*), *appear, become,* and *seem,* and at times *smell, taste, feel, sound, look, act, grow.* Also called *linking verb.*

storyboarding   A technique for planning presentation slides; involves depicting the ideas by dividing a horizontal sheet of paper into two columns and putting text in one and a sketch or a graphic in the other.

strategy   An approach to solving problems or accomplishing a vision that consists of developing goals, objectives, and action plans.

strengths perspective   An approach that focuses on the strengths and capacities of people and their organizations to achieve a sense of well-being.

stress interview   An interview characterized by intense questioning and quick subject changes; intended to test an applicant's response to pressure.

style   In writing, the overall manner of presentation in a document; determined by many individual writing decisions that contribute to the total effect.

subheading   See **side heading**.

subject   Together with the verb, the core of a sentence; can be a noun, phrase, or clause. See also **grammatical subject, real subject**.

subjective case   The form of pronouns that function as subjects of verbs. Subject pronouns must be followed by a verb (either real or implied). Also called *nominative case.*

subordinating conjunctions   A word or phrase (for example, *if, when, as, although, because, as soon as, before*) used to connect a dependent clause to an independent clause; defines the relationship between the ideas in the clauses.

subjunctive mood   The form of the verb that is used to express a condition that is improbably, highly unlikely, or contrary to fact; also used with certain requests, demands, recommendations, and set phrases.

subsystem   A component element of focal system that displays all the attributes of a system, but can be located within a larger designate system; for example, a married couple functions as a system and is a subsystem of the total family unit.

summary   On a résumé, the section that highlights one's experience, achievements, and greatest skills and abilities.

superlative form   The form of an adjective that is used when three or more items are compared; for regular adjectives, formed by adding the suffix *est* or by using *most* or *least* before the adjective.

suprasystem   A part of the social environment to which a subject system is functionally linked; for example, birth families are relevant parts of a family's suprasystem.

survey   A research tool in which a questionnaire is administered to a number of people; designed to elicit responses about a specific topic being studied.

synergy   The energy created in team dynamics that leads to the whole becoming more than the sum of its parts.

synopsis   A short, written statement that gives and an overview of a report, study, or proposal; used in academic writing but equivalent to an abstract or executive summary.

syntax   The orderly arrangements of words. Also called *grammar*.

T

table   A graphics tool that displays data in columns and rows.

tag-on   An unnecessary preposition at the end of a phrase or clause; for example, "Where do you live *at*?"

team   A group of people who come together to work on a common goal.

theory   A logically derived set of assumptions and concepts used to explain something; for example, social systems theory.

theory/practice method   A learning technique that involves first learning a principle and then applying it; enables a learner to connect how something is used with the principle that defines how it should be used and develops analytical, critical thinking skills.

thesis statement   a one- or two-sentence summary of the problem being discussed or argument being made in a paper.

topic sentence   A broad, general sentence that gives an overview of the paragraph.

topic string   A series of sentences that develop the specific idea presented in a topic sentence.

transferable skills   Qualities, skills, and expertise that characterize a person regardless of his or her job description or profession and thus transfer with the person from one job to another.

transitional paragraph   In a document, a paragraph that summarizes the key ideas of the current section and indicates how the major theme of the document will be developed in the next section.

transitional sentences   A sentence that provides a logical connection between paragraphs.

V

validity   In research, whether a study examines what it is intended to examine.

value   A belief pertaining to what is right and good, comprising the normative structure of a social system; for example, values form the foundation on which social systems develop.

verb   Together with the subject, the core or nucleus of a sentence; conjugated on the basis of subject and tense. Verb usage indicates whether an event happened in the past, is happening in the present, or will happen in the future. See also **action verb, intransitive verb, state-of-being verb, transitive verb.**

verb parts   The basic forms of a verb; for example, *past*, *past participle*.

visual persuasion   Incorporating special features such as bold, underline, italics, numbering, and bullet points so that key points are instantly visible for the reader.

voicemail   Recorded phone messages.

W

"we" viewpoint   In written messages, a pronoun point of view that expresses teamwork and indicates that the ideas are those of the company as well as the writer; frequently used in business today.

works-cited list   In the MLA reference style, the end-of-document references list; equivalent to a bibliography.

Y

"you" viewpoint   In written messages, a pronoun point of view that helps the writer connect with the reader and focus on the reader's needs.

INDEX

Made in the USA
Columbia, SC
28 February 2018